The Political Effects of Entertainment Media

The Political Effects of Entertainment Media

How Fictional Worlds Affect Real World Political Perspectives

Anthony Gierzynski

LEXINGTON BOOKS
Lanham • Boulder • New York • London

Published by Lexington Books
An imprint of The Rowman & Littlefield Publishing Group, Inc.
4501 Forbes Boulevard, Suite 200, Lanham, Maryland 20706
www.rowman.com

Unit A, Whitacre Mews, 26-34 Stannary Street, London SE11 4AB

British Library Cataloguing in Publication Information Available

Library of Congress Cataloging-in-Publication Data Available

ISBN 978-1-4985-7398-6 (cloth : alk. paper)
ISBN 978-1-4985-7399-3 (electronic)

∞™ The paper used in this publication meets the minimum requirements of American National Standard for Information Sciences—Permanence of Paper for Printed Library Materials, ANSI/NISO Z39.48-1992.

Printed in the United States of America

For Joe, Paul, Gene, Mary, Sue, and Jenny

Contents

Acknowledgments

While the limited resources available to faculty at the University of Vermont put constraints on the research contained in this volume (no public opinion lab, no grad students), it also opened up the opportunity to engage my undergraduates directly in this research. I thank my now retired colleague Frank Bryan for demonstrating the positives of engaging students directly in one's research work—the benefits for the students and for the research.[1] As the notes throughout this volume will document, I have benefited from Bryan's model and from the intelligent and engaged students who have taken my classes and participated in the development and implementation of the research projects I report on in this book. I want to thank those students here. They include (students are grouped by the class and project they worked on) William Andreycak, Jake Brudney, Antonia David, Mitchell Hansen, Kevin Kennedy, Frederick Knight, Eric Schwarzbach, Sarah Simmons, David Thal, Erik Tidmon, Marissa Bucci, Mac Cleary, Daniel Cmejla, Nicholas Ingersoll, Kelly Joyce, Anastasia Kopp, Luca Piccin, Macie Rebel, Connor Seitchik, Emma Stern, Ashley Szilvassy, Nicholas Usen, Sarah Weichselbaum, Matthew West, Lauren Willigan; Hayley Aydelott, Evyn Banach, Kevin Cafferky, Matthew Donovan, Emmett Hoskin, Sean McEwan, Stewart Micali, Jacob Mitchell, Tyler Mogk, Scott Pavek, Emily Queiroz, Galen Stump, Allie VanSickle, Jack Vest, William Andreycak, Ben Brownstein, Fernando DeOleo, Adam Elias, Michael Gibson, Matthew Holleb, Katherine Ida, Alison Kelly, Sara Lindstrom, Evan McDaniel, Patrick Milliken, Scott Olsen, Emily Pijanowski, Alexandra Raymond, Alexander Rosenblatt, Jordan Tahami, Julia Wejchert, and Jordan White.

I would also like to thank the wonderful staff of the Political Science Department at the University of Vermont, Candace Smith and Carol Tank-Day, who were always quick to help with producing materials for this research. And, my colleagues Jennifer Barnes-Bowie, F. Gregory Gause, and Heather Yates for encouraging their students to participate in some of the studies in this volume. I would like to thank my daughter and son, Kelsey and Chay, with whom I enjoyed, and from whom I learned about many different entertainment media of their choice—from *Star Trek: Voyager* to *Adventure Time* to *The Legend of Zelda: Breath of the Wild*. And, finally, I would like to thank my siblings, to whom I dedicate this book. We spent many hours not just watching and reading—*M*A*S*H*, *Star Trek*, *The Lord of the Rings*, *The Chronicles of Narnia*, *The Twilight Zone*, and so on—but discussing these books, shows and movies. Thanks to my brother Gene, who brought home *The Hobbit*—the book that got me reading as an adolescent—my brother Paul, who drove some of us to see the first *Star Wars* movie in 1977, the discussions we all had about whether they would ever make a good movie version of *The Lord of the Rings*, and the family trips to see movies (one year we, with our spouses and children, took up a whole twenty-five-seat row at the movie theater for *Star Trek: Generations*).

NOTE

1. Bryan, Frank M. 2004. *Real Democracy: The New England Town meeting and How it Works* (Chicago, IL: The University Press of Chicago).

Introduction

Our stories often show us, for better or worse, how everything can be solved by the rise of an individual hero, and that the "best way" to deal with a bad guy with a gun is a good guy with a gun. Our stories portray individuals along the lines of gender, racial, and ethnic stereotypes; offer us villains who are one-dimensional characters driven by evil; and show us politicians who are almost always corrupt, self-serving, and/or incompetent. They offer up models for how to deal with unreasonable and/or oppressive authority and typically portray worlds that are just, where those who do the right thing come out on top and those who do not meet undesirable ends. Entire entertainment genres, with their shared storytelling conventions and common plot devices, provide lessons and perspectives that are relevant to how the public sees political issues. Science fiction, for example, by its very nature deals with technology and its effects, the implications of the existence of other forms of intelligent life, and the vastness of space-time. Our stories show us all these things and more, but to what effect? That is the central question of this volume.

The skeptical reader may believe that they already have an answer to that question and stop reading. They may accept that our stories *do* contain many political lessons, but counterargue that stories are just that, stories—ways to escape our world and entertain ourselves with the lives and events of imagined worlds—and, thus dismiss the notion that fiction might affect real world political beliefs. No one turns to fiction in order to learn about politics and government, after all. The flaw in the position of such a skeptic is that their argument is based on the faulty presumption that people consciously build their political positions through the active and reasoned acquisition of political information. The extant research in multiple disciplines (psychology, sociology, and political science to name a few) shows that presumption to be false, especially with regard to the foundations of political beliefs. The other problem with that skeptical argument dismissing entertainment media effects is that it assumes that we consume all media containing political messages in the same way. We do not. Research on story immersion has provided a strong body of evidence that people's mental state when transported by a story is very different from their state when processing information (I will elaborate on this in chapter 2). In that transported state, characteristic of story immersion, it turns out that we are in no condition to just dismiss information and perspectives because they are made up.

Other skeptics may accept the point that fictional narratives can influence political perspectives but argue that people's choice of entertainment will reflect their preexisting political views, thus making it unlikely that entertainment will have a unique, or independent, effect on those views. This position, rooted in the notion of selective exposure and acceptance—the assertion that we only consume media that is congruent with our existing beliefs and only accept messages that we already believe in—has its flaws when it comes to entertainment media. First, it undervalues belief reinforcement as a media effect. When beliefs are reinforced, they are stronger, more resistant to change, and more predictive of behavior.[1] So, were entertainment media found to merely reinforce beliefs, that would actually be an important finding in and of itself. But, as a small but not unsubstantial body of research has shown,[2] a body of research I attempt to add to here, entertainment media effects do go beyond reinforcement.

The second problem with the selective exposure/acceptance argument is that there are good reasons to argue that the selective exposure model is far less applicable to entertainment media than it is to news media. For most people, the reasons behind exposure to entertainment media will have nothing to do with their existing political views. We may be drawn to certain entertainment media because of their popularity among friends, family, and co-workers, or because of attention given to them in the news and social media, critical reviews of the programs, or the visual appeal of their special effects. The advertising for the movie, show, or game might draw us in. It may be that we may just be bored and have nothing better to do, or we are inadvertently exposed when we have little choice, such as when roommates or family are watching (chapters 3 and 4 contain evidence supporting these as the reasons for exposure to entertainment media). Once exposed, the reasons we continue to consume entertainment media also have little to do with preexisting political views, and the state of narrative transportation means that we are unlikely to be selective about the lessons we accept from the stories. We may continue to watch, read, or play for the same reasons that drew us to the entertainment and in the process we may become immersed in the book, TV program, film, or game, and/or come to identify with a certain character. Once that happens, we are, as scholars in psychology, political science, and communications have demonstrated, unlikely to counterargue politically relevant messages and instead likely to internalize the lessons of the narrative and emulate the qualities of those with whom we identify.[3]

Selective exposure and acceptance is also complicated by the fact that the politically relevant lessons of a narrative or the personal qualities of fictional characters are not always evident early on in the story, and, they may evolve throughout it. Take the story of Darth Vader, a cultural icon of evil, for example. The initial portrayal of him as pure evil is muddled as the story progresses from *A New Hope* to *The Empire Strikes Back*, and in *The Return of the Jedi* we see that his son's belief that there was still some good in him proved true. Another example can be found in the Cylons of the 2004–2009 reimagining of *Battlestar Galactica*. The Cylons (a form of artificial intelligence created by humans) are portrayed in the initial season as genocidal robots bent on destroying their creators; but, as the story progresses, the leading human characters come to see the Cylons as a form of intelligent life deserving acceptance and tolerance.

The combination of the points made above—the evident political content of entertainment media, the reasons why the selective exposure model is unlikely to apply to entertainment media, and the unique mental state that occurs when we are transported by a story—give us good cause to expect that fictional television shows, movies, books and games could be a source of some of the political views held by the public. Thus, if scholars wish to understand fully how citizens come to see the political world the way they do, we may want to look beyond the traditional sources of political information and explore how those things that the public chooses for entertainment shape political views as well.[4] This is especially true in today's high-choice media environment that allows people to opt for entertainment and avoid the news altogether, which millions do.[5] After all, with all the "tales of war and of waste," why not "turn right over to the TV page"?[6] That option to eschew news in favor of entertainment is even greater now, in the early decades of the twenty-first century, with a media environment where the volume of entertainment available (and selected) overwhelms the amount of time devoted to news and public affairs. The potential for entertainment media to affect political perspectives is also greater these days given the thin substance of most news stories—the result of the media businesses' need to hold on to their audience with trivia and entertainment packaged as news.[7] One has only to consider how many scenes of torture audiences have seen in movies and television shows versus how many good journalistic news stories they have been exposed to on the subject (investigative reports that analyze the effectiveness of the various interrogation methods) in order to get a sense of the potential entertainment media have to shape our views on political topics.

Up until recently, scholars have paid scant attention to entertainment media as a source of political views. Some scholars have argued for the importance of studying entertainment media effects before.[8] And, a number of political scientists published pieces on explicitly political shows such as the 1980s made-for-TV movie *The Day After*,[9] the TV miniseries *Amerika*,[10] and the movies *Wag the Dog*[11] and *JFK*.[12] Several scholars have published pieces on the overtly political entertainment shows *The Daily Show* and *The Colbert Report*[13] or the effects of the portrayal of governmental institutions.[14] It hasn't been until very recently that work has emerged on the effects of pure entertainment media. By "pure entertainment" media, I mean programs, movies, books, and video games with storylines about something other than politics or government. Research examining the political effects of pure entertainment media now include works on: the effects of the *Harry Potter* series;[15] the effects of fictional narratives on the belief in a just world;[16] the way fictional framing of abortion in the movie *The Cider House Rules* affected opinions on abortion;[17] agenda setting and priming effects on issues of crime and healthcare from the television dramas *Without a Trace* and *ER*;[18] the impact of *Law & Order* on attitudes about criminal justice and the death penalty;[19] the impact of science fiction on attitudes about autonomous military weapons;[20] and the impact of the authoritarian-dystopian genre on attitudes justifying the use of radical forms of political action.[21]

My purpose in this book is to build on that previous work, extending the exploration of entertainment media's political effects. To that end, the chapters that follow are dedicated to the analysis of the impact that entertainment media—both pure entertainment media and entertainment with obvious political content—have on the way we see the political world. I start in the next chapter with a discussion of how to identify the political and politically relevant content in television shows, movies, books, and video games that has the potential to influence political perspectives. In chapter 2, I develop a broad theory of entertainment media's political effects, drawing from theories and research on media effects and public opinion, in order to specify *how* entertainment media affect political perspectives and *when* that is likely to happen. Then the rest of the book is devoted to a series of studies that test for the impact of entertainment shows such as *Game of Thrones*, *House of Cards*, *The Daily Show*, and *The Colbert Report*, genres like science fiction, and character types such as villains or leaders.

In chapter 3, I examine the impact of the relentless injustices perpetrated in the first five seasons of HBO's *Game of Thrones* on audiences' levels of belief in a just world. Two experiments and one survey offer evidence that suggests that when people are exposed to a show that repeatedly defies the "just world" script norm of most stories (the happy endings), audiences are less likely to see the real world as just. In chapter 4, I continue to examine the impact of shows depicting unjust worlds by examining the effect of exposure to Netflix's *House of Cards*. Two surveys and an experiment offer evidence to suggest a similar effect as *Game of Thrones*. These studies of *House of Cards* also examine whether the show affected its audiences' attitudes about whether means justify ends, their levels of cynicism, and whether a prominent issue in the third season led to an agenda-setting effect. In chapter 5 I take the first look at an entire genre, using an experiment and survey instrument to examine the impact of the common story themes of science fiction on attitudes about technology and human diversity. In chapter 6, I report on an online experiment that focuses on a category of fictional character types—villains—and whether the portrayal of fictional villains is related to how the public views real world villains. In chapter 7, I report on a series of surveys that examine the relationship between exposure to two news parody shows—*The Daily Show* and *The Colbert Report*—on viewers' level of cynicism versus skepticism. The survey suggests that these shows, unlike *House of Cards*, actually promoted a healthy level of skepticism as opposed to cynicism. And, finally, in chapter 8 I return to categories of characters—in this case characters in a position of leadership—to assess the impact of the stereotyped gender traits exhibited by fictional leaders on those traits audiences deem as important in a leader. Two online experiments suggest that portrayals of fictional leadership in which traits stereotypically associated with women are evident and effective can elevate the importance of those traits to peoples' conception of good leadership. In the conclusion, I situate this research in the context of our understanding of the development of citizens' political perspectives and discuss the implications of the research and avenues for future research.

NOTES

1. For the arguments as to why reinforcement is important, see Michael D. Slater, "Reinforcing Spirals: The Mutual Influence of Media Selectivity and Media Effects and Their Impact on Individual Behavior and Social Identity," *Communications Theory* 17 (2007): 281–303.

2. See the discussion and references below.

3. I will discuss the literature on this more fully in chapter 2. For a summary of the research on this matter, see Jordan M. Carpenter and Melanie C. Green, "Flying with Icarus: Narrative Transportation and the Persuasiveness of Entertainment," in *The Psychology of Entertainment Media: Blurring the Lines Between Entertainment and Persuasion*, edited by L. J. Shrum (New York: Routledge, 2012).

4. I am not the first to make this argument. See, for example, Diana C. Mutz and Lilach Nir, "Not Necessarily the News: Does Fictional Television Influence Real-World Policy Preferences?" *Mass Communication and Society* 13 (2010): 196–217; Kenneth Mulligan and Philip Habel, "The Implications of Fictional Media for Political Beliefs," *American Politics Research* 41, no. 1 (2013), 122–46; and R. Lance Holbert, "A Typology for the Study of Entertainment Television and Politics," *American Behavioral Scientist* 49, no. 3 (2005): 436–53.

5. See Markus Prior, *Post-Broadcast Democracy: How Media Choice Increases Inequality in Political Involvement and Polarizes Elections* (Cambridge: Cambridge University Press, 2007); and, Mindich, David T. Z., *Tuned Out: Why Americans Under 40 Don't Follow the News* (New York: Oxford University Press, 2005).

6. Crowded House, "Don't Dream It's Over," *Crowded House*, 1988.

7. See Alison Dagnes, *Politics on Demand: The Effects of 24-Hour News on American Politics* (Santa Barbara, CA: Praeger, 2010); an, Anthony Gierzynski, *Saving American Elections: A Diagnosis and Prescription for a Healthier Democracy* (Amherst, NY: Cambria Press, 2011).

8. See Michale X. Delli Carpini and Bruce A. Williams, "Constructing Public Opinion: The Uses of Fictional and Nonfictional Television in Conversations about the Environment," in The *Psychology of Political Communication*, edited by Ann N. Crigler (Ann Arbor, MI: University Michigan Press, 1996), p. 171; and R. Lance Holbert, "A Typology for the Study of Entertainment Television and Politics," *American Behavioral Scientist* 49, no. 3 (2005): 436–53.

9. Stanley Feldman and Lee Sigelman, "The Political Impact of Prime-Time Television: 'The Day After,'" *The Journal of Politics* 47, no. 2 (June 1985): 556–78.

10. Silvo Lenart and Kathleen McGraw, "America Watches 'Amerika': Television Docudrama and Political Attitudes," *The Journal of Politics* 51, no. 3 (August 1989): 697–712.

11. Mulligan and Habel, "The Implications of Fictional Media for Political Beliefs."

12. Lisa D. Butler, Cheryl Koopman, and Philip G. Zimbardo, "The Psychological Impact of Viewing the Film *JFK*": Emotions, Beliefs, and Political Behavioral Intentions," *Political Psychology* 16, no. 2 (1995): 237–57.

13. See Jody Baumgartner and Jonathan S. Morris "The Daily Show Effect: Candidate Evaluations, Efficacy, and American Youth," *American Politics Research* 34 (May 2006): 341–67; Lauren Guggenheim, Nojin Kwak, and Scott W. Campbell, "Nontraditional News Negativity: The Relationship of Entertaining Political News Use to Political Cynicism and Mistrust," *International Journal of Public Opinion Research* 23 (2011), 287–314.

14. Michael Pfau, Patricia Moy, and Erin Alison Szabo, "Influence of Prime-Time Television Programming on Perceptions of the Federal Government," *Mass Communication & Society* 4, no. 4 (2001): 437–53.

15. See Anthony Gierzynski and Kathryn Eddy, *Harry Potter and the Millennials: Research Methods and the Politics of the Muggle Generation* (New York: The Johns Hopkins University Press, 2013); Loris Vezzali, Sofia Stathi, Dino Giovannini, Dora Capozza and Elena Trifiletti, "The Greatest Magic of Harry Potter: Reducing Preju-

dice," *Journal of Applied Social Psychology* 45, no. 2 (2015): 105–21 and Diana C. Mutz, "Harry Potter and the Deadly Donald," *PS: Political Science and Politics* 49, no. 4 (October 2016): 722–29.

16. Markus Appel, "Fictional Narratives Cultivate Just-World Beliefs," *Journal of Communication* 58, no. 1 (2008): 62–83.

17. Kenneth Mulligan and Philip Habel, "An Experimental Test of the Effects of Fictional Framing on Attitudes," *Social Science Quarterly* 92 no. 1 (2011): 79–99.

18. Andrew R. Holbrook and Timothy G. Hill, "Agenda-Setting and Priming in Prime Time Television: Crime Dramas as Political Cues," *Political Communication* 22, no. 3 (2005): 277–95.

19. Michael D. Slater, Donna Rouner and Marilee Long, "Television Dramas and Support for Controversial Public Policies: Effects and Mechanisms," *Journal of Communication* 56 (2006) 235–52; and Diana C. Mutz and Lilach Nir, "Not Necessarily the News: Does Fictional Television Influence Real-World Policy Preferences?" *Mass Communication and Society*, 13 (2010): 196–217.

20. Charli Carpenter, "Rethinking the Political Science Fiction Nexus: Global Policy Making and the Campaign to Stop Killer Robots," *Perspectives on Politics* 14, no. 1 (2016): 53–69.

21. Calvert W. Jones, "It's the End of the World and They Know It: How Dystopian Fiction Shapes Political Attitudes," paper selected for presentation at the Southern Political Science Association Annual Meeting, San Juan, Puerto Rico, January 9, 2016.

Chapter 1

The Potentially Influential Political Content of Entertainment Media

The first step to understanding the power of entertainment media to influence political perspectives is to make visible the content of films, TV shows, books and games that has the potential to influence. The content that has the real potential to influence opinions is not the obviously political—not portrayal of ideologies, parties, and politicians or overt attempts to persuade audiences on an issue. Obvious attempts at persuasion along ideological or partisan lines are likely to activate audiences' predispositions, leading them to counterargue or be selective about what they take from such overt attempts at persuasion. Additionally, most entertainment media, even that which uses real world political settings, actually avoid, or are ambiguous about ideological labels and positions so as not to turn off audiences of one stripe or the other.[1]

The real potential for entertainment media to influence political perspectives lies in the politically relevant content that is not so obvious, not likely to be intentional on the part of the producers, and about which audiences may not be aware. As Gadi Wolfsfeld put it in his 2011 book *Making Sense of Media and Politics*, the most important media effects are unintentional and unnoticed.[2] Researching media effects in these unintentional and little noticed areas, as Wolfsfeld documented, has proved fruitful for scholars studying news media effects. It is in these areas of the unintentional and unnoticed that research on entertainment media is also likely to prove fruitful.

Beyond obvious ideological or partisan content of entertainment media, observers might be tempted to simply differentiate between what one might call "political entertainment" media and "pure entertainment" media, and look only for political effects in the former. Such a simple dichotomy, however, has its limits. For the purpose of discussion (and a convention I will use at times in this book), "political entertainment media" includes those books,

1

movies, and television shows set in the real political world and which focus
on the actions of politicians and public officials within political institutions.
This category would include shows such as *The West Wing, House of Cards,
Scandal, Veep,* or *The Newsroom,* movies like *Mr. Smith Goes to Washington,
The American President,* or *Bulworth.* Political entertainment media also includes those entertainment outlets that use(d) real politics for their material,
namely comedy shows such as *Full Frontal with Samantha Bee, The Daily
Show, The Colbert Report, The Nightly Show with Larry Wilmore,* and *Last
Week Tonight with John Oliver.* "Pure entertainment media" is typically a
broad category that includes all entertainment media that does not fall into
the political entertainment media category. This dichotomy is limited in its
usefulness for identifying politically relevant content because not all entertainment media fit nicely into these two categories. There are often elements
of politics in pure entertainment (stories, regardless of settings, often have
governments, leaders, institutions, etc., like the president in *Independence
Day* or the Center for Disease Control in *The Walking Dead*); and the plots
or subplots of political entertainment often involve, and sometimes focus on,
nonpolitical narratives (such as a romance, like that between Olivia Pope
and the president in *Scandal*). Recognizing that complexity, Holbert created
a nine-part typology of entertainment media based on the degree to which
audiences expect the content to be political and the degree to which the programs' political messages were explicitly political, with categories such as
fictional political dramas, political satire, and lifeworld content (what some
might call the pure entertainment category).[3] While that categorization serves
to give scholars a good broad overview map of the territory of entertainment
media, what we need to assist us in identifying potentially influential political
content is a more detailed guide (the street map within and across territories)
to steer the search for politically relevant content in any type of entertainment
media. In table 1.1, I propose such a guide.

In table 1.1, I divide political content found in entertainment media into
two areas—the *political* and the *politically relevant* content with examples
of both. The political content includes the content that on the surface is obviously political—characters that are politicians or leaders, settings that are
clearly political institutions, such as a deliberative legislative bodies, and issues, such as environmental degradation or the role of guns. It also includes
material on the fundamentals of politics—the role of government, ideology,
partisanship and the nature of political conflict. The "politically relevant"
content includes material that, while not always obviously political, has a
bearing on political views. This sort of content can usually be found in the
lessons that the stories teach as the narrative unfolds (like whether torture
works or whether doing the "right thing" is wise or foolish) and in the traits

Table 1.1.   Guide for Identifying Political Content of Entertainment Media

Political Content	• The nature of political conflict, the role of ideology and political parties
	• Hero storyline versus the role of government
	• Leaders/politicians
	   ◦ Engendering cynicism toward
	   ◦ Action-hero presidents
	   ◦ Stereotypes and the characteristics of "good" leaders
	• Institutions
	• Satire and parody of political discourse/modeling skepticism versus cynicism
	• Issues—agenda setting, priming and framing

Politically Relevant Content	• Lessons learned by characters (modeling) that have political implications
	   ◦ Tolerance and acceptance
	   ◦ Proper orientation toward authority (authoritarianism)
	   ◦ Treating others as equal
	   ◦ Use of deadly force and torture
	   ◦ "The only way to beat a bad guy with a gun is a good guy with a gun"
	   ◦ Doing the "right thing" and just world beliefs
	   ◦ Skepticism versus cynicism
	   ◦ Dangers of technology
	   ◦ Conspiracy Theories are True
	   ◦ The needs of the many versus the needs of the few, or the one
	• Lessons intrinsic to particular genres
	   ◦ Science fiction and fantasy: tolerance and diversity
	   ◦ Science fiction: the dangers of technology
	   ◦ Westerns: rugged individualism and the need to maintain order
	   ◦ Vampire: "sexual deviants," foreigners, and parasites
	   ◦ Zombie: mindless consumerism and obliteration of nonconformity

that characters exhibit (such as tolerance and respect for those who are different), which are either rewarded or punished. In the rest of this chapter I show how this guide can be used to uncover political content, both that which is in plain sight as well as that which can be found in the most unlikely places. Before I continue, however, it is important to take a moment to note that there are other scholarly disciplines whose researchers expend a great deal of effort on identifying the meaning of literature, film, and television. I do not adopt the work and models that they have produced because the task for the research presented here is a bit different from that which those scholars pursue. In investigating the potential political impact of entertainment, we do not need to know the author's intent, or the subtlety of meaning, the use of metaphors, and symbolism in fictional works and how that all creates distinct genres and subgenres. This is not to devalue such work, it is simply to say that what we need is a different sort of model to identify that content which has a potential to have a political influence through the lessons and perspectives that an audience can take away from the stories they consume.

THE POLITICAL CONTENT WITH THE POTENTIAL TO INFLUENCE

Returning to the framework for identifying the political content of entertainment media that has the potential to influence the public's views (table 1.1), I'll start by focusing on the political messages that grow out of the portrayal of politicians in fictional stories or in comedy shows. The real potential of such portrayals is not to engender sympathy or animosity for specific politicians or for sets of politicians from one party or ideological bent (such attitudes are unlikely to be altered by any form of media). The financial imperatives of the entertainment industry mean that most fictional stories on television or in film will shy away from party labels or ideologies (even while portraying historical figures) so as to avoid losing segments of their audience.[4] And again, even when sympathetic or derisive portrayals of politicians of one ideology appear (as they do in political comedy shows), the ability of most audiences to counterargue such content makes it less likely that stories or shows with such portrayals would change the partisan attitudes of their audiences (though, as Baumgartner and Morris show, it can increase the negative views of the specific politicians portrayed[5]).

The true potential in the portrayal of politicians, leaders, and political institutions in entertainment media lies in other areas that audiences may be unaware of and thus cannot counterargue. Take the fact that instead of promoting one ideology or party, most fictional political stories play down, ignore, oversimplify, avoid, and/or denigrate ideology and partisanship. A good illustration comes from the popular Netflix series, *House of Cards*, which portrays those who hold principled positions as weak or disingenuous. "Leave ideology to the armchair generals—it does me no good,"[6] Frank Underwood smirks to the camera after manipulating a liberal member of his party into handing over the management of an education bill to him. Does such a pervasive negative attitude about parties and ideology engender or enhance negative beliefs and feelings about these political tools that are so important for a functioning democracy? Does the fact that political conflict tends to be portrayed as good versus evil, right versus wrong, or one side motivated by greed or personal ambition versus the other side trying to "do what is right" shape our understanding of, and the way we engage in political conflict? Do the protagonists of fictional political stories who are devoid of that which defines real world political conflicts—the real differences in opinion over ideas and the values government should pursue—distort how we see politics? Do these portrayals have anything to do with the fact that political polarization in the US has gone from disagreements over ideas (a healthy form of polarization) to an unhealthy "villainification" of those with whom we disagree, to the point that partisans on one side see the other party as a threat to the nation's well-being?[7]

It is also all too common that movies, television shows, and books portray politicians and their motives in a negative way. Could this affect the public's level of trust in politicians and in the political system? The Frank Underwoods of fictional political worlds are unlikely to make audiences sympathetic or hostile to Democrats or liberals. The real effects of shows such as *House of Cards* will more likely be found in the fact that the charismatic lead character is a corrupt and scheming politician who denigrates ideology and partisanship as mere tools to his own self-centered ends. Such fictional political characters have the potential to either engender or reinforce audiences' cynicism about the character of those who serve in politics and the nature of the political system overall, encouraging people to drop out of the actual political process.

Another spinoff from the portrayal of politicians and leaders can be found in the ubiquitous plotline in which the problems at the heart of the narrative get solved by a heroic individual who arrives on the scene to save the day. The most compelling story line in any drama is this hero-centric one. Plotlines typically follow the formula: something goes wrong—a government becomes oppressive or dysfunctional, or war breaks out, or aliens invade, or environmental hazards sicken people, and so on—and someone (the hero[8] or "chosen one") steps forward to fight the oppressive regime, fix the dysfunction, win the war, defeat the aliens, or take down the polluting companies in court. Such plotlines are "teaching" us that problems are solved by individuals, a lesson that resonates with the "cult of the individual" dominant in US political culture.[9] As Delli Carpini and Williams argue, by "emphasizing individualism to the exclusion of collective or political action" these plotlines actually promote a conservative view on the role of government, which most audiences don't pick up on in a conscious manner.[10] The message of this stock narrative is that it is up to individual heroes to take things into their own hands because governments are either incompetent or corrupt. Indeed, many stories involve the protagonist having to deal with corrupt or incompetent governments that just impede the progress of the hero. Think of *The Dark Knight*, *Avatar*, and the *X-Men* series as illustrations of this plotline. The US political culture has long been one with a strong strain of individualism, but one has to wonder what impact the repeated individualistic storyline has on reinforcing this value and transmitting it to successive generations. Take the Millennial Generation, whose values are more liberal on almost every attitude than any generation alive today. The one exception is that they see little value in the role of government to pursue their liberal agenda.[11] Could this set of attitudes have somehow been shaped by the ubiquitous messages in our fiction regarding the futility of government as a positive force?[12]

The hero narrative structure that is common in both political entertainment and pure entertainment media also has implications for how we view our political leaders and whether we actually participate in the collective action of democracy or sit on the sidelines, waiting to cheer on the next individual who we believe will save the day. Barack Obama's powerful charisma and his arrival on the scene at the end of the disastrous Bush years could not have fit the heroic narrative better. Making vote choices based on expectations inherent in such thinking about leaders is a double-edged sword. While it can propel certain figures into office and give the public hope, it can also lead to disillusionment with government. Indeed, the disillusionment that set in shortly after Obama's inauguration in 2009, when the economy didn't miraculously turn around and peace break out all over, was undoubtedly due in part to the expectations created by our fictional stories. Recessions, wars, and the other problems that governments confront are not solved so easily as in the movies—they require negotiations with the other actors in the political system or internationally, compromise, and patience. The real work of politics and governance, which is like a long slog through a murky swamp, is just not exciting or simple enough for our stories (apparently not even so for the profit-ergo-entertainment-driven news media). Because problems in fictional worlds are easily fixed by the heroes (as opposed to the way it truly is), political entertainment leads us to a never-ending search for the next savior and engenders the unreasonable expectations we have for political leaders, which then leads to the disillusionment with politics that follows when those unreasonable expectations are not met.

The dominance of the individualistic storyline should not be surprising since stories by their nature focus on individuals. The need of storytellers to focus on individuals means that the source of problems that arise in stories are typically individuals, as well. Villains cause the troubles for the hero to address, not political institutions or systems. The story goes: bad people mess up the system and it takes a hero to come along, defeat the villain, and thus solve the problem. Ignored in these tales is the fact that, at least in the political realm, problems often arise due to flaws in the system, the political structure or institutions. This villain-as-culprit narrative feeds the view that all that is needed is the heroic individual to vanquish the villain(s) as opposed to institutional or systemic reform. There certainly seems to be little appetite among the bulk of the American public for addressing the real systemic/institutional problems in the US[13] with reforms to the system in the areas such as campaign finance or redistricting.

The nature of the individuals who play leaders and how they fare in our stories may also have a political effect. This is true whether the story is set in real world political systems or in purely fictional settings. How much have entertainment media portrayals of presidents shaped our expectations (role schema) of what a president is supposed to be like? Take the films that represent one of the few exceptions to the negative portrayal of politicians— the president-as-action-hero movies, such as *Independence Day*, *Air Force One*, *Abraham Lincoln: Vampire Hunter*, and *White House Down*. Do these fictional presidents in anyway influence the character traits we look for in real presidents? Research on the effect of *The West Wing* found that the show primed positive thoughts about the presidency, which carried over to attitudes about Presidents George H. W. Bush and Bill Clinton.[14] Is it possible then, as Manohla Dargis and A. O. Scott asserted in their *New York Times* article back in 2009, that "the presidencies of James Earl Jones in *The Man*, Morgan Freeman in *Deep Impact*, Chris Rock in *Head of State* and Dennis Haysbert in *24*, helped us imagine Mr. Obama's transformative breakthrough before it occurred" and "in a modest way, they also hastened its arrival"?[15] With regard to the 2016 election, could the portrayals of female presidents (or lack thereof) have had any impact on Hillary Clinton's fortunes? The TV series *Veep*, the rebel president in *The Hunger Games* series, and President Laura Roslin of *Battlestar Galactica* offer fascinating and contrasting possibilities. Or, could the stereotypically male traits exhibited by our fictional leaders shape our expectations about what traits are important in leaders in a way that puts women contending for executive positions at a disadvantage? We turn to a study of this possible effect in chapter 8.

So, while it is clear to audiences that they are consuming something political, the potential areas of influence from this form of entertainment go far beyond what most audience members may be alert to. In chapter 4 I report on a study that digs even deeper, looking at the various ways *House of Cards* influences its audience, including their sense of whether the world is just and their levels of cynicism about political institutions.

Speaking of cynicism, political entertainment includes more than just dramas based in real world political settings. It also includes comedies that use politics for their material. Jon Stewart and Stephen Colbert hosted popular shows that used the inanity of political discourse and the news media as fodder to keep their audiences entertained. Both have been accused of liberal bias, but, again, that is not the area where important media effects are likely. As Geoffrey Baym argued in his 2009 book *From Cronkite to Colbert*, both Stewart and Colbert model a form of skepticism that set them apart from the cynicism pervasive in the dominant postmodern news media outlets.[16] As Baym noted, Stewart hosted lengthy interviews that modeled a rational form of discourse with serious content in addition to the jokes. The discussions Stewart had with President Obama offer a prime example of this potential for rational discourse. The president during these lengthy interviews (even lengthier on the extended versions of the episode offered to viewers on the show's website) was able to lay out his view on the bigger picture of government and politics in a way that is just not allowed for in the actual "news" media.[17] Colbert, as Baym argued, parodied the irrational nature of public discourse in many of his segments, especially in "The Word" segment. Check out his first edition of "The Word," in which he coined the term "truthiness."[18] There isn't a better parody of the inane nature of political discourse in the US when it was aired, offering some insight on how we got to the age of Trump.

Additionally, both Stewart and Colbert devoted most of their attention mocking or parodying the postmodern news media. Research has demonstrated that audiences of *The Daily Show* and *Colbert Report* (henceforth *TDS* and *TCR*) were better informed, politically, than audiences of most other news outlets. The National Annenberg Election Survey found that those who regularly watched *TDS* had higher levels of campaign knowledge than national news viewers and even newspaper readers.[19] Further evidence of the important role *TDS* and *TCR* play in our political discourse appeared in a 2007 Pew Center Study—a greater percentage of *TDS* and *TCR* viewers scored as high or higher on a political knowledge test than regular viewers of any other television program, internet site, or newspaper.[20] How much of it is due to the structure and content of these shows? In chapter 7, I report on studies that my students and I conducted in an attempt to discern whether *TDS* and *TCR* audiences adopted a more skeptical (as opposed to cynical) approach to politics, government, and the media that Baym argues these shows modeled.

In a spin-off of *TDS*, John Oliver's *Last Week Tonight* models the same sort of skepticism as is evident on *TDS*, but adds another dimension by doing in-depth investigative pieces that are so rare in modern profit-conscious news media outlets. The pieces are around fifteen minutes long and include investigations that have delved into the tobacco industry's threats to nations regarding cigarette package warning labels, the misleading claim that state lottery money increases support for education, the inadequacies of maternity leave in the US, and blockchain currencies.

These investigative pieces include plenty of humor (usually in the form of outrageous metaphors), but the content and approach is journalistic. Because he is exploring issues that are typically under the radar of "serious" news media outlets, the potential for these pieces to affect its audience's awareness of problems (and have a possible agenda-setting effect) seems to be quite high.

The fact that entertainment media (overtly political or pure entertainment) often utilize issues as plot devices also opens up the door to other forms of political media effects. As discussed in the Introduction, more people have undoubtedly seen a multitude of scenes involving torture in fictional shows (which typically show torture working for the "good guys") than have read good journalism on the known inefficacy of the methods from experts. How do all those fictional instances of torture shape the public's understanding of the issue? Do the lessons the public learns from fictional torture scenes help to explain the public's reaction to the torture policies of the Bush administration or the statements of candidate Donald Trump on the matter?

The fact that Wayne Lapierre (the President of the National Rifle Association) was not publicly laughed off stage by his claim that "the only way to stop a bad guy with a gun is a good guy with a gun" is probably because that is how all the "bad guys" in American entertainment media are stopped (whereas, over the last thirty years of mass shootings, not one was prevented by a "good guy" with a gun). Indeed, it is ironic that the gun lobby likes to blame Hollywood for violence and the misuse of guns while much of what Hollywood produces could serve as a long running pro-gun commercial showing "good guys" with guns winning the day. When is the last time you saw a conflict solved in fictional narrative without a gun? It is rare. Perhaps superheroes who use their fists, a hammer, or spiderwebs. There is the Doctor, who often exhibits a disdain for guns, but, that is, perhaps, because he is a character created by British media (the BBC).

If you look, you can find political issues in almost any entertainment media outlet. Not only can these issues affect our understanding of the issues, but it is possible the use of issues in popular entertainment media could have an agenda-setting effect and, possibly, a priming effect.[21] The agenda-setting effect, put simply, is the way in which media mentions of certain issues elevate the importance of those issues in the public's mind. The priming effect is a dynamic in which those issues that are elevated by the media become *the* issues that we use to make political judgments. Researchers have uncovered some evidence of agenda-setting and priming effects for entertainment programs—Holbrook et al. found that exposure to crime dramas increased the salience of the issue of crime among audiences and increased the use of the issue to evaluate President Clinton.[22] An example of agenda setting in entertainment from the studies in this volume can be seen in the focus on jobs in the third season of *House of Cards* as President Underwood pursues his "America Works" program. In chapter 4 I report on research that shows how those who watched the third season of *House of Cards* were more likely to select jobs and the economy as the most important problem facing the US than those who hadn't seen the show or who hadn't seen the third season of the series. If this phenomenon made those people more likely to judge President Obama on the basis of how he is dealing with the issue of joblessness, that would be a priming effect.

Additionally, we know from the research on the news media that how an issue is framed—that is, what aspects of the issue are emphasized—can affect attitudes on the issue.[23] Taking the gun example from above, guns are almost universally portrayed as good in entertainment media, because they are presented in a guns-as-defense frame—the protagonist of action movies always seems to need a gun of some sort to defeat the villain. Whereas the reality is that guns are rarely used successfully in self-defense while the greatest number of deaths by guns in the US, by a wide margin, actually comes from suicides.[24] There is no reason to assume that framing effects that researchers have found due to news story frames would not also likely surface in entertainment media issue frames. And, indeed, there is one piece of research that provides evidence to support this assumption of framing effects for entertainment media: Mulligan and Habel's experimental study of the impact of the framing of the abortion issue in the movie *The Cider House Rules*.[25]

POLITICALLY RELEVANT
CONTENT IN ENTERTAINMENT

Moving the discussion to the bottom half of table 1.1, fictional narratives, no matter what the subject or setting, are likely to have *politically relevant* lessons that fictional characters learn, lessons we are likely to take away from the story, especially if we are transported by the narrative and/or identify with the characters. The nature of storytelling is such that the characters, as they move through the arc of a story, learn lessons from how the things that they do play out and from how they overcome obstacles in their story. In other words, the fictional worlds in which they exist teach the characters what they need to do to attain their goals. Many of these lessons involve values and attitudes—such as those related to prejudice, equality, political tolerance, authoritarianism, and just world beliefs—that have been demonstrated to affect other political values, political attitudes, ideology, and ultimately political behavior.[26]

Diversity and Political Tolerance

An example from the immensely popular *Harry Potter* series should serve to illustrate. Throughout the series Harry Potter exhibits a willingness to accept others who are different from him, even radically different—from the half-giant (Hagrid) who breaks down the door to take him to his first year at Hogwarts School of Witchcraft and Wizardry, to a werewolf teacher (Professor Lupin), to house elves (even nasty ones like Kreacher), and goblins (Griphook). In essence, Harry seems to hold no prejudices against others just because they are different. The villains who Harry and his friends fight in the story are just the opposite in this regard; they believe in the superiority of wizards and discriminate against, and attempt to dominate any who are not pure-blood wizards—from "mudbloods" to "muggles" to sentient magical creatures. As the narrative unfolds, these accepting and tolerant traits serve Harry well again and again (and the opposite proves true for the villains). For example, near the end of the tale Harry receives some critical assistance from a goblin named Griphook in the form of help breaking into the goblin-run wizarding bank (in whose vaults is a cup that contains a piece of the evil wizard Voldemort's soul that Harry and his friends must destroy in order to defeat Voldemort). Griphook's willingness to help is due in part to what he has witnessed of Harry's character (and also because Harry is willing to give the goblin-made Sword of Gryffindor to Griphook and the goblins). *later paying off.*

> "If there was a wizard of whom I would believe that they did not seek personal gain," said Griphook finally, "it would be you, Harry Potter. Goblins and elves are not used to the protection or the respect that you have shown this night. Not from wand-carriers."[27]

This tendency to accept those who are different (the opposite of prejudice) is politically relevant because it is strongly related to the willingness to extend political rights and freedoms to all, that is, a person's level of political tolerance.[28] The political impact of the politically relevant lesson develops when readers (or viewers) who identify with Harry and/or become transported by the story emulate Harry's level of acceptance of diversity, which, in turn, makes them more politically tolerant. In *Harry Potter and the Millennials*,[29] we showed that this is indeed what happened—fans of the *Harry Potter* series seem to have internalized this lesson on diversity and exhibited higher levels of political tolerance (a finding that has been backed up by additional experimental research[30]).

Not only does fiction offer lessons relevant to politics in the rewards and punishments dealt out to the characters of the stories, politically relevant lessons are also embedded in the very nature of certain genres. Take fantasy and science fiction. The conventions of these two genres generally include the idea that humans are not the only sentient beings. That notion, in of itself, has the potential to shape audiences' perspectives on diversity and political tolerance. Discrimination and intolerance have their roots in the definition of in-groups (my side) and out-groups (the others). What would happen if, all of a sudden, humans were confronted with a completely new species of intelligent/sentient life? Would such a discovery alter perceptions of the in-group and out-groups in such a way that all humans become the in-group and the other form of intelligent life the out-group, increasing acceptance of human diversity and reducing the conflict among humans? It is a given in most science fiction that we, humans are not alone in the universe (think *E.T.*, Klingons, Vulcans, Wookies, the alien in *Alien*, the Na'vi of *Avatar*, etc.) The same can be said for stories in the fantasy genre—elves, dwarves, wizards, talking animals, fairies, goblins, and succubae. What effect does exposure to this imagining that we, humans, are not alone have? Does it make us more accepting of those humans who are different and increase our levels of political tolerance?

It is worth noting here that recent research has uncovered some evidence of genre effects, albeit on other politically relevant attitudes. Calvert Jones's research on the "authoritarian-dystopian" science fiction genre showed that exposure to content unique to stories in this genre increased support for radical, even violent political action.[31] Charli Carpenter found evidence of science fiction shaping attitudes about autonomous weapons, or "killer robots."[32]

Other genres carry different sets of inherent messages. Classic westerns placed a great deal of value on rugged individualism and the need to maintain order, crime dramas usually involve law enforcement protecting victims from heinous criminals, coming-of-age movies always seem to involve rebellion against unreasonable authority, and so on.[33] In a *Cracked* article, S. Peter Davis pointed out a correlation between the popularity of the vampire and zombie genres with the party affiliation of the occupant of the White House—the vampire genre seems more popular during Democratic presidencies and the zombie genre during Republican presidencies.[34] Davis explains the correlation by arguing that the nature of each genre resonates in some way with the fears of partisans of the out-party. He argues that the vampire genre typically includes aspects that "horrify" Republicans— vampires are sexual deviants, foreigners, and parasites. The zombie genre includes aspects that "horrify" Democrats—zombies are mindless consumers and "are here to stamp out all nonconformists."

Authoritarianism

In addition to attitudes about diversity and tolerance, entertainment media is rife with other lessons and implicit messages that could lead audiences to alter beliefs, attitudes, and even values that are important to their overall political perspective. Back to the *Harry Potter* series—in *Harry Potter and the Millennials* we identified a number of politically relevant lessons in addition to acceptance of diversity and political tolerance. The *Harry Potter* series contains repeated lessons about the use of deadly force and torture, lessons about equality, and lessons about dealing with authorities that could influence subjects' levels of authoritarianism.

As was the case in the *Harry Potter* series, most narratives contain situations where the protagonists have to deal with someone in a position of authority. It could be a school principal like the principals in *Matilda*, *Ferris Bueller's Day Off*, or *Rock 'n' Roll High School*, or the head of a government, such as the president in *The West Wing* or *The Hunger Games*, the prime minister in *V for Vendetta*, *Doctor Who*, or *Love Actually*, congressional committees as in the Intelligence Committee in *Mission Impossible: Rogue Nation*, or police officers as in *NYPD Blue* or *Fargo*, or prison officers as in *Orange is the New Black* or *The Shawshank Redemption*, or military leaders as in any of the Star Trek series or *Top Gun*, or group leaders when there is no government structure around such as Rick and "The Governor" in *The Walking Dead* or Jack and John Locke in *Lost*. Not only do these fictional portrayals of authority model "right" and "wrong" types of leadership, they also offer lessons in what to do when confronted with different types of authority (as well as the social order those authorities enforce). The manner in which the interaction between the story protagonist and the story authority plays out teaches audiences about dealing with authorities and societal order and because of that offer lessons which can have important implications for a democracy.

Much of our entertainment is filled with protagonists who defy undemocratic/absolute authority and refuse to conform to an unreasonable societal order, a defiance that typically leads to the downfall of that authority and a change in the social order. Think of the fate of the school principals in *Matilda*, *Ferris Bueller's Day Off*, or *Rock 'n' Roll High School*, or the two presidents in *The Hunger Games*. Such portrayals of rebellion against unreasonable authority and defiance of a rigid societal order are common in our fictional stories and model a democratic response to authority. The opposite reaction to authority—an uncritical acceptance of authority and rigid social order characteristic of those disposed to authoritarianism—is usually found among the less desirable characters in our fictional narratives. Could fictional stories in which the protagonist defies unreasonable authority enhance democracy and protect us to some degree from authoritarianism? If so, the political impact of antiauthoritarian narratives on politics is obvious because authoritarianism is potentially dangerous to a democratic society. That danger was realized in the horrific fascist regimes that arose in Europe and Japan in the 1930s and is what motivated scholars in the US to determine why some people support such fascist regimes and are willing to conform to a social order that leads to extreme intolerance and genocide. Their research led to the identification of a personality type, the Authoritarian Personality.[35] In recent years, the research into this predisposition has been refined and improved by Karen Stenner and Stanley Feldman.[36] Stenner and Feldman conceived of the authoritarian dynamic as a product of a stable individual predisposition that is activated by fears engendered by political dissent and diversity, "moral decay," social disorder, and national decline.

> Authoritarian fears are alleviated by defense of the collective normative order: positive differentiation of the in-group, devaluation and discrimination against out-groups, obedience to authorities, conformity to rules and norms, and intolerance and punishment of those who fail to obey and conform.[37]

When such a dynamic is played out in fictional stories, the authoritarian types are typically portrayed in a negative light and that, as well as the protagonists' reactions to authoritarians, models a more democratic way of being. This is illustrated clearly in the *Harry Potter* series. In addition to fighting against the authoritarian types in the series—the Dursleys and Malfoys, Dolores Umbridge, and, of course, Voldemort—Harry, Ron, and Hermione, and the rest of the "good" characters in the books display characteristics that are the opposite of the authoritarian predisposition. The characters on the good side are open to new experiences, try different things, they do not fear the unusual or the different, and, are extremely tolerant and accepting of everyone, regardless of their bloodlines or outward appearances. And, there is some evidence that suggests that Millennials learned these lessons about authority. As reported in *Harry Potter and the Millennials*, fans of the *Harry Potter* series registered a lower predisposition to authoritarianism than those who were not fans (even when controlling for other known predictors of levels of the predisposition).[38] Stories I heard from fans reinforced this idea that antiauthoritarian lessons were picked up from exposure to the series. A good example is the story told by a Middlebury College student in the question-and-answer period of a talk I gave at her school in 2014. She related how her Texas high school had banned the *Harry Potter* books, but that she and her friends followed the lead of Harry and his friends and formed their own Dumbledore's Army to defy school authorities' ban on everything Potter.

Belief in a Just World

Another fascinating area of fictional stories is what they say about justice, whether the way the world works means that good people are rewarded and that bad people are punished (those who believe that good things happen to good people and bad things happen to bad people are said to hold what is known as a *belief in a just world*). Scholars have shown that a tendency to believe in a just world has political implications—those who believe the world is just are less likely to support government action to address societal ills and more likely to support harsh punitive approaches to dealing with those who do wrong.[39] And, one scholar has shown that consumption of fictional narratives, with their typical happy endings, is associated with a greater likelihood to believe the world is just.[40] In chapter 3 we examine the popular HBO show *Game of Thrones* to test the possibility that its brutal and unjust plotlines shake viewers' belief in a just world.

Fictional and Real World Villains

Fictional stories require conflict to make the story compelling, and conflict necessitates antagonists. The news, because it is now told to us in story form, also requires antagonists. Is it possible that the portraits of antagonists in former affect perceptions of, and attitudes toward those who are cast as antagonists in the later? And, when does the way entertainment media portray villains have any effects on levels of political tolerance?

In science fiction, fantasy and superhero genres antagonists are much more than just an adversary for the protagonists, they are some combination of extremely wicked, clever, powerful, egomaniacal, bloodthirsty and brutal villains. Villains in these genres come in many different forms and any story line may include a number of different villain types. There are the singular villains, like Sauron of *The Lord of the Rings* or Voldemort of the *Harry Potter* series, who are pure evil and whose single-minded purpose is domination and destruction. Then there are the individual villains who are painted in a more complex way, such as Magneto of the *X-Men*, whose experience in a World War II concentration camp drives his distrust of, and ultimately his preemptory violence against nonmutant humans. Villains also come in groups (Klingons, The First Order, Daleks, the Others in *Lost*) who may be either evil like Sauron (Daleks and the aliens in *Independence Day* would fit this category) or more complex (Klingons and the Others), motivated by concerns that while not justifying the villains' actions, may at least be understandable in some way. Sometimes the nature of a villain (or villains) evolves as the story progresses, usually going from one-dimensional evil characters to tragic figures or, at least, more complex characters, as we learn more about them. This is perhaps best illustrated by the tale of Darth Vader. Other examples include the Klingons of the *Star Trek* universe and the Cylons of the universe of *Battlestar Galactica*. In surveying the nature of villains in science fiction, fantasy, and superhero stories, it seems that villains can be categorized based on three dimensions—whether they are singular villains or a group, whether the villains are portrayed as simply pure evil or more complex, and, finally, based on that which motivates the villain(s).

To assess the frequency of the types of villains in science fiction, fantasy, and superhero genres, some of my students[41] and I identified and categorized the top villains in the most popular books, movies, television shows, and video games in these genres.[42] The results can be found in figures 1.1 and 1.2. As figure 1.1 indicates, most villains come in individual form and those are equally split between being pure evil and complex villains. Group villains tend to be portrayed as more complex. By far the most common motivation for villains was power, followed by destruction, greed, and ideology (see figure 1.2).

Clearly, fans of these genres are exposed to a variety of villain types. If they subconsciously draw on fictional models to understand antagonists in the real world, then the fictional will certainly have an impact on the real. Taking this a step farther, if fictional villains affect how we understand real world "villains," then it is possible to see how fiction can affect attitudes regarding government policies to combat real world "villains," as well as how much tolerance we have for real world antagonists. Does exposure to pure evil villains make audiences more likely to support harsh and punitive approaches to dealing with real world bad guys and be more intolerant of out-groups? In chapter 7 we look into this question and report on research that examined the impact of villain portrayals on attitudes about fighting terrorism and criminal justice.

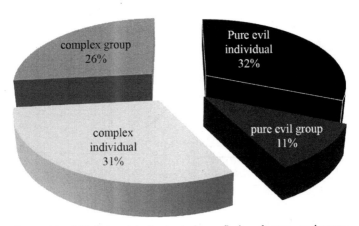

Figure 1.1.   Villain types in the top science fiction, fantasy, and super-hero books, movies, television shows, and video games. n = 105.

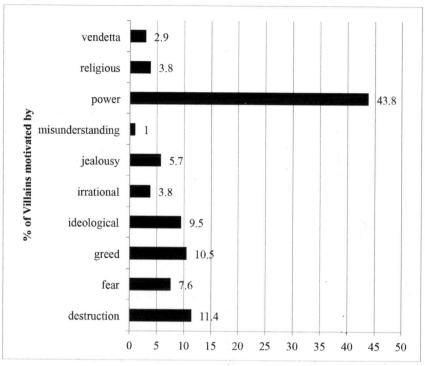

Figure 1.2. Villain motivation in the top science fiction, fantasy, and superhero books, movies, television shows, and video games.

Science and Technology

While the genre of science fiction has allowed us to imagine the seemingly impossible, out to the edges of space-time, it also typically offers a cautionary tale of the dangers of technology. Indeed, a subgenre of science fiction, dystopian science fiction, usually involves technology run amok in some way. In these stories, the artificial intelligence we create rises up and destroy us (such as in the works of Isaac Asimov, *2001: A Space Odyssey*, *Battlestar Galactica*, and the *Terminator* movies) or we use technology to ruin our future and/or destroy ourselves (nukes in the original *Planet of the Apes* movies, an experimental drug in the newer version; viruses in *Twelve Monkeys*; the direct wiring of the internet in our brains that makes us mindless consumers in the book *Feed*; science gone awry in zombie movies, etc.), or ruin other races/planets (*Avatar*). Even in more optimistic tales of the genre, humans are often endangered by technology. In what is one of, if not *the* most optimistic imagined futures of science fiction, the *Star Trek* shows and movies, humans have rebounded after World War III nearly destroys the planet. In the second installment of the series, *Star Trek: The Next Generation*, one of the biggest challenges the crew of the Enterprise must confront is an alien race called the "Borg," a species which is a hybrid of human and machine, in which individuality is extinguished in a hive-like collective (each Borg "drone" is plugged into the collective), and whose goal is to assimilate (and effectively destroy) all other species to add their biological and technological distinctiveness to the Borg collective. In what is probably the other most optimistic science fiction series—the BBC's *Doctor Who* series—the Doctor confronts similar technology-gone-awry races such as the Daleks and the Cybermen.

Whether it is a component of the main plotline or just appears in various episodes, fans of science fiction are likely to be exposed repeatedly to such morality lessons about the dangers of technology. Now, early in the twenty-first century, there are a myriad of government policies dealing with technology, from the space program, to the development of military technology (drones and "killer robots"), from issues of privacy in the cybernetic world to cyber warfare, to government financing for, and regulation of, research in genetics and artificial intelligence. Is it possible that the lessons from science fiction affect our positions on technology and these sort of policies in a way that could shape public policy on the subject and, ultimately, future scientific advances? There is at least one piece of research that suggests it does;[43] in chapter 5, I report on a study my students and I ran that provides some additional evidence of such an effect.

Conflict Resolution: The Use of Deadly Force

Conflict is an essential ingredient in all stories. How the protagonists in stories resolve that conflict naturally tells us something about how conflicts are to be resolved. The *Harry Potter* series and *Doctor Who* stand out as different from most stories in that the protagonists of these stories attempt to resolve conflict without the use of deadly force. Harry repeatedly refuses to use the killing curse, *Avada Kedavra*, even when confronting Voldemort (he uses a disarming curse instead). This resistance to using deadly force was echoed in the attitudes of Millennials who were fans of the series.[44] The Doctor typically outsmarts the villains as a way to resolve story conflicts, his only "weapon" a sonic screwdriver. Contrast these forms of conflict resolution with the way conflicts are resolved in much of the rest of our entertainment media. It usually comes down to violent conflict, with the hero killing off the villain. There are variations in this and it might be useful to think of stories fitting on a continuum of the use of deadly force to resolve the conflict. Sometimes the antagonists are portrayed as unredeemable villains, and we, the audience, can see no other solution than killing them (how often have you whispered under your breath "kill the bastard" while immersed in such a story?). Sometimes the protagonists simply capture the villain(s) after varying amounts of violence. Sometimes the protagonists try to negotiate, but oftentimes negotiation is portrayed as a failure that puts the protagonists at a disadvantage when the inevitable violence breaks out. All, however, feature violence of some sort. Add these fictional lessons to the news media coverage of war versus their coverage of peace negotiations[45] and one has to wonder what impact this all has on public attitudes about war and diplomacy.

The costs associated with violent conflict are also portrayed along a continuum. At one end of the continuum the toll of violence and death are vividly shown to be high and portrayed gruesomely as in the "Battle of the Bastards" episode of *Game of Thrones* or the movie *Saving Private Ryan*; at the other end the costs and horror are not portrayed. Do the different portrayals of the toll war takes have any effect on support for military solutions?

Torture

Scenes of torture are common in entertainment media. While the TV show *24* is probably the most prominent example, scenes of torture abound in many places and in a variety of ways. It shows up in light-hearted ways, such as in *Shrek* when Lord Farquaad takes apart the Gingerbread Man. It can be the heroes being tortured, as happened to James Bond in *Casino Royale*, or Harry Potter forced to carve "I must not tell lies" onto the back of his hand with a magical pen, or Captain Picard when captured by the Cardassians. These torture scenes almost universally play out in ways that suggest that torture is an efficacious tactic to extract needed information from the villains, while the heroes successfully resist. The portrayal of torture as effective is contrary to the bulk of real world evidence and does not include any consideration of the blowback from the use of such tactics.[46] Given the public's media consumption patterns and their failure to seek out good journalistic pieces on torture, the ratio of fictional torture scenes viewed by the public to the number of serious news analyses of the tactic in the real world consumed by the public is undoubtedly tilted overwhelmingly in favor of the fictions of torture. What role does this sort of repeated exposure to misleading portrayals of torture have in the formation of the public's opinion about torture and support or opposition to the use of tactics like waterboarding?

Conspiracy Theories

Conspiracies are a great plot device. The notion that there are secret sinister machinations behind the scenes, that things aren't what they seem, that reality is hidden from us, makes for a compelling story and is often a springboard to plots that send fictional heroes on their quests to reveal the truth and free us from the illusions and those who manipulate us. Because of that, fictional stories are rife with conspiracies and hidden realities or truths. This plot device is the very foundation of fictional movies like *Fight Club, The Matrix*, the *Men in Black* series, *Wag the Dog, Captain America: The Winter Soldier, Capricorn One, JFK, 24*, and *The Manchurian Candidate* as well as TV shows like *Burn Notice, The X-Files*, and *The Prisoner*. The conspiracy plot device is also used as a less-central device in many other fictional narratives, often as a subplot. Season 6 of *Doctor Who*, for example, contains a running subplot that the world has been controlled by a secret alien race, The Silence. The Silence have the psychic ability to make anyone immediately forget that they have seen members of The Silence, so the group can remain in the shadows keeping people from ever knowing of their presence or their manipulations. Multiple examples of the use of conspiracy theories can be found in the *Law & Order* series. A cursory review of fictional narratives will lead one to uncover many additional examples of the use of conspiracies as a plot device and, as a result, many heroes who are, in effect, conspiracy theorists.

In the real world, conspiracy theories and the mode of thinking that leads to belief in conspiracy theories is problematic for a democracy. Such thinking inhibits our understanding of political systems, policy making, and historical events and figures by engendering a deep cynicism about knowledge and the sources of knowledge. Conspiracy theory thinking leads many to dismiss information that might contradict their political beliefs or their understanding of how the world operates. This is because a fundamental principle of all conspiracy theories is the belief that the truth is being covered up and is inaccessible to all but true believers of the theory (and these theories *do* require faith since reason and evidence are irrelevant). This notion that the truth is hidden intentionally from us allows believers to dismiss any evidence that contradicts the conspiracy theory, often claiming such evidence is a ruse perpetuated by those who are secretly in control, designed to throw us off the trail that would lead to the "truth." Evidence from any source, no matter the source's expertise or track record, is dismissed as part of the conspiracy, part of the cover up. Evidence that purportedly supports the theory is valued above all other evidence no matter how much of that contradictory evidence exists. Conspiracies also offer a simplistic way to understand the complexity of the world—political and otherwise. They boil down complex systems into a single determinant cause and are thus easier to understand. This is not unlike the way ancient cultures used gods to explain natural world phenomena. Furthermore, conspiracy thinking breeds more conspiracies—it is a habit of thinking and dealing with evidence that leaves one without any means to discern what is real in and what is not.

While humans have long been prone to conspiracy thinking,[47] one needs only to do a simple search of the internet (or listen to Trump[48]) to discover how popular conspiracy theories are. Listing the classic ones, like the JFK assassination, claims that the moon landing was fabricated, that the government controls the weather, to more modern ones such as the claim that the George W. Bush administration was behind the attacks of September 11, only skims the surface of the body of conspiracy theories people believe in the twenty-first century. The popularity of conspiracy theories and the willingness of segments of the population to believe them is clearly reflected in our popular entertainment media, even spawning TV and radio shows that purport to examine conspiracy theories while actually promoting them. The question for my purpose here is, how much of a role does the fictional world have in shaping the real world tendency to believe conspiracy theories? The public is clearly bombarded with conspiracy theories throughout their journeys in popular fictional worlds and have plenty of heroes who are conspiracy theorists with whom they can identify. Does this make us, or at least segments of the population, more susceptible to conspiracy theory peddlers? Does this fascination in fiction with secret worlds and secret plots reinforce and promote the human penchant to look for scapegoats and simple explanations in their complex world that are the hallmark of conspiracy theories? Research on the impact of overtly political entertainment—the movies *Wag the Dog* and *JFK*—has shown that these political dramas affect belief in conspiracy theories and participation in politics.[49] The question as to whether these findings extend more broadly to other pure entertainment media outlets remains for future research.

CONCLUSION

At this point the reader should have a good sense of how much politically relevant content pervades our fictional stories. The cataloguing of such content could continue and fill up this entire book, but that is not my purpose here. My purpose in going over this politically relevant content was to illustrate how the framework in this chapter can assist in identifying the types of political content that are most likely to affect public opinion, and to lay down the foundation of the research into the effects of specific content I present later in this book. Now it is time to move on to the discussion of why we should expect any of this content to have an actual and significant impact on the political perspectives of those who are exposed to such stories.

NOTES

1. Elizabeth Haas, Terry Christensen, and Peter J. Haas, *Projecting Politics: Political Messages in American Films*, second edition (New York: Routledge, 2015).

2. Gadi Wolfsfeld, *Making Sense of Media and Politics: Five Principles in Political Communication* (New York: Routledge, 2011).

3. R. Lance Holbert, "A Typology for the Study of Entertainment Television and Politics," *American Behavioral Scientist* 49, no. 3 (2005): 436–53.

4. Haas, Christensen, and Haas, *Projecting Politics*.

5. Jody Baumgartner and Jonathan S. Morris, "The Daily Show Effect: Candidate Evaluations, Efficacy, and American Youth," *American Politics Research* 34 (May 2006): 341–67.

6. *House of Cards*, season 1, episode 1.

7. Pew Research Center, "Political Polarization in the American Public: How Increasing Ideological Uniformity and Partisan Antipathy Affect Politics, Compromise and Everyday Life," June 12, 2014, accessed July 23, 2015 from http://www.people-press.org/2014/06/12/political-polarization-in-the-american-public/.

8. I will use the term "hero" in a gender-neutral way throughout the book.

9. For a discussion of this theme in American films, see Daniel P. Franklin, *Politics and Film: The Political Culture of Television and Movies* (New York: Rowman & Littlefield, 2017).

10. Michale X. Delli Carpini and Bruce A. Williams, "Constructing Public Opinion: The Uses of Fictional and Nonfictional Television in Conversations about the Environment," in The *Psychology of Political Communication*, edited by Ann N. Crigler (Ann Arbor, MI: University of Michigan Press, 1996), p. 171.

11. See the research on Millennials by the Pew Research Center.

12. For an interesting piece in which the author makes this argument with regard to the *Harry Potter* series, see Benjamin H. Barton, "Harry Potter and the Half-Crazed Bureaucracy," *University of Michigan Law Review* 104 (2006): 1523–38.

13. For a discussion of the systemic problems in US elections see Anthony Gierzynski, *Saving American Elections: A Diagnosis and Prescription for a Healthier Democracy* (Amherst, NY: Cambria Press, 2011).

14. R. Lance Holbert, Owen Pillion, David A. Tschida, Greg G. Armfield, Kelly Kinder, Kristin L. Cherry, and Amy R. Daulton, "*The West Wing* as an Endorsement of the American Presidency: Expanding the Domain of Priming in Political Communications," *Journal of Communications* 53 (September 2003): 427–43.

15. Manohla Dargis and A. O. Scott, "How the Movies Made a President," *New York Times*, January 16, 2009, accessed July 21, 2015, http://www.nytimes.com/2009/01/18/movies/18darg.html.

16. Geoffrey Baym, *From Cronkite to Colbert: The Evolution of Broadcast News* (New York: Oxford University Press, 2009).

17. See his July 21, 2015 appearance, http://thedailyshow.cc.com/full-episodes/skawjk/july-21—2015—-barack-obama, (accessed July 23, 2015), and his October 18, 2012 interview at http://thedailyshow.cc.com/extended-interviews/w2pk0y/barack-obama-extended-interview (accessed July 23, 2015).

18. Originally aired October 17, 2005, accessed June 16, 2017, http://www.cc.com/video-clips/63ite2/the-colbert-report-the-word—-truthiness.

19. Annenberg Public Policy Center, "*Daily Show* Viewers Knowledgeable About Presidential Campaign, National Annenberg Election Survey Shows" (Philadelphia, PA: Annenberg Public Policy Center, 2004).

20. Pew Research Center for the People & the Press, "Public Knowledge of Current Affairs Little Changed by News and Information Revolutions: What Americans Know: 1989–2007," April 15, 2007, http://people-press.org/reports/display .php3?ReportID=319, accessed May 30, 2007.

21. For a discussion of and research on these effects, see Shanto Iyengar and Donald R. Kinder, *News that Matters: Television and American Opinion* (Chicago: University of Chicago Press, 1987).

22. Andrew R. Holbrook and Timothy G. Hill, "Agenda-Setting and Priming in Prime Time Television: Crime Dramas as Political Cues," *Political Communication* 22, no. 3 (2005): 277–95.

23. See Shanto Iyengar, *Is Anyone Responsible? How Television Frames Political Issues* (Chicago: University of Chicago Press, 1991); and, for an overview of framing, see Dennis Chong and James N. Druckman, "Framing Theory," *Annual Review of Political Science* 10 (2007): 103–26.

24. Margaret Sanger-Katz, "Gun Deaths are Mostly Suicides," *The Upshot*, October 8, 2015, accessed June 16, 2017, https://www.nytimes.com/2015/10/09/upshot/ gun-deaths-are-mostly-suicides.html.

25. Kenneth Mulligan and Philip Habel, "An Experimental Test of the Effects of Fictional Framing on Attitudes," *Social Science Quarterly* 92, no. 1 (2011): 79–99.

26. Instead of citing all of the research supporting the relationships between these politically relevant views and political views, I will note the research connecting the politically relevant and political beliefs/behavior throughout the book when dealing separately with each politically relevant view.

27. Rowling, *Harry Potter and the Deathly Hallows* (New York: Scholastic, Inc, 2007), 488–89.

28. See John L. Sullivan, James Piereson, and George E. Marcus, *Political Tolerance and American Democracy* (Chicago: University of Chicago Press, 1993).

29. Anthony Gierzynski and Kathryn Eddy, *Harry Potter and the Millennials: Research Methods and the Politics of the Muggle Generation* (New York: The Johns Hopkins University Press, 2013).

30. See Loris Vezzali, Sofia Stathi, Dino Giovannini, Dora Capozza and Elena Trifiletti, "The greatest magic of Harry Potter: Reducing prejudice," *Journal of Applied Social Psychology* 45, no. 2 (2015): 105–21.

31. Calvert W. Jones, "It's the End of the World and They Know It: How Dystopian Fiction Shapes Political Attitudes," paper selected for presentation at the Southern Political Science Association Annual Meeting, San Juan, Puerto Rico, January 9, 2016.

32. Charli Carpenter, "Rethinking the Political Science Fiction Nexus: Global Policy Making and the Campaign to Stop Killer Robots," *Perspectives on Politics* 14, no. 1 (2016): 53–69.

33. See Robert Savage, "The Stuff of Politics through Cinematic Imagery: An Economic Perspective," in Robert Savage and Dan Nimmo (editors) *Politics in Familiar Contexts*.

34. S. Peter Davis, "6 Mind-Blowing Ways Zombies and Vampires Explain America," *Cracked*, September 6, 2011, accessed September 14, 2015 http://www .cracked.com/article_19402_6-mind-blowing-ways-zombies-vampires-explain -america_p2.html.

35. Theodor Adorno, Else Frenkel-Brunswik, Daniel J. Levinson, and R. Nevitt Sanford, *The Authoritarian Personality* (New York: Harper & Row, 1950).

36. See Stanley Feldman and Karen Stenner, "Perceived Threat and Authoritarianism," *Political Psychology* 18 (1997): 741–70; and Karen Stenner, *The Authoritarian Dynamic*.

37. Karen Stenner, *The Authoritarian Dynamic* (Cambridge: Cambridge University Press, 2005), 33.

38. We used the measure of the predisposition developed by Stenner and Feldman; see Gierzynski and Eddy, *Harry Potter and the Millennials* for more details.

39. Zick Rubin and Letitia Anne Peplau, "Who Believes in a Just World," *Journal of Social Issues* 31 (1975): 65–89; Lauren D. Appelbaum, Mary Clare Lennon and J. Lawrence Aber, "When Effort Is Threatening: The Influence of the Belief in a Just World on Americans' Attitudes toward Antipoverty," *Political Psychology* 27, no. 3 (2006): 387–402; Vicky M Wilkins and Jeffrey B. Wenger, "Belief in a Just World and Attitudes Toward Affirmative Action," *Policy Studies Journal* 42 (2014): 325–43.

40. Markus Appel, "Fictional Narratives Cultivate Just-World Beliefs," *Journal of Communication* 58 (2008): 1, 62–83.

41. This study was developed with Gierzynski's "Film, TV and Public Opinion" (POLS237) University of Vermont class in the fall 2012 semester; students in the class who contributed to the development and implementation of this project were Jake Brudney, Antonia David, Mitchell Hansen, Kevin Kennedy, Frederick Knight, Eric Schwarzbach, Sarah Simmons, David Thal, and Erik Tidmon.

42. For movies we choose the top seven grossing films in each genres using box office receipts from IMDB.com, for television shows we used the top seven televisions shows in each genre using IGN's ranking of the top fifty science fiction shows, for books we selected the top five from each genre based on book sales, and, finally we used the top five of the best-selling video games.

43. Carpenter, "Rethinking the Political Science Fiction Nexus."

44. See Gierzynski and Eddy, *Harry Potter and the Millennials*.

45. See Gadi Wolfsfeld, *Making Sense of Media and Politics*.

46. For a review of the research on torture see Mark A. Costanzo and Ellen Gerrity, "The Effects and Effectiveness of Using Torture as an Interrogation Device: Using Research to Inform the Policy Debate," *Social Issues and Policy Review* 3, no. 1 (2009): 179–210.

47. See Joseph E. Uscinski and Joseph M. Parent, *American Conspiracy Theories* (Oxford: Oxford University Press, 2014); and, Richard Hofstadter's 1964 article "The Paranoid Style in American Politics" in *Harpers*, accessed September 28, 2016, http://harpers.org/archive/1964/11/the-paranoid-style-in-american-politics/.

48. Charles Homans, "The Conspiracy Theorists' Election," *New York Times Magazine*, September 27, 2016.

49. See Kenneth Mulligan and Philip Habel, "The Implications of Fictional Media for Political Beliefs," *American Politics Research* 41, no. 1 (2013): 122–46; and Lisa D. Butler, Cheryl Koopman, and Philip G. Zimbardo, "The Psychological Impact of Viewing the Film *JFK*: Emotions, Beliefs, and Political Behavioral Intentions," *Political Psychology* 16, no. 2 (1995): 237–57.

Chapter 2

The How and When of Entertainment Media Effects

Consider the previous chapter as the answer to the "what" question of entertainment media effects. In this chapter I address the how and when of those effects. To start, no one expects the political content of entertainment media to be internalized in the simplistic way in which exposure equals influence. Nor does anyone think that people intentionally learn from fiction or that everyone acquires politically relevant views in line with the entertainment media they consume in every instance. As scholars who study media know, media effects are much subtler and more complex than that. This chapter is dedicated to explaining those subtle and complex paths from entertainment media content to political beliefs, laying out the reasoning as to why fiction is more than "just a story" when it comes to political learning. The explanation contains two components: one, the mental processes through which people acquire political views from entertainment, that is, the "how," and, two the conditions under which this sort of political learning occurs, or the "when."

THE HOW:
NARRATIVE TRANSPORTATION
THEORY AND IDENTIFICATION

The reasoning that leads me to hypothesize that entertainment can shape political perspectives starts with the wealth of evidence from a number of disciplines that demonstrates that the acquisition of political beliefs is not a rational process. It is not the simple process that most assume goes on in political learning—the acquisition, assessment and storage of information arranged in a coherent political worldview. That's not to say that we don't learn that way sometimes, but research that models how we process overt attempts at persuasion, such as the Elaboration Likelihood Model (ELM), the Cognitive-Transactional Model, and Learning Models, have all demonstrated that there are pathways to the development of political views that are not conscious and/or direct, such as the peripheral route (in the ELM) and passive learning.[1] The fact that most people do not approach entertainment thinking that the stories that they enjoy are attempts at persuasion means that the direct or active routes to learning spelled out in these models are not relevant to what happens when we are being entertained and immerse ourselves in a story. That is, we do not enter into a story thinking we will learn something, we are doing it to be entertained. Furthermore, research on our states of mind when we are following stories (as opposed to following an argument) demonstrates that even the peripheral or passive processes that are modeled in these dual-process models of persuasion and learning don't exactly capture how the mind works when we are immersed in stories or narratives.[2] Research in psychology has shown that when we are being entertained by stories something qualitatively different is going on than when we process rhetoric or overt attempts at persuasion (either directly or peripherally).[3] Neuroscientists have even found that fiction and reality engage different parts of the brain.[4] These research findings have led to the development of a theory that explains the unique ways the mind works when audiences are enjoying stories.[5] The theory is the theory of narrative transportation (formally known as the Transportation-Imagery Model), which was developed by Gerrig,[6] empirically verified first in a series of experiments by Green and Brock,[7] and supported by subsequent research.[8] It is this theory that provides us with the best insights into how it is that we end up acquiring political perspectives from the imaginary worlds with which we entertain ourselves. Once acquired from stories while in the state of narrative transportation, other models—such as the Cognitive-Transactional Model, attitude theory, attribution theory, value acquisition theories such as political socialization—are of value to map out how the internalized beliefs from fictional worlds interact with perspectives acquired from other processes and manifest themselves in current political opinions and behavior.

When we follow a story—whether in print, on TV, in a video game, a streamed video or a movie in a theater—we can become immersed in the story in ways that take us away from our physical environment and mental state. In other words, the narrative transports us away from our world and into the world of the story. This "transportation," it is argued, is a "unique subjective state characterized by deep focus on a narrative."[9] In the state of narrative transportation the reader/viewer/player is engaged in imaginative imagery within their minds, becomes emotionally attached to the characters and the world of the story, accepts the story's reality, and loses awareness of the real world. To get a sense of the nature of the state of transportation, think about your own responses to stories and you will likely find personal evidence of narrative transportation. Have you ever yelled "watch out" to a character on the screen or cheered when a villain is killed? Or physically reacted to a fear (like a fear of heights or spiders) that is activated by the story? Have you felt anxiety regarding the outcome of a story, even when you know what will happen? Or, have you found yourself thinking of ways to change the fate of the characters or the outcome of the story while watching or reading? These phenomenon—labeled participatory responses, anomalous suspense, and anomalous replotting by Gerrig—should give you an indication of the nature of the state of transportation.[10] It is not a rational state. In the transported state, you have left the real world behind—including the known facts that are stored in your mind (such as, I can't possibly fall off that imagined drilling platform in orbit around Vulcan, I cannot actually prevent President Lincoln from being assassinated, etc.)—and you react as though you are truly in the world of the story.

Narrative transportation has been demonstrated to lead to belief change through a number of processes, the combination of which, scholars argue, make attitude change via transportation even more likely than through persuasion or rhetoric.[11] Because stories evoke often powerful emotional responses and can create emotional connections to characters, narrative transportation can impact attitudes through affective responses to story messages. Think of how emotionally attached you get to certain book series, television shows, or movies. Many people go so far as to emulate their favorite story characters by dressing as the character (in what is known as cosplay), often carrying it beyond just wearing the costume, to behavior and attitudes. During the 2004 presidential election, for example, a group of people who dress and talk like Klingons from the *Star Trek* series endorsed John Kerry because his opponent, George W. Bush, had "no honor" (for those who don't know the series, honor is of utmost import to Klingons).[12] Additionally, the fan communities that are built up around certain stories—*Harry Potter*, *Star Wars*, *Star Trek*—show how powerful those attachments can be and how fans find a lot of different ways to revisit the worlds of the stories they enjoy. Such revisiting fictional worlds can now include playing video games based on the stories or visits to theme parks built based on these fictional worlds, such as Universal Studio's Wizarding World of *Harry Potter* and Paramount's forthcoming *Star Trek* theme park. Such strong affect and continued emersion in those fictional worlds facilitates the acquisition of the perspectives of the stories and the emulation of the behavior of the characters.

The strong focus on the events of a story, the primacy of emotional reactions, the state of enjoyment, and the focus on imagery that are characteristic of transportation, all mean that there is little motivation, and few cognitive resources to devote to counterarguing or negative cognitive responding to the messages of the story. Think of the last time you were really enjoying a movie, book or television show and said to yourself "no, that's not possible." So, not only is it true that people are unaware of a great deal of the politically relevant content of entertainment as discussed in the previous chapter, but even if they do notice political content, people are highly unlikely to question the lessons, values exhibited, or even basic facts incorporated into the story plots when transported. With one's cognitive defenses down, such messages in fictional stories are more likely to be internalized.

The mental imagery that is a component of narrative transportation (whether mentally generated while reading or imprinted in one's mind while watching) can also have a powerful and lasting effect, not only evoking emotions while immersed in the narrative but "may also re-evoke story themes and messages when recalled."[13] This phenomenon, along with people's tendency to retain the content and forget the source of information they have acquired can result in what scholars call a "sleeper effect" for content learned from fictional stories. Researchers testing this sleeper effect have actually found that this dynamic means that the persuasive effects of fiction increase over time.[14] Additionally, the imagery aspect of transportation (images conjured while reading or exposed to when consuming visual entertainment) may be more resistant to verbal counterarguing than rhetoric because of the mental status of images—it is hard to argue with a visual. A good illustration of this, used by a number of those who have written about narrative transportation, is the ability of the fear-evoking power of the visual imagery of the movie *Jaws* to overwhelm the factual evidence regarding the rarity of shark attacks for most ocean swimmers.

Finally, the concrete and specific nature of narratives makes it difficult to argue against their conclusions even if we thought to do so. Think of the conclusions about the justice system that are inherent in crime shows like *Law & Order* and *The Wire* or the vigilante need to take justice in your own hands that is at the heart of *Daredevil, Jessica Jones*, or any number of entries in the superhero genre. These stories offer fictional portrayals of aspects of our world that are very real and substantial to us while we are in a transported state, whether it be the functioning of institutions like courts, the police, or jails, or cause-and-effect lessons, such as failed criminal justice institutions that make vigilantism necessary.

In short, stories transport us to another world where we are open to (oftentimes new) perspectives and ideas that are then driven home and retained thanks to the powerful conventions of storytelling—the evocative imagery, concreteness of the events, and emotional engagement. Altogether, this makes fictional stories a powerful driver of how we see the world around us in ways that we are unaware of and that have important implications for our politics.

In addition to these characteristics of transportation that suggest a powerful effect for stories, a companion process, "identification," provides another reason to expect that exposure to stories could lead to belief change. When one identifies with a character in a narrative, they come to see the events of the story from the perspective of that character.[15] Identification "involves losing track of one's own identity and then subsequently adopting the character's goals and perspectives as one's own."[16] Identification makes it even more likely that when we exit a narrative we will come away from it with altered perspectives. One of the reasons that the *Harry Potter* series had such a powerful impact on the Millennial Generation was that the main characters of the books were the same age as the target audience of the books. The characters grew at a pace with the fans (as did the complexity of the story and the reading level of the books). Harry, Hermione, Ron and the rest of the Hogwarts students in the narrative were dealing with many of the same issues/problems of growing up as were the readers. The parallel timing of the growth of the readers and characters made it almost inevitable that the young fans would identify strongly with the characters of the books. One only needs to refer to media accounts of how many Millennials dressed as characters for the series when attending the releases of each successive book. Those Millennials saw themselves in the characters and adopted some of the characters' values in the process.

Not surprisingly, then, a body of research has demonstrated the power of narrative transportation and identification to encourage the internalization of story messages, adopt values, evoke belief change, and even accept false facts.[17] The empirically verified psychological processes described in the Transportation-Imagery Model and in the dynamic that occurs when we identify with characters thus provides us with the explanation of the process that takes place when the values and lessons of stories and the characters become adopted by audiences. It is a process that most people are unaware of, which makes it an even more powerful avenue of learning politically relevant views.

Those things that are acquire in this process—whether it be facts (true or otherwise), values (how one should act in this world and what goals or end-states are preferred), emotional attachments, beliefs, and ways of thinking—then become part of a person's belief system. How they then manifest themselves in terms of political perspectives and behavior can be explained by other theories developed by psychologists, anthropologists, sociologists, and political scientists. To illustrate, suppose a person's notions of authority are modified (or reinforced) by being transported by a story where the protagonists challenge and defy arbitrary exercise of authority and the demands to conform to a dominant view of society promoted by that authority. This could happen with fans of Katniss of the *Hunger Games* series or, as I demonstrated in a previous book, fans of Harry Potter and his friends. The audiences of these stories learn the lessons and adopt the values of the characters coming away from the story being less predisposed to authoritarianism. As Karen Stenner's work shows, this then leads the individuals to be less likely to be caught in the authoritarian dynamic. That is, when perceived threats to the social order occur, those who are less predisposed to authoritarianism, thanks in part to the lessons they learned from the stories they have been transported by, would be less likely to fall into the dynamic of differentiating between in- and out-groups, and the corresponding increase in intolerance toward out-groups. Thus, transportation theory explains how the story modifies the belief, the authoritarian dynamic theory explains how the acquired belief is then manifest in political views and behavior, in this case prejudice or political intolerance.

For another example, suppose a person acquires some new information about how Congress operates from being transported by the first season of *House of Cards*. Cognitive-Transactional Theory (or schema theory) can then explain how that new information is stored in a person's schema and drawn upon in other situations. When asked how much they trust Congress or are deciding how to vote (or not to vote) in an election, the most readily accessible exemplar may just be the Congress of the *House of Cards* world as opposed to some other source, say CSPAN coverage. Or, imagine a person's sense of how much justice there is in the world is modified by watching the endless string of injustices perpetrated by characters in the first five seasons of *Game of Thrones*. This reduced level of just world belief then, as the research shows, manifests itself in higher support for government programs to address the real injustices in society.[18] In summary, Narrative Transportation theory shows how the ideas get into the public's belief systems, other theories can then show how these beliefs manifest themselves and become politically important.

THE WHEN

While the mental states of narrative transportation and identification show us the mechanics of *how* entertainment media can influence our perspectives, the extant research on the development of political views tells us that it is also important to consider *when* learning from entertainment media is likely to happen. That is to say, entertainment media's political effects do not happen all the time or in the same way to everyone. *When* it is likely to happen and *to whom* depends on the status of three different dimensions of media effects: the individual, group, and cultural dimensions. Briefly, within the individual dimension, the potential for entertainment to shape one's political values and beliefs varies depending in large part on a person's age, the personality of an individual, and the presence of other influences. Within the group dimension, the impact of entertainment media on politics will vary depending on whether one is part of social groups that influence access to media and the extent to which social groups can block media messages the group finds undesirable. And, finally, the character of the broader culture will make the internalization of certain perspectives more or less likely depending on the state of the culture—its level of homogeneity, its technological development, and its openness to change.

Individual Dimension

We are more (or less) likely to acquire political values and perspectives from fiction and entertainment depending on our personality traits and the stage of political socialization we are going through. Research on personality indicates that "there is something intrinsic in each of us, largely present at birth, that defines who and what we are, and shapes how we behave,"[19] that is, our personality. Personality is an internal psychological structure that can be defined by a number of traits—such as, openness to experience, conscientiousness, extroversion, agreeableness, and emotional stability.[20] Personality as reflected in these traits is not an absolute determinant of political perspectives or behavior, but plays an important role in shaping how we interact with other environmental influences on the development of political perspectives. Take how open a person is to different experiences. Such a trait likely effects the types of entertainment that a person chooses; though, other environmental factors also play a role, such as the shows/movies/books that friends are watching and talking about. So, when theorizing about entertainment media effects it is important to take into consideration the role of personality traits in both the exposure to the types of entertainment and the interaction between relevant traits and the messages of the stories. In the research on the Harry Potter effect we did consider that exposing oneself to a fantasy series with wizards and witches and other fantastic beasts required a certain amount of openness to experience. So, we included a measure of openness to experience in the empirical model to test whether fans of the *Harry Potter* series were different because they were just those who were open to experience or whether the series had an independent impact on political views such as authoritarianism. We found exposure to the *Harry Potter* series was inversely related to the authoritarian predisposition independently of this trait.[21]

While research shows that personality is set early in life arising from biological factors, I can't help but believe that the stories that we are exposed to early in life also play some role in encouraging (or depressing) the development of these traits. One only needs to read through children's books and watch children's shows to see the repetition of lessons related to some of these traits, like conscientiousness, openness to experience, or agreeableness. Take Eric Carle's *The Very Grouchy Ladybug* and the trait of agreeableness, for example, or Doctor Seuss's *Green Eggs and Ham* or *The Cat in the Hat* and openness to experience (or indeed all Seuss's [Geisel's] wonderful and silly worlds). Most characters in children's stories are conscientious in some way, like *Thomas the Tank Engine*. Additionally, the extent to which one is read stories or exposed to stories in shows and movies, regardless of the content of those stories, must have some role in the development of openness to experience. Being transported by stories, after all, is one of the main avenues in one's early years for new experiences.

Political socialization—a theory about how we acquire the values and beliefs of our political culture—posits that we learn different types of perspectives at different times of life and that there are certain times when people are more politically malleable—namely, adolescence and the formative years (late teens, early adulthood).[22] Core values (beliefs about the proper modes of behavior and desired end-states of existence) are developed early on in life, largely from the dominant role models in one's life—parents, siblings, friends, grade school teachers, authority figures, and, yes, fictional characters. In adolescence and into the formative years, when a person's cognitive capabilities grow to allow for the abstract thinking necessary for the development of political views, adolescents and young adults will re-examine the values they've acquired in the context of the political environment of the times to construct their own belief system.[23] Consequently, the time of adolescence and the formative years are periods during a person's life when messages and role models regarding values and other political perspectives could prove very influential. And, there is no reason that those messages cannot come from entertainment or that the role models cannot be fictional characters with which one identifies, such as Harry Potter. It was the fact that a large segment of the Millennial Generation was continually being transported by the *Harry Potter* series throughout their adolescence and formative years that made me theorize that the series likely had an impact on that generation's political orientations.[24]

The acquisition of political perspectives from one's political culture, or political socialization, continues throughout a person's lifecycle and entertainment media is there throughout it. While one's core values may solidify by adulthood, those values are not set in stone. That said, it is unlikely entertainment media could engender fundamental changes in values later in adulthood unless it is part of broader changes in a person's culture or social grouping. Aside from those core values though, entertainment media may play a role by shifting beliefs and attitudes that are less central to an individual's belief system but still politically important, or by adding facts or altering basic understandings of history and reality.[25] Take the belief in a just world, for example, a belief that has been demonstrated to have very real political effects.[26] While the extent to which you believe the world is just—that good things happen to good people and bad things happen to bad people—is shaped by a number of factors throughout your life including personal experience and religious beliefs, it is possible for that belief to shift and for entertainment media stories to play a role in that change. After all, aren't many stories morality plays about what happens to characters who do, or do not do the right thing? Or tales of why things go so wrong for some people? In chapter 3 I show how exposure to *Game of Thrones*—a show that so powerfully contradicts this belief and general trend in the culture—is capable of affecting people's sense of how just the world is. Or, for another example, consider people's views about what makes a good leader or president. What traits do people associate with good leadership? Is it possible that the portrayal of leaders in fictional stories, including presidents, shape the traits that we associate with successful leadership? Those who consume a lot of entertainment probably witness more cases of fictional leadership than real world cases. What implications might this have for the types of candidates we support? Chapter 8 explores just such a dynamic. For more such examples of the various content of entertainment that could shape political beliefs, I refer you back to the previous chapter. In short, during the adult years entertainment media effects may take a number of different forms. Fictional stories may add information to a person's schema or attitudes; stories may alter attitudes and beliefs on a short-term or long-term basis depending on the level of reinforcement; or the content of stories may interact with existing views in ways that research on media effects have demonstrated have political consequences—by enhancing the salience of certain issues or perspectives in decision-making (the priming effect)[27] or by framing issues in a particular way.[28]

In sum, when considering the role of entertainment media in the way the public sees politics it is important to be aware that the timing of exposure to political perspectives affects the sort of perspectives an individual will acquire. Fundamental political values and beliefs are most likely to be affected by entertainment media in the early years of political socialization and during the adolescent and formative years. Other, less fundamental perspectives may potentially be affected throughout the lifecycle.

In addition to considering the human lifecycle when hypothesizing about entertainment media's political effects, it is important to take into account the presence or absence of other potential sources of politically relevant perspectives—agents of political socialization—at the time of exposure to fictional messages. Agents of socialization are individuals, institutions, and the media that transmit cultural values from one generation to the next.[29] Parents tend to be the most influential of these agents, though research has demonstrated that peers, schools, communities, and media play a role, too.[30] The cluster of political socialization agents surrounding an individual can vary in its character from one in which all the agents tend to share similar outlooks to one in which the agents have a diverse set of perspectives.

Individuals who are socialized in an environment that is homogeneous—one in which one's parents, friends, community, school, and media exposure share the same values—will be greatly influenced by those agents who continually reinforce each other, until and unless alternative perspectives are somehow introduced to the individual. One may think that entertainment media would play mainly a reinforcing effect in this circumstance, which is not to say that such effects are unimportant. Beliefs and values that have been reinforced by multiple agents are more likely to guide future behavior and resist change.[31] Such socialization environments, however, do not completely prevent change. In such circumstances fictional stories may have a good chance to influence an individual because they are not obviously political and the politically relevant content is not obvious. So, with the exception of zealously closed groups, alternative perspectives are unlikely to be completely filtered out by the other agents (see the discussion of the group dimension below for more on this). The easy access afforded by the media technology of the twenty-first century makes the filtering out of media messages in entertainment even more difficult.

Thus, due to the nature of entertainment media and our approach to it, entertainment can have an effect even in homogeneous political socialization environments, acting as a Trojan horse in our political socialization, carrying alternative values and perspectives into the transported individual's belief system in ways that have the potential to alter one's beliefs or draw out a part of a person's personality. My personal political history includes one such example. I grew up in an environment in which authority figures were to be honored and deferred to, and in which absolute reverence given to religious beliefs. Somehow I ended up with the opposite views. How? While all my socialization agents were similar with regard to this orientation, some of the entertainment I consumed was not. *Saturday Night Live*, *Monty Python*, and *M*A*S*H* (the first two of which my brother, Gene, and I watched without our parents' knowledge because they would not allow us to watch a show that "made fun of the president") were the opposite with regard to this value—they were highly irreverent when it came to authority and cultural institutions. As there was no other similar source, I can only conclude that my irreverent disposition and regular defiance of authority (and my taste for shows that exhibit such irreverence today, like *South Park*) has its origins in large part in those late nights watching *SNL*, *Monty Python* and those episodes of *M*A*S*H*.

For individuals whose political socialization is characterized by a more diverse set of perspectives the path from entertainment media to belief system is a bit different. In these situations, entertainment media is one of many competing agents and thus its influence will depend on how connected the individual is to those other agents versus their connection to fictional worlds and characters, or, the level and frequency of transportation and identification. Parents, siblings, friends, and teachers may introduce the individual to certain entertainment media resulting in a reinforcement effect, but only if the recommendations are somehow based on the politics of the entertainment as opposed to other reasons, like wanting a child to learn to enjoy reading or because all of an individual's friends are talking about a show. And, again, as discussed in the Introduction, the politically relevant content of fictional stories is usually not evident.

So, fictional stories have the potential to influence the politics of people who have been socialized in homogeneous environments or in heterogeneous environments with transportation and identification making such influence possible in both situations. In homogeneous environments entertainment may introduce unique perspectives which adoption will depend on the level of transportation and identification engendered by the stories; and, in heterogeneous socialization environments entertainment competes with a diverse set of agents of socialization, which, in this case as well, will be more or less influential depending on the extent to which an individual is transported by the stories and identifies with the characters.

Group Dimension

Individuals do not exist independent of social groupings—religious, political, racial, lifestyle—within society. So, in order to accurately theorize about when entertainment media is likely to have an effect on beliefs we need to understand when group membership and identity affects the types of entertainment media consumed and its effects. In his essay, "Reinforcing Spirals," Michael Slater mapped out the interaction between social groups, media exposure, and media effects in a way that applies to entertainment media as well as news media.[32] With regard to social group membership and media choices, Slater proposes that:

> In general, those individuals who identify with a given set of religious, ideological, or lifestyle beliefs and values (i.e., a shared group or communal identity) will have certain preferred media outlets, and will selectively attend to content that reflects and shares the values of that social identity group.[33]

Furthermore, not only will some groups have preferred media outlets, but they will also vary with regard to the extent that they attempt to manage exposure to media whose messages are not congruent with the values of the group—labeled exposure avoidance—by the outright banning of certain media, by engendering suspicion of media incongruent with their beliefs, and/or by creating their own media. Some groups maintain a more closed media environment for their members through these techniques, other groups are more open. Fundamentalist religious movements, for example, represent a type of group that is most likely to maintain closed media systems.

The closed versus open nature of a group media system has some obvious, and perhaps not-so-obvious implications for theorizing when entertainment media may have an effect on beliefs. The obvious being that relatively closed group media system will block, or at least attempt to block, exposure to fictional stories that don't conform to the group's existing beliefs. A good example of this is the reaction of some fundamentalist Christian groups to the *Harry Potter* series. Those fundamentalist Christian groups encouraged parents and schools to block access to the *Harry Potter* series because of the central role of magic in the books and the positive portrayal of witches and wizards, which the fundamentalist Christians believed to be evil. But, the filtering out or blocking of messages contrary to a group's values can never be absolute for a number of reasons. For one, as argued throughout this book, the politically relevant content of entertainment and its effects are not always obvious. For another, modern media technology makes the closing off of alternative perspectives nearly impossible—access to the internet, handheld devices, etc., open up the world to individuals in ways that weren't possible in the past and in ways which cannot be completely controlled. And, finally, some media become so popular and well-known that it overwhelms all groups' defenses. The story of the student from Texas related earlier illustrated this nicely. The student and her friends got copies of the *Harry Potter* series despite the books being banned by their high school, and formed their own "Dumbledore's Army" (in the series this was a group of students who rebelled against the authoritarian control of their Hogwarts education in the defense against the dark arts) to actively thwart the school's ban on all things Potter. In this case, the *Potter* series was just too popular in the overall culture and easy enough to gain access to, to allow the Christian groups to successfully implement exposure avoidance to it.

In short, entertainment media effects will be more likely to happen when one's exposure to media is not manipulated—through outright bans, the creation of culture of suspicion, and/or alternative media—by the social, religious, or cultural groups to which one belongs. When technology allows easy access to entertainment—through streaming video, eBooks, and information about entertainment media—group control of the content of media viewed by its members is weakened. It is important to note that there is some evidence that social media (mainly Facebook) may be narrowing exposure to perspectives that exist outside of one's social groups, but this applies mainly to overtly political media and is unlikely to apply to popular entertainment. Entertainment media do have an advantage over more explicitly political media because the fact that it is not overtly political makes it less likely that group will flag it and block exposure to it. Applying the same metaphor I used for those who are socialized in homogeneous environments, entertainment media can be seen in these circumstances as a political Trojan horse, introducing new ideas and perspectives, getting through group defenses in a way that overtly political media cannot. Finally, the subculture of any group can never be fully isolated from the greater influences of the broader culture, which come, in part, from entertainment media.

Cultural Dimension

A culture is comprised of a shared set of values and beliefs. Those values and beliefs will permeate the stories that members of a culture compose for each other. As a consequence, one will find in stories of a culture similar lessons promoting a common set of values or perspectives. In the US culture in the twenty-first century, for example, common politically relevant themes that are repeated in story after story include: the notion that the best way to beat a bad guy with a gun is a good guy with a gun; that problems are solved by the arrival of a heroic individual; that criminals are heinous, evil individuals who deserve death; that torture works; that the world is just; that effective leaders are the ones who exhibit what are mostly stereotypical male traits; and, that those who may be different from us still deserve respect and political tolerance. Stories include these common themes in part because of storytelling conventions (these storylines are most engaging), but more importantly because such stories will resonate with beliefs that already exist in a culture.[34] The ubiquity and repetition of such messages increases the odds that members of a culture will acquire the values and perspectives contained within the stories of a culture. This notion is at the heart of the media effects theories such as the Cumulative Effects Model and Cultivation Theory, which argue that when the stories that we tell ourselves—in books, television shows, and movies—share common messages, it is likely that followers of those stories will internalize the ideas imbedded in the stories' messages.[35] Stories with common cultural themes and values resonate with members of the culture, transmit cultural beliefs from one generation to the next, and act to reinforce the beliefs throughout the culture. In this way, entertainment media act as an agent of socialization, transmitting cultural perspectives through the values and beliefs that are conveyed through story lessons and modeled by story characters.

But cultural values change over time, and entertainment media can play a role in fostering and even leading cultural change as well. Fictional stories may pick up on a thread of cultural values that exist in only some segments of the population and make those values popular through the story's own popularity. As other stories pick up on and spread the theme larger segments of the population may adopt those new values and the culture may change. The point here is that entertainment media not only reinforce existing values in a culture, but also play a role in spreading new perspectives that can lead to changes in the culture. That is, media, including and perhaps most especially entertainment media, are agents of cultural change. So, when looking for entertainment media effects, it may prove most productive to look for emerging trends in a culture and study the effect of the entertainment media that are promoting such trends in their narratives. It is at these times that entertainment media may be found to affect perspectives held by the audience and give a hint at cultural shifts that may come. The mechanism for such cultural shifts will be the formation of new generations that form out of age cohorts uniquely socialized by these entertainment-media-magnified trends in the culture,[36] which takes us back to the potentially important role of entertainment media during individuals' formative years of political socialization as discussed above.

Because media technologies determine the extent to which fictional stories are spread and cut across cultural boundaries, they too help to determine when entertainment media will have an effect on any given culture. Indeed, when media technology allowed Hollywood to widely disseminate US-created movies and television shows, concerns were raised in other countries about US cultural hegemony and the erosion of other cultures throughout the world.[37] Thanks to the technologies that have more recently emerged, blockbuster movies, television shows, and popular books are now most likely to be worldwide phenomena that cut across cultures. And, while US production still dominates, that production is often done in collaboration with artists, producers, and facilities, in other countries—such as *District 9*, large parts of which were made in South Africa—or even produced mainly in other nations, such as *The Lord of the Rings* movies which were filmed and produced in New Zealand. Furthermore, the economic imperatives of the entertainment industry, with large markets such as China playing a big role in box office receipts, mean that entertainment is produced with an eye toward appealing to audiences of different cultures around the world. As entertainment media is globalized along these lines, avenues for the dissemination of new perspectives and values open up in cultures around the world, including the US.

CONCLUSION

As the material in this chapter suggests, our political selves are ultimately a product of a mix of influences that interact with our basic personality traits to form our own cluster of perspectives, values, beliefs, and attitudes that comprise the foundation of our politics. The purpose of this chapter, and, indeed, the entire book, is to show that those fictional stories we read for fun, or watch at the cinema, or stream on our smart televisions, etc., play an important (and perhaps increasingly important) part of our political development. The unique state of mind that occurs when we are transported by stories and identify with characters makes fictional stories (perhaps especially those most disconnected from our current reality, such as fantasy and science fiction) a more potent agent of political learning than overt attempts to teach politically relevant values. The circumstances under which individuals are more or less susceptible to acquiring new perspectives through transportation and identification vary depending on their individual state or the state of the groups and cultures to which they belong. All of this, in combination with the discussion of how to identify politically relevant content in the previous chapter, gives us a map that tells us where to look for entertainment media effects on the development of perspectives that shape our political selves.

NOTES

1. For a good summary of these theories and the supporting research, see Elizabeth Perse, *Media Effects and Society* (Mahwah, NJ: Lawrence Erlbaum Associates, Inc, 2001).

2. Markus Appel and Tobias Richter, "Persuasive Effects of Fictional Narratives Increase over Time," *Media Psychology* 10 (2007): 113–34.

3. See Richard Gerrig, *Experiencing Narrative Worlds: On the Psychological Activities of Reading* (New Haven, CT: Yale University Press, 1993); and Melanie C. Green and Timothy C. Brock, "In the Mind's Eye: Transportation-Imagery Model of Narrative Persuasion," in *Narrative Impact: Social and Cognitive Foundations*, eds. Melanie C. Green, Jeffrey J. Strange, and Timothy C. Brock, (Mahwah, NJ: Lawrence Erlbaum Associates, Inc., 2002), 315–41.

4. Anna Abraham, D. Yves von Cramon, and Ricarda I. Schubotz, "Meeting George Bush Versus Meeting Cinderella: The Neural Response When Telling Apart What is Real from What is Fictional in the Context of our Reality," *Journal of Cognitive Neuroscience* 20, no. 6 (2008): 965–76.

5. While I focus on the Transportation-Imagery Model, it is important to note the contribution of Gamson's theoretical work on "lifeworld content" effects that identifies a similar state of mind as that in transportation theory (see William A. Gamson, "Policy Discourse and the Language of the Life-World," in *Eigenwilligkeit und*

Rationalität sozialer Prozesse, J. Gerhards, Hitzler R. editors (Opladen, Germany, 1999), 127–44.

6. Gerrig, *Experiencing Narrative Worlds.*

7. Melanie C. Green and Timothy C. Brock, "The Role of Transportation in the Persuasiveness of Public Narratives," *Journal of Personality and Social Psychology* 79, no. 5 (2000): 701–21.

8. For a meta-analysis of the extant research on narrative transportation see Tom Van Laer, Ko de Ruyter, Luca M. Visconti, and Martin Wetzels, "The Extended Transportation-Imagery Model: A Meta-Analysis of the Antecedents and Consequences of Consumers' Narrative Transportation," *Journal of Consumer Research* 40, no. 5 (February 2014): 797–817. For a summary of the theory and research see Jordan M. Carpenter and Melanie C. Green, "Flying with Icarus: Narrative Transportation and the Persuasiveness of Entertainment," in *The Psychology of Entertainment Media: Blurring the Lines Between Entertainment and Persuasion*, edited by L. J. Shrum (New York: Routledge, 2012).

9. Carpenter and Green, "Flying with Icarus," p. 170.

10. Gerrig, *Experiencing Narrative Worlds.*

11. Appel and Richter, "Persuasive Effects of Fictional Narratives Increase over Time," Carpenter and Green, "Flying with Icarus."

12. "Klingons Commit to Kerry," *Blogcritics Magazine,* September 29, 2004, accessed June 14, 2017, http://blogcritics.org/klingons-commit-to-kerry/.

13. Carpenter and Green, "Flying with Icarus," p. 175.

14. Appel and Richter, "Persuasive Effects of Fictional Narratives Increase Over Time."

15. Keith Oatley, "Emotions and the Story Worlds of Fiction," in *Narrative Impact: Social and Cognitive Foundations*, eds. Melanie C. Green, Jeffrey J. Strange, and Timothy C. Brock (Mahwah, NJ: Lawrence Erlbaum Associates, Inc., 2002), 39–69.

16. Carpenter and Green, "Flying with Icarus," p. 181.

17. For a summary of this research, see Carpenter and Green, "Flying with Icarus"; also see Appel and Richter, "Persuasive effects of fictional narratives increase over time."

18. Zick Rubin and Letitia Anne Peplau, "Who Believes in a Just World," *Journal of Social Issues* 31 (1975): 65–89; and Lauren D. Appelbaum, Mary Clare Lennon, and J. Lawrence Aber, "When Effort Is Threatening: The Influence of the Belief in a Just World on Americans' Attitudes toward Antipoverty," *Political Psychology* 27, no. 3 (June 2006): 387–402.

19. Jeffery J. Mondak, *Personality and the Foundations of Political Behavior* (New York: Cambridge University Press, 2010), p. 20.

20. These are the traits of the "big five" model and are the ones used by Mondak in his research.

21. Anthony Gierzynski and Kathryn Eddy, *Harry Potter and the Millennials: Research Methods and the Politics of the Muggle Generation* (New York: The Johns Hopkins University Press, 2013).

22. Richard E. Dawson, Kenneth Prewitt, and Karen S. Dawson, *Political Socialization*, second edition (Boston: Little, Brown and Company, 1977).

23. M. Kent Jennings and Richard G. Niemi, *The Political Character of Adolescence: The Influence of Families and Schools* (Princeton, NJ: Princeton University Press, 1974).

24. Gierzynski and Eddy, *Harry Potter and the Millennials.*

25. See Carpenter and Green, "Flying with Icarus."

26. See, for example, Lauren D. Appelbaum, Mary Clare Lennon and J. Lawrence Aber, "When Effort Is Threatening: The Influence of the Belief in a Just World on Americans' Attitudes Toward Antipoverty," *Political Psychology* 27, no. 3 (June 2006): 387–402.

27. Andrew R. Holbrook and Timothy G. Hill, "Agenda-Setting and Priming in Prime Time Television: Crime Dramas as Political Cues," *Political Communication* 22, no. 3 (2005): 277–95.

28. Kenneth Mulligan and Philip Habel, "An Experimental Test of the Effects of Fictional Framing on Attitudes," *Social Science Quarterly* 92, no. 1 (2011): 79–99.

29. Dawson, Prewitt, and Dawson, *Political Socialization.*

30. M. Kent Jennings and Richard G. Niemi, "The Transmission of Political Values from Parent to Child," *American Political Science Review* 62, no. 1 (March 1968): 169–84; M. Kent Jennings, Laura Stoker, and Jake Bowers, "Politics across Generations: Family Transmission Reexamined," *Journal of Politics* 71, no. 3 (July 2009): 782–89.

31. Michael D. Slater, "Reinforcing Spirals: The Mutual Influence of Media Selectivity and Media Effects and Their Impact on Individual Behavior and Social Identity," *Communications Theory* 17 (2007): 281–303.

32. Slater, "Reinforcing Spirals."

33. Slater, "Reinforcing Spirals," p. 290.

34. For an extended discussion on the relationship between culture and entertainment media with a focus on film, see Daniel P. Franklin, *Politics and Film: The Political Culture of Television and Movies* (New York: Rowman & Littlefield, 2017).

35. George Gerbner, Larry Gross, Michael Morgan, and Nancy Signorielli, "Growing Up with Television: Cultivation Processes," in *Media Effects: Advances in Theory and Research* second edition, eds. J. Bryant and D. Zillmann (Hillsdale, NJ: Lawrence Erlbaum Associates, 2002), 43–68. For a summary of this literature in the context of entertainment media, see L. J. Shrum and Jaehoon Lee, "The Stories TV Tells: How Fictional TV Narratives Shape Normative Perceptions and Personal Values," in *The Psychology of Entertainment Media: Blurring the Lines Between Entertainment and Persuasion*, edited by L. J. Shrum (New York: Routledge, 2012), 147–67.

36. For a good discussion of media and generation formation see Goran Bolin, *Media Generations: Experience, Identity and Mediatised Social Change* (New York: Routledge, 2017).

37. For a discussion of this see Jack Lule, *Globalization and Media: Global Village of Babel*, second edition (Lanham, MD: The Rowman & Littlefield Publishing Group, 2015).

Chapter 3

Game of Thrones and the Belief in a Just World

When we are transported by stories[1] that share common messages, messages that are repeated across media and within narratives, there is a good chance that we will internalize the ideas imbedded in the stories' messages.[2] Stories come to share common messages because of storytelling conventions and because the messages reflect beliefs that already exist in a culture;[3] as such, the stories resonate with members of the culture, transmit the cultural beliefs from one generation to the next, and act to reinforce the beliefs throughout the culture. What happens then when stories containing messages contrary to those dominant in the culture become popular? Can those stories alter the previously held cultural belief among those who are exposed to, and become transported by the stories? To address that question, this chapter focuses on a highly popular television show—HBO's *Game of Thrones*—testing whether the show's defiance of the typical just world story outcome affects its audience's level of belief in a just world. Referring back to the previous chapter, this chapter tests for entertainment media effects arising from narrative transportation (the *how*) *when* messages in popular entertainment contradict the messages dominant in the culture.

The cultural belief common to fictional stories that is the primary focus of this chapter is the politically relevant belief in a just world (BJW), a belief that we "live in a world where people generally get what they deserve."[4] This belief allows individuals to make attributions of responsibility for adverse social outcomes in ways that alleviate the discomfort of being confronted with victims of abuse, crime, economic conditions, war, and other conditions that put individuals in need of help. The just world belief is in many ways a dynamic (not unlike the authoritarian dynamic as described by Stenner[5]) in which people's tendency to believe in a just world has its consequences when

it is activated by being confronted with victims of injustice whose suffering
they cannot alleviate. Those who are more likely to believe in a just world
have been found to be more likely to derogate the victims of injustice in order
to alleviate the psychological discomfort engendered by being a witness to
suffering they can do nothing about.[6] If something bad happens to someone,
the just world thinking goes, they must have deserved it in some way. Adopting that line of thinking reassures the individual that such misfortune is not
likely to happen to them. In other words, "[t]he belief that the world is just
enables the individual to confront his physical and social environment as
though they were stable and orderly."[7] Since this belief deals with perspectives on justice, people's level of belief in a just world has political implications. Researchers have shown that the degree to which one believes that
world is just affects a number of political attitudes, including attitudes toward
redistributive policies, feelings toward the poor, affirmative action, general
conservatism, authoritarianism, and social activism.[8]

   Evidence that entertainment media have a tendency to promote and reinforce
the belief that the world is just was found by Appel.[9] Appel's research findings
should not be surprising given the fact that most fictional stories take place in
just worlds—the good "guy"[10] always wins out in the end, the evil, corrupt, and
self-serving are punished or destroyed, those with honorable and good qualities,
who work hard and persevere, win the day. It is the core of the fairy-tale happy
ending that is the stock in trade of almost all of our modern narratives, regardless of the twists and turns that the plot takes. If one follows the news of the real
world, it is clear that most of our stories do not reflect the real world when it
comes to justice. Indeed, in two separate studies in Germany and Austria, Appel
found that those who watched entertainment TV were more likely to subscribe
to the belief in a just world than those who watched TV news.[11]

   For most of us the stories we wish to enjoy for entertainment represent
an escape from the real world, and research has shown that people are more
likely to enjoy (and thus watch) stories with just outcomes.[12] But, as Appel
has shown, that escapism has its cost, and perhaps even more so in an era of
endless media choices where large portions of the public choose to ignore the
news altogether (and its tales of woe and injustice) in favor of entertainment[13]
with its happy endings. The cost of that escapism is a delusion that the world
is just, that people generally get what they deserve. Such a delusion would
be harmless if it was merely a matter of personal belief systems, but it isn't.
As research on the belief in a just world shows (cited above), views about
the justice in the distribution of rewards and punishments in society can have
a powerful effect on politics and public support (or lack thereof) for certain
policies, because "if people get what they deserve, why should I support government policies to improve their situation?"

Some recent trends in popular entertainment media, however, have bucked the tendency to promote a belief in a just world, stories whose plotlines instead show an unrelentingly cruel and *un*just world. The most extreme version of this trend can be found in HBO's immensely popular show *Game of Thrones*; Netflix's *House of Cards* represents another, albeit less graphic case in point (other shows, such as *The Wire*, could also be considered part of this trend). These shows could be considered part of a trend, picking up and promoting a new cultural development in how we see the world in terms of justice. Given the previous research tying culturally dominant happy-ending entertainment fare to a greater tendency to believe the world is just, is it possible that shows such as these that defy the fairy-tale endings actually reverse that effect and weaken the belief in a just world? In this chapter I report on three studies of varying methodology that test whether this is the case with regard to exposure to *Game of Thrones*.

THE UNJUST WORLD OF *GAME OF THRONES*

The first five seasons HBO's *Game of Thrones* stand out in popular entertainment for their repeated and powerfully dramatic lessons that the world is *not* just.[14] Indeed, the producers of *Game of Thrones* seem to delight in cruelly defying our expectations of justice in story narratives. Seasons 1 through 5 of *Game of Thrones* are in many ways the antithesis of *The Lord of the Rings* series (as if to signify this, the actor who appeared in both series, Sean Bean, plays the most honorable and just character in *Game of Thrones* and is shockingly and unjustly beheaded in the first season). Despite defying happy-ending storytelling conventions, the show has enjoyed immense popularity and become a cultural phenomenon. While about three million people tuned in to the series premiere of *Game of Thrones* in 2011, the number jumped to 5.4 million for that season's final episode;[15] and, the audience has continued to grow with each subsequent season. Indeed, it became so popular that the release of the first episode of season four crashed the streaming service HBOgo. Furthermore, in this modern era of streaming video and illegal downloads, it should be noted that the number of people viewing the show via HBO account for just part of the show's audience—it has been estimated that people downloaded 5.9 million illegal copies of the final episode of the third season.[16]

HBO's *Game of Thrones* (*GoT* henceforth) is based on George R. R. Martin's book series *A Song of Ice and Fire*, but the television series has outpaced the books, taking the story beyond the last published volume. *GoT* is set in the imaginary world of Westeros and the nearby lands across the Narrow Sea. The plotlines revolve around a struggle for the Iron Throne of Westeros (the "game" for the throne) and the coming of the world's winter, which brings longer, colder nights and the "White Walkers" and their army of the dead. On its surface GoT appears to be a standard fantasy series complete with knights, kings and queens, dragons, elves (the Children of the Forest), giants, and beastly creatures (icemen known as the "White Walkers" and the army of zombies they created), but it is anything but your typical fantasy narrative. Repeatedly throughout the first five seasons of the television show and the five books of the series (and in the multiple storylines of the tale), those who exhibit good and honorable qualities and who strive for justice are either killed off or forced to suffer and struggle endlessly, while characters who are self-serving, cunning, and twisted thrive. Fans of the fantasy genre are used to plotlines that allow the antagonists to get the upper hand early in the story only to be vanquished by the hero, but the first five seasons of GoT is unrelenting in destroying its good and noble characters and brutally extinguishing any flicker of hope for a just or happy outcome until much deeper into the story. A brief summary of some of the events in the saga should serve to illustrate (for those who haven't completed either series, we give the obligatory warning of spoilers).

In the first season, Sean Bean's character, Eddard (Ned) Stark, is the pivotal character. Ned Stark is a just and honorable lord who takes the position of the "King's Hand" to administer the kingdom for King Robert, his long-time friend. He plays fair and is a selfless character who is always trying to do the right thing. When he uncovers the true parentage of the King's children—that they are actually a product of incest between the queen and her brother—what unfolds is a series of events with dramatically unjust outcomes. Ned Stark does the honorable thing by warning the Queen, Cersei, that he is about to reveal the true parentage of her children and gives her a chance to take her children to a safe place outside the capital city. While this is going on, King Robert is mortally wounded by a boar in a hunting accident (Robert was impaired by drink fed to him by one of his Queen's cousins under direction of the Queen). Before the King dies, he hands power to Ned Stark in a writ, making him regent until the king's heir is of age. Everything seems in order; but, when King Robert ultimately dies from his hunting wounds, Cersei outmaneuvers Stark, telling him "when you play the game of thrones, you win or you die." Cersei accuses Stark of being a traitor and convinces the city guard to betray him. She has his household soldiers and staff slaughtered, and then, after Stark provides a false confession in order to protect his daughters and spare him execution, Cersei's son, King Joffrey, orders him beheaded. He is executed publicly and in front of his young daughters and his head is mounted on the castle wall.

Stark's eldest son, Rob, rallies his father's bannermen to avenge his father and seek justice. As such, the character of Rob becomes a major protagonist of the series. After Rob wins a number of battles, the audience, use to the normal conventions of storytelling, is led to believe that Rob is one of the heroes of the story. Rob is a lot like his father—a noble and just character trying to do the right thing and bringing justice to Westeros. Again, everything seems to be following our expectations for this type of story. But, Rob doesn't last long. In what has to be one of the most shocking and brutal television episodes of any popular show, Rob, his pregnant wife, and his mother, along with all his knights, are slaughtered at a wedding feast (known as "The Red Wedding"). It was shockingly brutal and outrageously unjust. Personally, I had to watch several episodes of another television show and read a book to get the scenes of "The Red Wedding" out of my head (didn't get much sleep that night). Social media was immediately flooded with people's horrified reactions (many fans who had read the books, and thus knew what was coming, filmed their friends, who didn't know what was coming, while their friends watched the episode and then shared their reactions).

Another line in the narrative that draws the audience in their search for a hero to follow Tyrion Lannister, the dwarf brother of Queen Cersei, who, while flawed, tries, for the most part, to do the right thing throughout the story. Tyrion becomes the acting King's Hand following Stark's execution and, as King's Hand, he attempts to school his sadistic young nephew, King Joffrey. Additionally, Tyrion, as Hand, plays a critical role in defending the capital city, King's Landing, through his clever defense plan as well as his courage in the actual battle. His reward? One of the King's Guard attempts to murder him in the midst of the battle and after the battle Tyrion is stripped of his position, his lodgings, and is afforded no recognition for his deeds save being forced to marry Ned Stark's thirteen-year-old daughter, Sansa, in what Tyrion views as a horrible injustice for Sansa. Later, Tyrion is falsely accused of poisoning King Joffrey at Joffrey's wedding feast (in one morsel of justice, Joffrey dies from poison in his wine).

Plotlines like these, both major and minor, repeatedly shock the audience with lesson after lesson that the world is cruel and unjust. Followers of the story are offered a multitude of potential "heroes or heroines" with expectations that, surely this time justice will be done. But, in the first five seasons (when the research reported here was conducted) justice almost never seems to arrive. In season 4, we are led to follow Prince Oberyn's quest for justice for his sister, Elia, and her children. The charismatic Oberyn is, perhaps, one of the most likeable characters in the fourth season of the show. A soldier known as "The Mountain" (a brutal, lethal giant of a man), raped and murdered Oberyn's sister and killed her children. At this point, Tyrion and Oberyn's storylines come together. Oberyn offers to be Tyrion's combat champion to prove Tyrion's innocence in the killing of King Joffrey. Oberyn seeks to win justice with the chance to kill "The Mountain," and publicly reveal the name of the person who gave "The Mountain" the order to rape and kill his sister. As the combat unfolds Oberyn uses his skill with the spear and his acrobatic maneuvers to take down "The Mountain" all the while chanting, "you raped and murdered my sister and killed her children." Ah, finally justice, the audience is led to believe . . . but before delivering the final deathblow, Oberyn demands that "The Mountain" confess and reveal the name the person who gave him the order to kill his sister and her children. In doing so, Oberyn gets too close to the prostrate and dying "Mountain." The Moutain knocks Oberyn off his feet and crushes his skull with his bare hands. It happened again! The audience reels. Oberyn is denied justice and Tyrion is consequently sentenced to death for a crime we know that he did not commit.[17]

While horrifying things befall the "good" characters, the sadistic and self-serving thrive, a story dynamic best exemplified by the character known as the "Bastard of Bolton," Ramsey Snow. Ramsey is by far the most sadistic and twisted character in the series. Ramsay Snow loves to torture his captives (physically and psychologically) and uses them as hunting game. He wins his battles through deceit and betrayal. Due to the efficacy of his brutality and deceitfulness, Ramsey's father rewards Ramsey by giving him the full first-born rights to the Bolton family's holdings (Ramsey later murders his father and feeds his stepmother and infant stepbrother to his hounds). Other despicable characters who thrive in Westeros include Queen Cersei, Tywin Lannister, Walder Frey, and, most notably Peter Balish, known as "Little Finger," who repeatedly schools one of Ned Stark's daughters on the need for deceit in the game of thrones. Sometimes, the despicable characters do get a comeuppance in the first five seasons (more "justice" is dealt out in seasons 6 and 7), but it is usually a very twisted form of "justice"—as the case with Theon Greyjoy, whose betrayal of the Starks is answered with extreme levels of torture and castration by the sadistic Bastard of Bolton. As if to underscore it all, the religions of this world are either corrupt servants of the elite or simply cruel and twisted, preying on the fear of their followers while hiding behind their piety.

GoT characters often put their awareness of this cruel reality in words. In the fourth season, the character called "The Hound" is taking his captive, another of Ned Stark's young daughters, Arya, to her relatives to seek a ransom. In episode 4, The Hound and Arya are taken in and fed by a farmer and his daughter. In return for their charity, The Hound (who in previous episodes had been evincing some more admirable traits, possibly endearing him to the audience) strikes down the old man and steals his silver. Arya, outraged, calls him "the worst shit in the whole kingdom." The Hound responds, saying, "There are plenty worse than me. I just understand the way things are. How many Starks they got to behead before you figure it out?"[18]

I am not alone in noting this violation of the just world storytelling convention—it has caught the attention of those who write about television, as well. Calum Marsh, wrote of *GoT* in *Esquire*'s culture blog:

> I like, in a somewhat perverse sense, that the characters I like best are routinely punished while the characters I like least are invariably rewarded, not because I enjoy the result, but because I understand that this is exactly how the universe operates. The people who succeed aren't the most moral, or the most just, or the most affable. They tend to be the opposite: ruthless, cunning, shrewd.[19]

David Berry, in a piece for *Hazlitt*, wrote:

> Still, all of the deaths that occur inherently follow the show's own cold logic—that noble ideals and even a good dose of cleverness are no match for dispassionate scheming, passionate hurt, and the judicious execution of the power to act on the two. The deaths are not remotely shocking in retrospect; the surprise comes from an error in our understanding of the rules of the game, not their sudden change.[20]

As these writers point out (and as is evident in the discussion of the plot twists above), it is not only that the show defies the just world turns that we expect in our fiction (and especially in our fantasy fiction), but that the characters who use brutal and deceitful means are rewarded.

SPECIFIC REASONS TO EXPECT THAT *GAME OF THRONES* AFFECTS JUST WORLD BELIEFS

In chapter 2, I mapped out the *how* and *when* of entertainment media effects in a theoretical framework meant to guide us in developing expectations of entertainment media effects. Here, in this section, I will use that framework to explain in terms that are more specific to this show why I expect the unjust world of *GoT* to shape how audiences of the show see the real world.

The starting point is to think about the origin of people's belief in a just world. Why do some people think the world is likely to reward good behavior and punish bad behavior while other do not? As Appel pointed out in his 2008 article, while the belief in a just world has come to be an accepted and measureable tendency with stable variation among individuals, there has been scant research on the origin of the BJW (with what little there is focusing on family influences). Family and religious beliefs undoubtedly play a role (the latter of which is typically learned from former). Although media socialization is suspected to play a role in the BJW tendency, to the best of my knowledge, Appel's research is the only empirical exploration of the connection.

Appel utilized cultivation theory for the basis on which to develop his expectations about the relationship between media use and BJW. Cultivation Theory is in the tradition of the Cumulative Effects Model of media effects and contends that heavy consumers of media will come to see the world as the media presents it.[21] As such, cultivation theory offers the perfect foundation for hypothesizing that the ubiquitous just world themes of entertainment fare would lead consumers of entertainment media to be more likely to see the real world as just. It also offers a good starting point for our hypotheses that popular shows that counter the just world script might just break the spell of the fairytale ending of all those other stories and weaken the tendency to believe the world is just. But, to do so, such shows have to captivate audiences to get them to return again and again for a steady dose of the unpleasant antidote. As demonstrated by its popularity (documented above), *GoT* seems to do just that.

While cultivation theory has been shown to be valuable for identifying the impact of repeated exposure to media constructions of reality, it does not help us with situations when messages run counter to ubiquitous cultural themes, nor does it specify the psychological processes that result in learning from a fictional narrative, the "how" of entertainment media effects. For understanding that process, we turn to Narrative Transportation Theory, as discussed in chapter 2. To briefly summarize that discussion, Narrative Transportation Theory argues that when we follow a story—whether in print, on TV, in a video game, a streamed video or a movie in a theater—we become immersed in the story in ways that take us away from our physical environment and mental state. In other words, the narrative *transports* us away from our world and into the world of the story. Narrative transportation involves imaginative imagery when we are reading, emotional attachments, a lack of focus on the outside world, and an acceptance of the story's reality. People can become transported when reading, watching, or playing.[22] Narrative Transportation Theory tells us that audiences of *Game of Thrones* leave their world temporarily for Westeros, taken in by the powerful visuals of the show and caught up in the struggles of the characters. They buy into the story as it unfolds. Fans of the series will readily accept that this is what happens for them. What else can explain the magnitude of our shock at the "Red Wedding" scene or at the murder of Jon Snow? This transported state is the mental state of those who watch. In that state of transportation, according to the research on Narrative Transportation Theory, the audience is susceptible to the perspectives offered by the narrative and thus members of the audience may be led to rethink their notions about how just the world actually is.

Researchers have documented that narrative transportation can lead to belief change.[23] Transportation leads to belief change though a number of processes, the combination of which, scholars argue, make attitude change via transportation actually more likely than through persuasion or rhetoric.[24] Because stories can evoke powerful emotional responses and can create emotional connections to characters, narrative transportation can affect attitudes through affective (as opposed to cognitive/rational) responses to story messages. Take the power of the "Red Wedding" scene to affect audiences emotionally. The reaction is set up because we have come to like and/ or identify with Rob, his pregnant wife, and his mother to varying degrees and because we are wrapped up in their fight for justice. The brutality and betrayal engender powerful emotions. The strong focus on the events of a story, the primacy of emotional reactions, the state of "enjoyment," and the focus on imagery that is characteristic of transportation means there is little motivation and few cognitive resources to devote to counterarguing or negative cognitive responses to the messages of the story. That is, we are unlikely to think to ourselves that the betrayal of the "Red Wedding" just would not have happened, instead, we accept its reality and, perhaps, the reality that injustices like this *do* happen. The mental imagery that is a component of narrative transportation (whether mentally generated while reading or imprinted in one's mind while watching) can also have a powerful and lasting effect, not only evoking emotions while immersed in the narrative but "may also re-evoke story themes and messages when recalled."[25] In this way, entertainment such as *GoT* may actually have a longer lasting effect than those from the news media.[26] Certainly, the visual impact of the "Red Wedding" scene stayed with audiences, and a mere mention of the title of the episode will bring back a memory of the emotional impact and the appalling injustice of the scene. Finally, the concrete and specific nature of narratives makes it difficult to argue against their conclusions.

In addition to these characteristics of transportation that suggest a powerful effect for stories, the companion process of identification offers another reason to expect that exposure to *GoT* could lead to belief change. When one identifies with a character in a narrative (if one identified with Rob or his wife leading up to the "Red Wedding" for example), they come to see the events of the story from the perspective of that character.[27] Identification "involves losing track of one's own identity and then subsequently adopting the character's goals and perspectives as one's own."[28] Identification makes it even more likely that when we exit a narrative we will come away from it with altered perspectives.

In sum, narrative transportation theory (formally known as the Transportation-Imagery Model) and the extant research utilizing the concept

provide good reasons to expect that the fictional narratives of popular entertainment can have an effect on politically relevant predispositions. Appel's
research has provided evidence of a link between fictional television and the
belief in a just world. His research, the repeated themes of *in*justice in *GoT*,
and the Transportation-Imagery Model and concept of identification lead us
to hypothesize that exposure to *GoT* will be associated with a reduced tendency to believe that the world is just. That is, this is one of those times *when*
entertainment media may have an observable effect; narrative transportation,
again, gives us the *how* of it. In the following sections I describe some studies
I conducted with the help of my student researchers in order to empirically
test this expectation.

STUDY 1

Design and Measures

The first study was an online survey using the Qualtrics survey tool. The
study was part of a class project that the students in my "Film, TV and Public
Opinion" seminar and I designed in 2014.[29] The survey sample was a con-
venience sample, built by having the students in the seminar as well as 100
students in another one of my classes reach out to their contacts on Facebook,
Twitter, and via email.[30] While the fact that the sample was not randomly
selected limits our abilities to make descriptive claims about the population
as a whole, it should not be a problem for comparing respondents based on
exposure to *GoT*. Students in both classes were instructed not to take the
survey themselves or discuss the survey with their friends.

A total of 1,003 people completed the survey. As one might expect with
this tactic of reaching out to get respondents, the sample was predominantly
between the ages of 18 and 25 (79.5 percent were in this age category).
Because of the nature of the sample, our generalizations must be limited to
college-age students. It should be noted, however, that the findings of the
analysis did not differ whether it was run with the entire sample or just with
the younger cohort.

Our[31] primary focus of Study 1 was the relationship between exposure to
GoT (and *House of Cards*, which will be discussed in the next chapter) and
the belief in a just world (BJW). We did also look into the possibility that
the show might affect their audiences' views about whether ends justify the
means. This lesson, like the lesson on expecting just outcomes, is ubiquitous
throughout both shows—characters are either portrayed having to carry out
horrendous acts to survive or succeed and those that don't do so repeatedly
pay for it, often with their lives. In addition to looking at the effect of expo-

sure to these shows on this attitude, we also extended the analysis to include those attitudes that researchers have found to be related to the BJW—attitudes toward welfare and punitive criminal justice. We also included other attitudes that we expected both BJW and the ends-justify-means attitude to be related to—ideology and a posture on how to fight terrorism. The full model can be found in figure 3.1 (along with the results, which will be discussed below). Note that our main control variable for BJW is the importance of religion to the respondent (though we do also control for other variables such as gender).

I display the conditioning effects of transportation and identification with arrows pointing to the effect lines going from *GoT* to BJW and ends-justify-means attitudes in the figure. As discussed above, the extent to which an audience member is transported by the story and whether one identifies with characters in the story can condition the impact of the lessons of the story. For this study we used a series of questions designed to measure how much of a fan the respondent was of the show in order to have an indicator of how transported the respondent had been by the narrative. These fan-level questions included questions regarding the respondents' familiarity with characters, whether they watched the old episodes again in anticipation of the new season, and so on (see Q69 in appendix 1). For identification we measure the likelihood of the respondent to identify with characters using the Motivation and Mindreading scale developed by Carpenter, Green, LaFlam.[32] The

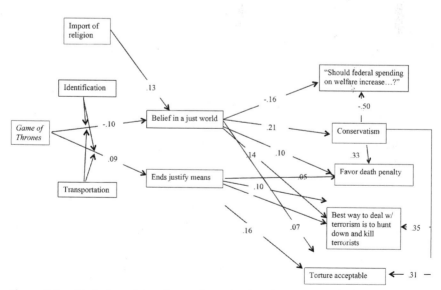

Figure 3.1. Study 1 model and overall results (numbers are standardized regression coefficients).

questions use a seven-point Likert scale asking whether respondents agree with statements such as "When I meet new people, I like wondering how they got to where they are in life." See Q58 in appendix 1 for all four items in the scale that we used.

The principal independent variable—exposure to *GoT*—was measured by asking respondents how familiar they were with the show (Q71); response options ranged from not having seen any of the show to having seen all of the episodes (we also asked whether they had read the book series). We used a feeling thermometer question to ask how respondents felt about a number of the principal characters. The primary purpose of asking for feelings about the characters was so we could include images of the characters next to the characters' names in order to re-evoke the feelings associated with the show/ activate respondents' schema of the show.

To measure the tendency to believe in a just world we used the standard BJW question asked by the American National Election Study (ANES), "Some people say that people get ahead by their own hard work; others say that lucky breaks or help from other people are more important. Which do you think is most important?" We also used the ANES question "How much of the time do people get what they deserve?" with the five response options ranging from "always" to "never." We recoded the responses so that the higher scores represented a greater tendency to believe in a just world. To measure the respondents' feelings about ends and means, we asked them to agree or disagree with the statement "Sometimes good people have to do bad things in order to attain a greater good."

Results

One of the biggest problems confronting researchers of media effects is the issue of selective exposure. We attempted to address this potential problem by including additional studies that used an experimental design (Studies 2 and 3). For this study, we attempted to check for selective exposure by asking respondents what got them to start watching *GoT*; and, for those who had only seen some of the episodes of *GoT*, we asked them why they hadn't watched all the episodes. For this second question, if the respondent selected "I didn't like the show" as the reason they didn't watch the all of the episodes, we asked them to indicate why they didn't like it in an open-ended question. Figure 3.2 shows the responses to the question "what got you to start watching *GoT*?" Figure 3.3 contains the reasons why those who had not watched all the shows disliked the shows.

As I argued in the prior chapters, selective exposure to politically relevant messages in entertainment media is less likely to happen than selective exposure to news media because people's selection of entertainment media

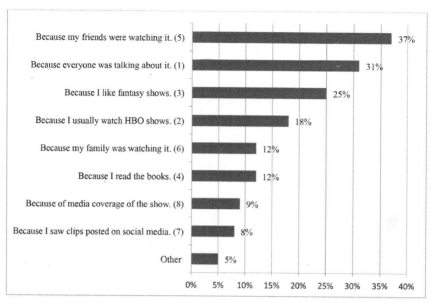

Figure 3.2. "What got you to start watching *Game of Thrones?*" Percentage of those who had at least some exposure (n = 808).

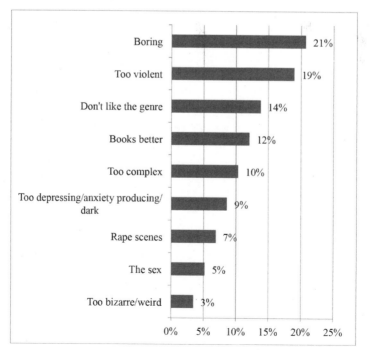

Figure 3.3. Reason given for not liking *Game of Thrones*.

is driven by media qualities other than the political nature of the media.[33] "We're often drawn to stories for reasons that may have nothing to do with our views. This may be its popularity, attention given to it in the media, critical reviews, special effects, advertising, boredom, inadvertent exposure when we have little choice."[34] Given that the politically relevant content in most entertainment (that which is not overtly political) is buried within the lessons that the story's characters learn, selective exposure based on the politics of the show or book is even less probable.

So, what got our respondents to watch *Game of Thrones*? The dominant factors in getting respondents to watch *GoT* were that their friends were watching it (37 percent) and because everyone was talking about it (31 percent). The "because my friends were watching it" may indicate that the politics of another socialization agent, friends, are influencing the selection of this media program, but it may also just be a reflection of the popularity of the show as indicated by the "because everyone is talking about it." We think that these first two reasons for watching are more about the buzz surrounding the show (a buzz that is easily and virally spread through social media) than it is some attempt on the part of friends (consciously or unconsciously) to politically socialize their friends. A quarter of those who watched *GoT* said they watched it because they liked the genre. This could pose selective exposure problems for our research if *GoT* was anything like the rest of the fantasy genre with regard to BJW, which, as discussed above, it is absolutely not. The reasons given for *not* liking *GoT* (see figure 3.3) indicate that while the buzz surrounding a show may get a lot of people to check it out, some of those who do so will stop watching it for reasons that may hint at some selectivity in the continued exposure to the show. The modal reason for not liking *GoT* was that it was too boring, and after that the level of violence portrayed was the second most cited reason. These two reasons do not seem to have anything to do with the just world beliefs. The "too depressing, anxiety-producing, and dark" reasons cited by 9 percent of those who did not like the show, however, hint at the possibility that the injustice prominent in the show's plotlines is too much for at least a few (a very small portion of our overall sample).

Overall, it seems that the buzz among social networks about *GoT* was what drew people to the show. Wanting to check out what everyone is talking about and be part of the conversations among friends and on social media seems to be the dominant factor leading to exposure. There is little indication that initial exposure is based on some understanding of the underlying politics of the shows. There does seem to be some selectivity in the continued exposure to the show, but it appears to be relevant for only a small portion of the sample. In the analysis that follows I examine the impact of any exposure to the show, which should eliminate the problem of selectivity associated with those who watched only some episodes and then stopped because they did not like *GoT.*

In figure 3.4 I present the breakdown of respondents on the just world response to the BJW question (that hard work is most important to getting ahead) for our sample based on exposure to the two shows. As can be seen from this preliminary cut at the data, a smaller percentage those who were exposed to *GoT* selected this option, a finding that offers some initial support for our hypothesis that exposure to the show can weaken the tendency to see the world as just. Additionally, the bivariate correlations between fandom of the shows and responses to the question about whether people get what they deserve lends some additional support to the relationship between the show and the BJW: the correlation for *GoT* and responses to whether people get what they deserve was -.093 (significant at better than .01).[35] On the question of means and ends as measured by the question as to whether sometimes

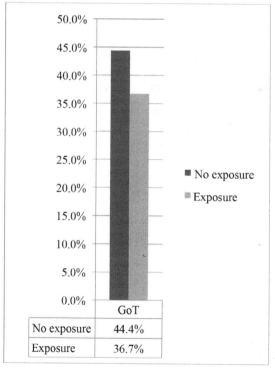

Figure 3.4. Exposure to *Game of Thrones* and the BJW. Bars represent the percent of respondents who believe that "Hard work is most important" to getting ahead.

people have to do bad things in order to attain a greater good, the correlation between those responses and the measure of fandom of *GoT* is .155 (significant at better than the .01 level).

To more rigorously test the relationship between exposure to *Game of Thrones* and the belief in a just world I ran a series of regression analyses in which I controlled for the importance of religion and the gender of the respondent. I did not control for ideology in these models because the research on just world beliefs suggest that just world beliefs precede ideological development and are more central to one's worldview than ideology; in other words, just world beliefs are more likely to shape ideology than the other way around.[36] To model the conditioning effects of transportation I ran the analysis with fan level instead of exposure. A respondent's level of fandom was a simple additive scale of responses to a set of questions such as "I watch *Game of Thrones* as soon as it airs," "I can name almost all of the characters in *Game of Thrones*," and "In anticipation of the new season, I re-watched previous episodes."[37] To model the conditioning effect of identification I included an interaction term that was the product of exposure and the Motivation and Mindreading scale (that measures tendency to identify). The equations for the analysis were as follows:

1. BJW = *GoT* exposure + religion + gender
2. BJW = *GoT* immersion + religion + gender
3. BJW = *GoT* exposure + (*GoT**identification) + religion + gender

BJW is the combined answers to the two "belief in a just world" questions—"Some people say that people get ahead by their own hard work; others say that lucky breaks or help from other people are more important. Which do you think is most important?" and "How much of the time do people get what they deserve?"—recoded so that the higher the score, the higher the BJW. *GoT* exposure was a simple dichotomous variable that equaled one for any exposure to *Game of Thrones*, zero for none (60 percent of our sample had some exposure to *GoT*). *GoT* immersion (my way of tapping into exposure and transportation) was measured by a scale created from responses to the fan questions. Religion was measured by responses to the ANES question "How important is religion in your life?" recoded so that the high score was "very important."

The regression results for these three equations can be found in table 3.1. The results lend additional support for our hypothesis that exposure to *Game of Thrones* could weaken its audience's belief in a just world. As can be seen in the table, exposure to *GoT* was associated with a lower level of BJW even when controlling for the importance of religion and gender. Indeed, the explanatory power of exposure to *GoT* (as measured by the standardized regression coefficient) was nearly equal to the explanatory power of the importance of religion. When we used fan level as the measure of exposure to

Table 3.1. Regression Results for *GoT* (Study 1)

	Equation 1	Equation 2	Equation 3
GoT Exposure	−.21*		.35
	(.10)		(.17)
GoT Fan Level		−.03*	
		(−.09)	
GoT Exp X Identification			−.03*
			(−.28)
Importance of Religion	.13*	.13*	.13*
	(.13)	(.13).	(.13)
Male	.01	.01	−.01
	(.01)	(.004)	(−.01)
Adjusted R²	.027	.026	.030

* significant at the .05 level or better, one-tailed test
Numbers in parentheses are the standardized regression coefficients.

GoT (in order to model transportation) we also find that the greater the fan, the lower the BJW. And, finally, when we consider the likelihood of identifying with the characters of the show, the regression analysis indicates (*GoT* Exp X Identification) that those who have a proclivity to identify with characters are the ones for whom the show seemed to have its greatest impact. The explanatory power of exposure to the show conditioned by identification was more than twice that of the importance of religion.

To further test the relationship between *GoT* and respondents' feelings about whether ends justify the means, I regressed the level of agreement with the statement "sometimes good people have to do bad things in order to attain a greater good" on exposure to the show or fan level and gender. The results can be found in table 3.2. Both exposure and fan levels are significantly related to believing that the ends justify the means.

Table 3.2. *GoT* and Ends/Means Regressions (Study 1)

	GoT	*GoT*
Exposure	.30*	
	(.09)	
Fan Level		.07*
		(.13)
Male	.52*	.50*
	(.16)	(.16)
Adjusted R²	.039	.045

* significant at the .05 level or better, one-tailed test

Finally, to extend the analysis to the more specific political attitudes such as those regarding welfare, criminal justice, conservatism, and the use of deadly force (as hypothesized in figure 3.1), I ran a series of regressions (full results available upon request) assessing the relationship between the various factors identified in the full model. And, as found in the literature, the tendency to believe the world is just was related to lower support for welfare spending and higher support for punitive criminal justice and terrorism policy, suggesting that the effect of *Game of Thrones* may go beyond affecting how just their audiences view the world or the extent to which ends justify the means, but also indirectly affect specific political attitudes as well.

STUDY 2

The second study to test the impact of *Game of Thrones* was an online experiment I designed with students in the fall 2014 version of my "Film, TV and Public Opinion" seminar.[38] Subjects for the experiment were recruited using Facebook, Twitter, and email by students in the class, students in my "American Political System" class, and by colleagues at Texas A&M and The University of Richmond.[39]

Enough people volunteered to create 5 groups of about 50 subjects; unfortunately, only about half of the volunteers followed through with the study, raising some concerns about selective exposure—did subjects not follow through because they had heard about and did not want to watch the show we assigned them? Or, were there other reasons, such of lack of access to shows, or that they did not have the time? For those who didn't watch any episodes or only watched a few we did include questions asking why, and only received a handful of responses (4), only one of which said they had heard about the show and didn't want to watch it. The other responses were that they could not get access to the show, one had already seen all the episodes, and one that it was "too boring!"

I sorted the subjects who volunteered into categories including whether they were UVM students, their gender, and their exposure to *Game of Thrones*. Then I randomly assigned subjects using an interval selection process with a random start into one of five groups for the experiment (two of the groups were used to study the effect of *House of Cards*, which will be discussed in the next chapter). We asked subjects in one of the groups to watch six episodes of *Game of Thrones*; we asked subjects in the second group to watch *True Blood*. We asked them to complete their viewing over a one-week period (hoping to encourage a bit of binge-watching). We did not ask those assigned to a third group to watch anything. We devised the experiment in this way to give us two different control groups for the experiment. The control group that was not asked to watch anything (and just asked to fill out the questionnaire at the end of the week) had 38 subjects complete the study. We intended the second control group to be one that watched a similar show, but one that had more just world themes. For that group we selected HBO's series *True Blood* and asked one group to watch six episodes of the series (eighteen subjects in this group completed the study). While set in the current time period, *True Blood* could be considered part of the fantasy genre since the plot revolves around creatures typically found in the fantasy genre—in addition to vampires, there are fairies and werewolves. The series unfolds along the lines of the just world script. The groups assigned *GoT* had twenty-six subjects who completed the study.

At the end of the week of watching *GoT* or *True Blood*, I emailed all subjects (and the group that was not asked to watch anything) a link to a questionnaire using the Qualtrics survey tool (see appendix 2 for the questionnaire). The questionnaire included questions about how many episodes the subject actually watched, manipulation check questions that asked about characters and the events of the shows (these questions included pictures of the characters so as to re-evoke themes of the program through the imagery), and measures of the key dependent variables and control variables. To measure the belief in a just world and attitudes regarding the ends justifying means we used the same questions as used in the survey in Study 1. For this study, we used a number of items from Green and Brock's narrative transportation scale to measure the extent to which subjects were transported by the show we asked them to watch.[40] The scale is composed of the responses to a number of questions that ask respondents to indicate the extent to which a series of statements described their viewing experience, statements such as: "I found myself worrying about what would happen to the characters as I watched," "While I was watching the show, activity going on in the room around me was on my mind," and "I found my mind wandering while watching the show." (For the full set of questions see Q73 in appendix 2). To measure identification for this study we asked them to tell us the extent to which the statement "As I watched, I found myself identifying with a character in the show" was accurate.

In figure 3.5 I present the simple breakdowns of the results. While those assigned to *GoT* scored lower on the belief in a just world scale than the subjects who we asked to watch *True Blood*, the differences in the means were not statistically significant. The subjects in the group that was not asked to watch any show scored lower on the BJW scale than the other two groups, though this difference was also not statistically significant. On whether the subjects believed the ends justify the means, the subjects assigned *GoT* scored higher on this than the *True Blood* group and the control group, though the difference was not statistically significant (see figure 3.6).

Chapter 3

To test whether those who were transported or who identified with a character were more affected by exposure to the shows, I ran an additional set of analysis with interaction terms included in the equations. Including interaction terms here allows me to model whether transportation or identification increases the impact of exposure to the show. So, I regressed the belief in a just world and attitude about ends/means on exposure to *GoT* and interaction variables—the products of the level of transportation and identification and exposure to show. The results can be found in table 3.3. The results for the belief in a just world lend support for the hypothesis that exposure to *GoT* reduces the tendency to believe in a just world—the coefficients for exposure to the show are all negative and statistically significant. The interaction term for transportation suggests that the effect of the shows on BJW weakened slightly as transportation increased. This result seems puzzling since narrative transportation theory suggests that the impact of the shows should be strengthened by transportation. The interaction term for identification and exposure was not statistically significant. The regression results for the impact of the experimental manipulations and the interaction terms for attitudes about ends and means failed to uncover any significant relationships for *GoT*.

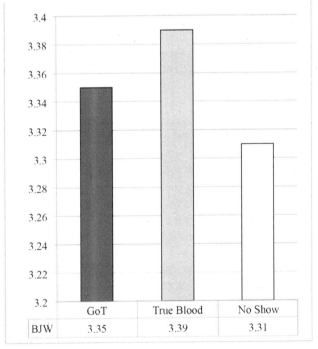

	GoT	True Blood	No Show
BJW	3.35	3.39	3.31

Figure 3.5. Mean BJW score for experimental and control groups in Study 2.

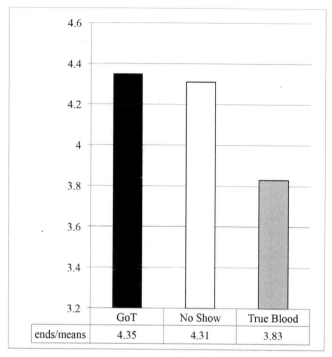

	GoT	No Show	True Blood
ends/means	4.35	4.31	3.83

Figure 3.6.   Mean score on ends justify means question by experimental group for Study 2.

In sum, once the conditioning effects of transportation and identification are taken into account, those in the *GoT* condition of the experiment scored significantly lower on the belief in a just world than both those in the *True Blood* group and those in the group who were not asked to watch anything.

Table 3.3.   BJW Regressed on Experimental Manipulations and Conditioning Effects of Transportation and Identification (Study 2)

	GoT v. TB	*GoT v. Control*
Exp. group	−1.45*	−1.27*
	(−.68)	(−.68)
Exp. Group X Transportation	.04*	.04*
	(.81)	(.90)
Exp. Group X Identification	−.36	−.36
	(−.11)	(−.12)
Adjusted R²	.015	.033

* significant at the .05 level or better, one-tailed test

STUDY 3

The third study was an experiment I ran in the first week of the 2015 spring semester using my students from my "Politics & the Media" course as subjects. This course does not focus on entertainment media effects, never the less, I ran the experiment in the first week in order to avoid any possible contamination of the subjects from course material. I offered students extra credit to participate in the study. I randomly assigned students who volunteered to participate into one of two groups. One group was asked to watch five episodes of *GoT* during the first week of classes; the other group, the control group, was asked to go to the theater to watch *The Hobbit: The Battle of the 5 Armies*. *The Hobbit* offered a nice contrast to *GoT* with regard to the just world lessons as it contained a number of dramatic instances in which justice was served. For example, the heroic character Bard, who exhibited a number of virtuous characteristics, bravely confronts the dragon Smaug as it was destroying his town. Bard slays the beast with a black arrow and the dragon crashes to earth on top of the Master of the town, who, instead of helping defend the city, was absconding with the gold from the city coffers. At the beginning of the following week, I sent the students a link to fill out a questionnaire. 89 students participated (out of the 103 enrolled in the class), with 45 assigned to *GoT* completing the study, 44 assigned *The Hobbit*.

The questionnaire (see appendix 3) contained the same measures for BJW as well as the measures of transportation and identification used in Study 2. I included manipulation check questions to make sure that the students actually watched the assigned show, questions asking about events of the show and accompanied by pictures (again, part of the purpose of this was to re-evoke the imagery from the shows). I asked subjects in the *GoT* group how many episodes of *GoT* they watched for the study as well as how much of the show they had seen in the past. Subjects in *The Hobbit* group were asked if they had seen the film prior to this study. I also included questions to filter out students who had had me in any previous class. I filtered out any subjects who had previously had me for a class in both the experimental and control group. For the *GoT* group I filtered out: those who did not get at least two of the three manipulation check questions correct, those who had not watched at least four episodes during the week of the study, those who had seen all the episodes of the show already. This left 23 subjects in this group. For *The Hobbit* group I filtered out those who did not get at least two of the three manipulation check questions correct and those who had seen *The Hobbit* before. This left 29 subjects in this group.

The mean belief in a just world score for the two experimental groups are presented in figure 3.7. Those who were assigned *GoT* scored lower on the

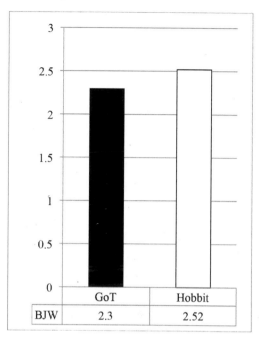

	GoT	Hobbit
BJW	2.3	2.52

Figure 3.7. Mean BJW score for *GoT* and *The Hobbit* groups (Study 3).

Table 3.4. BJW Regressed on Experimental Manipulations and Conditioning Effects of Transportation and Identification (Study 3)

	BJW
GoT	.70
	(.36)
GoT X Transportation (measured by enjoyed)	−1.21*
	(−.61)
GoT X Identification	.01
	(.04)
Hobbit X Transportation (measured by enjoyed)	.48**
	(.25)
Hobbit X Identification	−1.4*
	(−.34)
Adjusted R²	.072

* significant at the .05 level or better, one-tailed test
** significant at the .11 level, one-tailed test

BJW scale, though the difference is not statistically significant. To take into account transportation and identification I ran a regression using interaction terms for those dynamics. For narrative transportation in this analysis we simply utilized a dichotomous variable for whether the respondents enjoyed the show or not. The results of the regression can be found in table 3.4. The variable measuring baseline exposure to *GoT* was not significant, but the interaction terms that separate out those who enjoyed *GoT* was and in the correct direction—those reporting that they enjoyed *GoT* scored lower on BJW. The same interaction term for *The Hobbit*, that measures BJW for those who enjoyed *The Hobbit*, was also significant and in the right direction—those who reported enjoying *The Hobbit* scored higher on the belief in a just world measure.

DISCUSSION

All of the studies discussed here uncover, in some form, the expected relationship between the politically relevant content of *GoT* and the attitudes of the audiences of these shows. The audiences of these shows scored lower on the measure of the belief in a just world than those who were not exposed to the show. There is some evidence, too, that the audience of *GoT* seems to be more likely to believe that the ends justify the means, though the findings for this were not as strong. By utilizing different methods and a variety of questions I attempted to get at the issue of causality and generalizability. The findings indicate that there appears to be a causal linkage between exposure to these shows and the belief in a just world—exposure to the repeated lessons of *Game of Thrones* that the world is cruel and unjust seems to have dampened the tendency to believe the opposite, that the world is just. Given these pieces of evidence, as well as the findings of Appel of the opposite correlation with most other fictional narratives that promote just world beliefs,[41] I feel confident that exposure to *Game of Thrones* is responsible for the lower levels of the belief in a just world that we found in our studies. These findings mesh with the theoretical expectations mapped out in the previous chapters. They offer evidence of an entertainment media effect through fictional lessons on a politically relevant belief, lessons that the audience is unlikely to have noted as political lessons. The timing for the effect of *GoT* on BJW fits well with the "when" component of the theory, with the culturally dominant just world storyline opening the door for *GoT's* unjust world to challenge and dampen the belief in a just world. And, two of the three studies suggest that being transported by the narrative of *GoT* enhanced the internalization of the lesson on the BJW.

The fact that the different measures of transportation in Studies 2 and 3 (in Study 2 we used Green and Brock's scale, in Study 3 I used a simple measure of enjoyment) recorded opposite effects is puzzling, but may be explained by the differing research designs. While both studies were set up as experiments, with an attempt to control exposure to the experimental and control conditions, the design of Study 2 could not control exposure as well as Study 3. As a result, more subjects dropped out of Study 2 as compared with Study 3 (you can see this in the numbers reported above as well as some of the reasons offered for why subjects dropped out). The use of a quota sampling to insure that there were an equal number of subjects who had seen *Game of Thrones* in the experimental and control groups in Study 2 should have minimized this problem to a certain degree. Ideally, I would compare the respondents in the experimental and control groups on prior exposure to *GoT*. But, because we asked the questions about previous viewing of *GoT* when subjects registered for the experiment, and, because the surveys that we administered at the end of the week of viewing were anonymous, I cannot match the responses to questions subjects answered when joining the study with the subjects' responses after viewing. So, unfortunately, there is no way of knowing the differences between the experimental groups and control groups on prior exposure to *GoT*. If there were more subjects with prior exposure to *GoT* in the experimental group, that may explain the fact that those who reported being more transported by *GoT* actually scored slightly higher on the belief in a just world measure as measured by the interaction term in the equation (note: that the baseline of exposure to *GoT* is significant and in the correct direction). It may be that the effect of the show on the belief in a just world had already happened when subjects who had already seen the show had viewed it for the first time. This anomalous finding could also be due to the possibility that what matters for transportation is simply whether the respondent was transported (as measured in Study 3) as opposed to the extent to which the subjects were transported (as measured in Study 2). Slater et al. suggested this way of conceptualizing narrative transportation—as a threshold that had to be reached in order for story persuasion effects to take place—in an attempt to explain the anomalous findings regarding transportation in their experiments.[42]

As *GoT* moves into its final seasons (after the fifth season), Westeros (and surrounding territories) has become a bit more of a just world (this was written before the final season aired). A number of the most heinous and despicable characters—the "Bastard of Bolton," Walter Frey, and the slave traders of "Slaver's Bay"—have all had their comeuppance, sometimes with their victims dealing out the justice (the Stark daughters). It would be interesting to return to the effects of this show with the release of the final season in order to see how the show's effect on the BJW evolves with the resolution of the story.

CONCLUSION

The storytelling conventions of our time have up until recently followed Plato's mandate about the lessons that ought to be in our stories—lessons that justice will be served:

> I am afraid that we shall find that poets and story-tellers are in error in matters of greatest human importance. They have said that unjust men are often happy, and just men wretched, that wrong-doing pays if you can avoid being found out, and that justice is what is good for someone else but to your own disadvantage. We must forbid them to say this sort of thing, and require the opposite moral.[43]

The first five seasons of *Game of Thrones* stands out in defiance of those "moral" lessons ubiquitous in storytelling of our day and as the research here has shown can affect how we perceive the political world just as Plato feared. But, as research on the belief in a just world has shown that, contrary to Plato's thinking, such lessons may not be such a bad thing after all.

NOTES

1. Portions of this chapter appeared previously in a paper *"Game of Thrones, House of Cards* and the Belief in a Just World," presented at the 2015 Annual Meeting of the Midwest Political Science Association, April 16–19, Chicago, IL, with students Sarah Weichselbaum, Hayley Aydelott, Evyn Banach, Matthew Donovan, Allie VanSickle, and Jack Vest.

2. This follows from Cultivation Effects research; see George Gerbner, Larry Gross, Michael Morgan, and Nancy Signorielli, "Growing Up with Television: Cultivation Processes," in *Media Effects: Advances in Theory and Research* second edition, eds. J. Bryant and D. Zillmann (Hillsdale, NJ: Lawrence Erlbaum Associates, 2002), 43–68. For a summary of the literature on cultivation effects in the context of entertainment media, see L. J. Shrum and Jaehoon Lee, "The Stories TV Tells: How Fictional TV Narratives Shape Normative Perceptions and Personal Values," in *The Psychology of Entertainment Media: Blurring the Lines Between Entertainment and Persuasion*, edited by L. J. Shrum (New York: Routledge, 2012), 147–67.

3. Daniel P. Franklin, *Politics and Film: The Political Culture of Television and Movies* (New York: Rowman & Littlefield, 2017).

4. Melvin J. Lerner and Dale T. Miller, "Just World Research and the Attribution Process: Looking back and ahead," *Psychological Bulletin* 85 (1978): 1030–51, p. 1030; see also Melvin J. Lerner, "Evaluation of Performance as a Function of Performer's Reward and Attractiveness" *Journal of Personality and Social Psychology* 1 (1965): 355–60; and Melvin J. Lerner, *The Belief in a Just World: A Fundamental Delusion* (New York: Plenum Press, 1980).

5. Karen Stenner, *The Authoritarian Dynamic* (Cambridge: Cambridge University Press, 2005).

6. See Zick Rubin and Letitia Anne Peplau, "Who Believes in a Just World," *Journal of Social Issues* 31 (1975), 65–89; and, Lauren D. Appelbaum, Mary Clare Lennon and J. Lawrence Aber, "When Effort Is Threatening: The Influence of the Belief in a Just World on Americans' Attitudes toward Antipoverty," *Political Psychology* 27, no. 3 (2006): 387–402.

7. Lerner and Miller, "Just World Research and the Attribution Process," p. 1030.

8. See Rubin and Peplau, "Who Believes in a Just World," Appelbaum, Lennon and Aber, "When Effort Is Threatening," and Vicky M. Wilkins and Jeffrey B. Wenger, "Belief in a Just World and Attitudes Toward Affirmative Action," *Policy Studies Journal* 42 (2014): 325–43.

9. Markus Appel, "Fictional Narratives Cultivate Just-World Beliefs," *Journal of Communication* 58 (2008): 62–83.

10. And it is almost always a male, though that may be changing in the era of Katniss, Rey and Jyn (of the recent *Star Wars* movies), Wonder Woman, and most of the female characters in seasons 6 and 7 of *Game of Thrones*.

11. Appel, "Fictional Narratives Cultivate Just-World Beliefs."

12. A. A. Raney, "Punishing media criminals and moral judgment: The impact on enjoyment," *Media Psychology* 7 (2005): 145–63; D. Zillmann, "Empathy: Affect from bearing witness to the emotions of others," in J. Bryant & D. Zillmann (Eds.), *Responding to the Screen: Reception and Reaction Processes* (Hillsdale, NJ: Erlbaum, 1991), 135–68.

13. Markus Prior, *Post-Broadcast Democracy: How Media Choice Increases Inequality in Political Involvement and Polarizes Elections* (Cambridge: Cambridge University Press, 2007).

14. The research presented here took place before seasons 6 and 7 of *Game of Thrones*. These later seasons (which, interestingly enough go beyond the books of George R. R. Martin) feature more scenes of justice or revenge for the injustices that took place earlier in the story.

15. Jim Windolf, "The Gathering Storm," *Vanity Fair*, April 2014, accessed July 8, 2014 from http://www.vanityfair.com/hollywood/2014/04/game-of-thrones-season-4.

16. Windolf, "The Gathering Storm."

17. "The Mountain and the Viper," season 4, episode 8, aired June 1, 2014.

18. "The Breaker of Chains," season 4, episode 3, aired April 20, 2014.

19. Calum Marsh, "Why We Watch *Game of Thrones*: Because it gives us what we don't want, which is the rarest thing of all on TV," *Esquire*, Culture Blog, April 7, 2014, http://www.esquire.com/blogs/culture/why-we-watch-game-of-thrones, accessed July 8, 2014.

20. David Berry, "A World Where Death Matters: *On Game of Thrones* and *House of Cards*," *Hazlitt*, March 31, 2014, http://www.randomhouse.ca/hazlitt/blog/world -where-death-matters-game-thrones-and-house-cards, accessed July 8, 2014.

21. George Gerbner, Larry Gross, Michael Morgan, and Nancy Signorielli, "Growing Up with Television: The Cultivation Perspective," in *Media Effects: Advances in*

Theory and Research, edited by J. Bryant and D. Zillmann (Hillsdale, NJ: Lawrence Erlbaum Associates, 2002), 43–68; L. J. Shrum and Jaehoon Lee, "The Stories TV Tells: How Fictional TV Narratives Shape Normative Perceptions and Personal Values," in *The Psychology of Entertainment Media: Blurring the Lines Between Entertainment and Persuasion*, edited by L. J. Shrum (New York: Routledge, 2012).

22. For a summary of the research on this subject, see Jordan M. Carpenter and Melanie C. Green, "Flying with Icarus: Narrative Transportation and the Persuasiveness of Entertainment," in *The Psychology of Entertainment Media: Blurring the Lines Between Entertainment and Persuasion*, edited by L. J. Shrum (New York: Routledge, 2012). For more specific sources, see chapter 2 of this volume.

23. For a meta-analysis of the extant research on narrative transportation see Tom Van Laer, Ko de Ruyter, Luca M. Visconti, and Martin Wetzels, "The Extended Transportation-Imagery Model: A Meta-Analysis of the Antecedents and Consequences of Consumers' Narrative Transportation," *Journal of Consumer Research* 40, no. 5 (2014): 797–817. For a summary of the theory and research, see Jordan M. Carpenter and Melanie C. Green, "Flying with Icarus: Narrative Transportation and the Persuasiveness of Entertainment," in *The Psychology of Entertainment Media: Blurring the Lines Between Entertainment and Persuasion*, edited by L. J. Shrum (New York: Routledge, 2012).

24. Richard Gerrig, *Experiencing Narrative Worlds: On the Psychological Activities of Reading* (New Haven, CT: Yale University Press, 1993); Carpenter and Green, "Flying with Icarus"; Markus Appel and Tobias Richter, "Persuasive Effects of Fictional Narratives Increase over Time," *Media Psychology* 10 (2007): 113–34.

25. Carpenter and Green, "Flying with Icarus," p. 175.

26. Appel and Richter, "Persuasive effects of fictional narratives increase over time."

27. Keith Oatley, "Emotions and the Story Worlds of Fiction," in *Narrative Impact: Social and Cognitive Foundations*, eds. Melanie C. Green, Jeffrey J. Strange, and Timothy C. Brock (Mahwah, NJ: Lawrence Erlbaum Associates, Inc., 2002), 39–69.

28. Carpenter and Green, "Flying with Icarus," p. 181.

29. The students included Marissa Bucci, Mac Cleary, Daniel Cmejla, Nicholas Ingersoll, Kelly Joyce, Anastasia Kopp, Luca Piccin, Macie Rebel, Connor Seitchik, Emma Stern, Ashley Szilvassy, Nicholas Usen, Sarah Weichselbaum, Matthew West, and Lauren Willigan.

30. Students were asked to post/distribute the following message on Facebook: "Please help me and my fellow students with our project on the hottest TV shows by filling out a survey on the other end of this link [link was embedded here]. You can win a $100 Visa/MC gift card! The survey will only take you ten minutes or so to complete. Please share with your friends." For Tweets students used this: "Help UVM students by taking a survey on hot TV shows/win $100 Visa card. Takes about 10 min [link was embedded here]. Please retweet."

31. A note on pronouns: I alternate between plural pronouns and singular pronouns throughout this chapter and the following chapters because some aspects of the research were completed with my students as parts of class projects and other aspects were completed solely by me.

32. Jordan M. Carpenter, Melanie C. Green, and Jeff LaFlam, "People or Profiles: Individual Differences in Online Social Networking Use." *Personality and Individual Differences* (April 2011): 538–41.

33. See also Anthony Gierzynski and Kathryn Eddy, *Harry Potter and the Millennials: Research Methods and the Politics of the Muggle Generation* (New York: The Johns Hopkins University Press, 2013); and, Anthony Gierzynski, "Harry Potter Did Help Shape the Political Culture of a Generation," *The Conversation*, August 19, 2014, accessed March 19, 2015, http://theconversation.com/harry-potter-did-help -shape-the-political-culture-of-a-generation-29513.

34. Gierzynski, "Harry Potter Did Help Shape the Political Culture of a Generation."

35. Fandom was calculated by adding the affirmative responses to the series of questions about immersion into the show. See Q69 in appendix 1.

36. See Lerner, *The Belief in a Just World*, and material cited above in the discussion of BJW.

37. See Q69 in appendix 1.

38. Contributing students included Hayley Aydelott, Evyn Banach, Kevin Cafferky, Matthew Donovan, Emmett Hoskin, Sean McEwan, Stewart Micali, Jacob Mitchell, Tyler Mogk, Scott Pavek, Emily Queiroz, Galen Stump, Allie Van Sickle, and Jack Vest.

39. My thanks to Professor Greg Gause and Professor Jennifer Barnes-Bowie. The recruitment message read: "One of my UVM professors [A professor at the University of Vermont] is recruiting subjects for a study of some popular and critically acclaimed TV shows. Please consider volunteering. All subjects need to do is to watch several episodes of a specific TV show and answer some questions a week later. Those who participate in the study will be entered into a drawing for one of several cash prizes (they are giving away ten $25 visa cards and one $100 visa card). If you are interested in participating in this study follow this link: [link to an informational page, that included questions about exposure to *GoT*, a question about whether the volunteer was or had been a University of Vermont (UVM) student, and a place to sign up]."

40. Melanie C. Green and Timothy C. Brock, "The Role of Transportation in the Persuasiveness of Public Narratives," *Journal of Personality and Social Psychology* 79, no. 5 (2000): 701–21.

41. Appel, "Fictional Narratives Cultivate Just-World Beliefs."

42. Michael D. Slater, Donna Rouner and Marilee Long, "Television Dramas and Support for Controversial Public Policies: Effects and Mechanisms," *Journal of Communication* 56 (2006): 235–52.

43. Plato, *The Republic*, pp. 148–49, as quoted by Gerrig, *Experiencing Narrative Worlds: On the Psychological Activities of Reading* (New Haven, CT: Yale University Press, 1993) p. 196. A thank you to my student Allie Van Sickle for drawing my attention to this quote, which I later came across in Gerrig's book.

Chapter 4

House of Cards Effects

While the previous chapter on *Game of Thrones* discussed the impact of a fantasy world disconnected to the modern world in which we exist, the focus of the research in this chapter—Netflix's *House of Cards*—is set in the modern political world and plays out with characters filling recognizable political roles and operating in familiar political institutions. [1] As such, while some of the effects posited in this chapter parallel those examined in the previous chapter, the research in this chapter offers the reader the first look into the effects of politically relevant content on audiences' political perspectives from an explicitly political show. As mapped out in the discussion and framework in chapter 1, the effects of such a show on how we view politics are not necessarily the ones that might first come to mind. The political content with the potential to influence political perspectives lies not in portrayals of ideologies or political parties, but in more subtle ways, such as how just the world is portrayed, its ability to reinforce or engender cynicism, shape perspectives on means and ends, and make us think of certain issues that are used as plot devices. In this chapter, I report on a number of studies that my students and I designed to test the impact of *House of Cards* on just such political and politically relevant views.

THE UNJUST AND CYNICAL
WORLD OF *HOUSE OF CARDS*

Like HBO's *Game of Thrones*, Netflix's *House of Cards* stood out in popular entertainment when Netflix first released it for its repeated and powerfully dramatic lessons that the world is *not* just. *House of Cards* (based on the

BBC series and the book by Michael Dobbs by the same name) is the cynical antithesis of *The West Wing*. Just like in *Game of Thrones*, the cunning, self-serving, and often despicable characters seem to thrive in the *House of Cards* world, while the noble, selfless characters fail.

In an era characterized by extreme levels of cynicism about politics and government, it should not surprise anyone that Netflix's *House of Cards* became a cultural phenomenon. Netflix does not report viewership numbers, but it is estimated that about two to three million people watched *House of Cards* in the opening weekend of the second season (some estimates go as high as five million), which is impressive for a streaming-only program.[2] Netflix releases the entire season at one time, which has given many of those viewers the opportunity to binge-watch the series. This fact has some theoretical significance since binge-watching likely enhances the level of transportation experienced by the viewer and makes the viewing experience more akin to reading a novel. *House of Cards* has won a number of Emmys and Golden Globes, including nine Emmys in 2016.[3] Season 3 proved to be a disappointment to many fans (as reflected in reviews on Netflix and in social media), but the series built up fan loyalty that seems to have kept them watching. The popularity of the series is reflected anecdotally in the number of students that have told me that *House of Cards* inspired them to enroll in political science classes (a trend that I found a bit disturbing given the nature of the show). While the subject of the previous chapter, *Game of Thrones*, and *House of Cards* seem to have nothing in common—one is set in a fantasy world, the other is a political drama—they both seem to delight in cruelly defying our expectations of justice in story narratives.

House of Cards (henceforth *HoC*) tells the story of Frank and Claire Underwood (a married couple). At the start of the series, Frank, a Democrat, is the majority whip in the US House of Representatives and Claire is the head of a nonprofit charitable organization. The narrative follows the couple as they scheme and plot their way up the political ladder. Along the way, the couple exploits those around them and "dispose" of those who prove troublesome or in the way. Frank, for example, exploits a young reporter named Zoe Barnes in order to plant stories that undermine the nominee for Secretary of State (the post the incoming president had promised to Frank in exchange for his campaign support). Frank also uses fellow Congressman Peter Russo, whom he had helped avoid drunk driving and solicitation charges, to help undermine the nominee for Secretary of State with charges of anti-Semitism. (Underwood uses Russo in another scheme as well, one to get the Vice President out of the picture.) Congressman Russo acquires the "evidence" of anti-Semitism that sinks the nominee for Secretary of State. Then Frank gets the unstable Congressman Russo to run for governor of Pennsylvania, fully expecting him to fail (and he fails with a little push from Frank's henchman, Doug Stamper, who pays a prostitute to seduce Russo and get him drinking again). Underwood set up this scenario because he knows that when Congressman Russo fails it will create a vacuum that the Vice President (also from Pennsylvania) will be compelled to fill and thus relinquish the VP post (to run for governor in lieu of Russo). The plot works and Frank ends up becoming the Vice President. Next, Frank outmaneuvers the president's trusted adviser on trade policy with China, getting him exiled from the White House. Underwood also manipulates campaign contributions and lobbyists.

These plotlines may strike the reader as nothing more than a cynical take on our current politics (not to play down the effect such shows may have on audiences), but *HoC* takes it a brutal step further. When Congressmen Russo becomes a problem, not only does Frank have his henchman set Russo up for a fall, Frank kills Russo by closing the garage door on a drunk and passed-out Russo while Russo's car is still running. When the young reporter Frank was feeding stories to, Zoe Barnes, continues to question Frank on the death of Russo, he pushes Ms. Barnes in front of a Metro train. There is no justice for Frank's victims in the *HoC* world; indeed, instead of being punished Frank seems to be rewarded for his ruthlessness, ultimately manipulating his way to the presidency. It is a deeply cynical world in which the characters (and as a result we) are taught over and over again that if you wish to succeed (or even just survive) you need to do whatever it takes and not to put your trust in anyone or any institution. Through all of this (at least once an episode) the character Frank Underwood will pause from time to time, look directly into the camera to address the audience in monologues that reveal his cynicism, his means-justify-the-ends ruthlessness, and utter disregard for justice. For example, at the end of the episode in which Frank kills the reporter, Zoe Barnes, he looks in the camera and tells us

[D]on't waste a breath mourning Ms. Barnes—every kitten grows up to be a cat. They seem so harmless at first—small, quiet, lapping up their saucer of milk. But once their claws get long enough, they draw blood — sometimes, from the hands that feeds them. For those of us climbing to the top of the food chain, there can be no mercy. There is but one rule—hunt, or be hunted.[4]

It should be noted that this technique of having a character talking directly to the audience likely enhances transportation into the narrative and identification with Frank. It intimately connects the audience to Underwood's cynical machinations and encourages the viewer to actually identify with this vile, scheming, and brutal character.

The storylines of other characters in the *HoC* world reinforce the unjust world and ends-justify-the-means lessons and cynicism. Congressman Russo, for example, seemed to be one of those characters in standard narratives who clean up their acts and go on to succeed in something big—he stopped drinking, started AA, got into a stable relationship, and was working hard to do the right thing and win the governor's race. Instead of it working out for Russo, Frank Underwood destroys him. The same is true for Freddy Hayes, the proprietor of Frank's favorite rib place. Freddy, who had built a successful small business, was actually on the verge of great success when he is brought down by his criminal history (for which he *had* served time). Instead of helping Freddy, which, to be fair, Frank seems to want to do, Frank abandons Freddy because defending him would interfere with Frank's ambitions for the presidency.

A host of other characters who try to do the right thing are manipulated, framed, or outmaneuvered by Frank and/or his wife, Claire (who is his equal in ruthless ambition). A reporter digging into Zoe Barnes's death gets set up and imprisoned on false espionage charges. An artist friend and lover of Claire's is destroyed. Claire orders the administrator of her nonprofit organization to fire half of her staff (her organization loses a large donation when Frank is passed over for the Secretary of State post); after the administrator carries out Claire's order, Claire cruelly fires the administrator as well. Throughout the series the lesson that the world is not just and that the ends justify the means is driven home in one dramatic event after another. The promotional tagline under a picture of Frank for the second season was "Bad for a Greater Good." A dark tagline in and of itself, but the show makes it clear that all of Frank's machinations (and Claire's) are for their own benefit, not "the greater good." The promotional tagline also draws attention to the other politically relevant theme running throughout the show—that ends justify means. All of the plot twists discussed above drive home the same lesson—success comes with doing whatever it takes, no matter the legalities or morality.

These are not the only politically relevant themes of the show. In *HoC*, in what is in some ways an extension of the "ends justify the means" theme, the lessons that the characters learn and in the perspectives one might adopt from identifying with the characters, are extremely cynical about human nature and institutions. *HoC* also has the potential to have direct political effects because it portrays political institutions, politicians and the media in the U.S. (a number of real world journalists actually appear in the show) and deals with a variety of real world political issues.

Since at this point in the book the reader will have already been exposed to the theoretical reasons for expecting *House of Cards* to influence viewers along the lines hypothesized, I will not rehash the theory here. Suffice it to say that the Transportation-Imagery Model and the concept of identification, discussed previously in this book, explain *how* viewers of *HoC* could be influenced by the show. The show certainly has the potential to transport the viewer into the narrative and the performances of Kevin Spacey, Robin Wright, and the rest of the cast are notable for the way in which the actors draw you in and make it hard not to identify with them (though, the sexual harassment revelations about Kevin Spacey in 2017 have no doubt brought an end to identification for viewers of the show). As noted above, the show's practice of having Frank address the audience directly (and in the 2017 season Claire does the same) enhances the potential for audience transportation and identification. Netflix's practice of releasing the entire season at one time allows audiences to binge-watch, further enhancing the likelihood of transportation. Narrative transportation and identification lead us to hypothesize that viewers of the show will internalize the lessons and perspectives of the show, leaving them less likely to see the world as just, more likely to believe that the ends justify the means, and more cynical about human nature and U.S. political institutions. The nature of the effects hypothesized—the impact on the belief in a just world and cynicism—also feed our expectations of influence. We are not positing that the show would alter partisan or ideological perspectives. Underwood's status as a southern Democrat could be seen as a way to muddle partisan and ideological messages, since southern Democrats are rather rare and inert political forces, tending to straddle the ideological lines of the twenty-first century. Furthermore, as discussed in chapter 1, ideology and party are not the political attitudes likely to be influenced by such an overtly political show because viewers would be alert to such potential effects. We are focusing instead on cases involving political lessons that are less obvious and thus may escape the awareness of audiences and, consequently, be unlikely to provoke counter arguments while watching.

Finally, *HoC* arrived on the cultural scene at a time when the public was already very cynical about government institutions, politicians, and the media. Its arrival, however, was also at a time when there were other entertainment media, like *The Daily Show* and *The Colbert Report* (and just a few years after the end of *The West Wing*) which, while critical of politics, were less cynical, instead promoting a more skeptical take on politics.[5] As such, in contrast to these other shows, the effect of *HoC* on its audience was likely to push viewers further into cynicism. Analyses that allow for that contrast can be found in Study 3 of this chapter and the analyses of the effects of *The Daily Show* and *The Colbert Report* that I report on in chapter 7. The contrast can also be seen in two telling interviews that Jon Stewart and Stephen Colbert conducted with Kevin Spacey and Beau Willimon (the producer and writer of *HoC*) in 2015. In both interviews Stewart and Colbert asked whether their guests thought *HoC* depicted Washington as it is. Both Spacey and Willimon answered yes; Stewart and Colbert both reacted with incredulity.

In addition to the effects above, we also hypothesize that *HoC* could have a media-based agenda-setting effect. The agenda-setting effect occurs when the issues that the news covers become the issues that are on the public's mind. The agenda-setting effect is based on a different theory than what I have discussed thus far; it is based on the accessibility theory that is part of schema theory (or the Cognitive Transactional Model). Accessibility theory posits that the things that we are thinking about at any point in time are those that have been primed or activated by our environment (including the media, which has taken up more and more of our cognitive environment). A large body of research in political science—both experimental and survey-based—has provided evidence of the agenda-setting effect for news programs.[6] While there is only one instance of researchers having uncovered evidence of agenda-setting in entertainment media,[7] I expect that additional research on entertainment media will find more evidence that entertainment media can affect the public's political agenda. Entertainment media, after all, use real world issues as part of their plotlines; and, when the shows are set in the arena of modern-day politics, like *HoC*, the potential for agenda-setting may be even greater. The third season of *HoC* features an issue prominently throughout—unemployment. My thought was that viewers of that season who were constantly primed on this issue might have walked away from the story with a heightened sense of the importance of the issue.

To test all our hypotheses regarding the effect of *HoC* on its audience I, with the assistance of my students, carried out a series of different studies— two surveys and an experiment.

STUDY 1

Design and Measures

The first study was part of the online survey used to study *Game of Thrones*.[8] The methods used are the same as those for Study 1 discussed in the previous chapter. Our primary foci in Study 1 were the relationships between exposure to *HoC* and levels of belief in a just world (BJW) and views about whether ends justify the means. We also extended the analysis to include those attitudes that the literature has found to be related to the BJW—attitudes toward welfare and punitive criminal justices—and ones we expected both BJW and the ends-means attitude to be related to—ideology and views on how to fight terrorism. The full model (and results which will be discussed later) can be found in figure 4.1. Note that, as with the analysis of *GoT*, our main control variable for BJW is the importance of religion to the respondent (though we do also control for other variables such as gender).

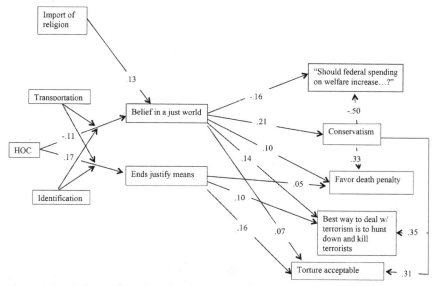

Figure 4.1. Full model (and results) for *HoC* Study 1.

As with the *GoT* study, we used a series of questions designed to measure how much of a fan the respondent was of the show in order to have an indicator of how transported the respondent had been by the narrative. These fan-level questions included questions regarding the respondents' familiarity with characters, whether they watched the old episodes again in anticipation of the new season, and so on (see Q69 in appendix 1). For identification we measure the likelihood of the respondent to identify with characters using the Motivation and Mindreading scale developed by Carpenter, Green, and LaFlam.[9]

The principal independent variable—exposure to *HoC*—was measured by asking respondents how familiar they were with the show; response options ranged from not having seen the show to having seen all of it. See appendix 1 for the full questionnaire. We used a feeling thermometer question to ask how respondents felt about a number of the principal characters. The primary purpose of asking for feelings about the characters was so we could include images of the characters next to the characters' names in order to re-evoke the feelings associated with the show and activate respondents' schema of the show.

To measure the tendency to believe in a just world (BJW) we used the same questions as in the *GoT* study—"Some people say that people get ahead by their own hard work; others say that lucky breaks or help from other people are more important. Which do you think is most important?" and "How much of the time do people get what they deserve?" I recoded the responses so that the higher scores represented a greater tendency to believe in a just world. To measure the respondents' feelings about ends and means, we asked them to agree or disagree with the statement "Sometimes good people have to do bad things in order to attain a greater good."

Results

As with the *Game of Thrones* study in the last chapter, we attempted to assess the level of selective exposure to *HoC* by asking respondents what got them to start watching *HoC*; and, for those who had only seen some of the episodes of *HoC*, we asked them why they had not watched all the episodes. For this second question, if the respondent selected "I didn't like the show" as the reason they did not watch the all of the episodes, we asked them to indicate why they did not like it in an open-ended question. Figure 4.2 shows the responses to the question "what got you to start watching *HoC*?" Figure 4.3 contains the reasons why those who had not watched all of *HoC* disliked the show.

So what got our respondents to watch *HoC*? *HoC*, being an overtly political entertainment show, poses more of a problem for selective exposure. The buzz about the show—from the constant advertising on Netflix (it was, after all, one of the company's first attempts at original programming), to friends watching it, to everyone talking about it—certainly accounts for most of the

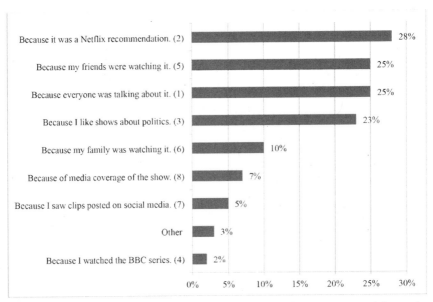

Figure 4.2. "What got you to start watching *House of Cards*?" Percentage of those who had at least some exposure.

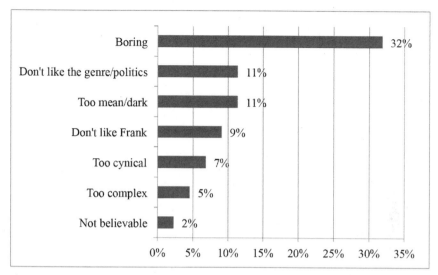

Figure 4.3. Reason given for not liking *HoC* among respondents who have not seen all of the shows because they did not like them. There were 44 written explanations for 44 respondents who said that they did not like *HoC* (of the 13% of the sample who had watched just some of the show, 28% said they disliked the show).

exposure. Almost a quarter of respondents, however, said they started watching it because they liked political shows, a finding that raises our concerns about selective exposure at least on the overtly political aspects of the show (not BJW or ends and means). This effect of the genre is also reflected in the reasons given for not liking the show among those who reported seeing just some of the episodes—"I don't like political shows" was cited by 11 percent (figure 4.3). Concerns about self-selection of the basis of BJW are reflected in the 11 percent who said they did not like the show because it was too mean or dark and the 7 percent who said it was too cynical.

Overall, it seems that the buzz among social networks about *HoC* was what drew people to the show, not unlike what we found with *GoT*. Wanting to check out what everyone is talking about and be part of the conversations among friends and on social media seems to be the dominant factor leading to exposure. There is little indication that initial exposure is based on some understanding of the underlying political values of the shows. There does seem to be some selectivity in the continued exposure to these shows, but it appears to be relevant for only a small portion of the sample. In the analysis that follows, I will examine the impact of any exposure to these shows, which should eliminate the problem of selectivity associated with those who watched only some episodes and then stopped because they did not like *HoC*.

In figure 4.4, I present the breakdown of respondents on the just world response to the BJW question (that hard work is most important to getting ahead) for our sample based on exposure to the *HoC*. As can be seen from this preliminary cut at the data, a smaller percentage of those who were exposed to *HoC* selected this option, a finding that offers some preliminary support for our hypothesis that exposure to *HoC* would be associated with a weaker tendency to see the world as just. Additionally, the bivariate correlations between fandom of the show and responses to the question about whether people get what they deserve lends some additional support to the relationship between *HoC* and the BJW. We measured fandom by asking respondents if they binge-watched the show, whether they had re-watched previous seasons in anticipation of the release of the new season, whether they had posted anything about the show on social media, discussed it with their friends, or would vote for Frank Underwood.[10] The correlation for this measure of *HoC* fan-level and responses to whether people get what they deserve was –0.08 (significant at

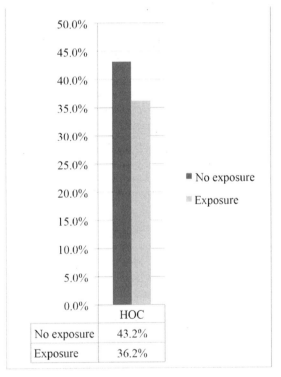

Figure 4.4. Exposure to *HoC* and BJW. Bars represent the percent of respondents who believe that "hard work is most important" to getting ahead.

better than .05). On the question of means and ends as measured by the question as to whether sometimes people have to do bad things in order to attain a greater good, the correlation with fandom was .234 (significant at better than the .01 level).

I conducted a series of regression analyses that more rigorously test the relationship between exposure to the shows and the belief in a just world. In those analyses, I controlled for the importance of religion and the gender of the respondent. I do not control for ideology in these models for the same reasons given in the previous chapter (according to the research, the causal direction is more likely to go from BJW to ideology than the other way around). To model the conditioning effects of transportation I ran the analysis with fan level instead of exposure. I included an interaction term that was the product of exposure and the MM scale (that measures tendency to identify) in order to model the conditioning effect of identification. The equations for the analysis were as follows:

1. BJW = *HoC* exposure + religion + gender
2. BJW = *HoC* fan level + religion + gender
3. BJW = *HoC* exposure + (*HoC**identification) + religion + gender

BJW is the combined answers to the two BJW questions recoded so that the higher the score, the higher the tendency to believe the world is just. *HoC* exposure was a simple dichotomous variable that equaled one for any exposure, zero for none (51 percent of our sample had some exposure to *HoC*). I used the interval-level fan scale as a surrogate for exposure to *HoC* enhanced by transportation. The logic in using fan questions as a surrogate for the interaction between exposure and transportation is that engagement in the series in multiple ways (which is how we measured fandom) should capture the respondents' level of transportation by the series. That is, the more the respondent reported having done things such as re-watch the show in anticipation of the release of the new season, binge-watch, or posting on social media about the show, the more likely they had been transported by *HoC*. Religion was measured by responses to the ANES question "How important is religion in your life?" recoded so that the high score was "very important."

The regression results for *HoC* (Equations 1–3) show the relationship between *HoC* and its audience's BJW (see table 4.1). As hypothesized, exposure to *HoC* and fan level (the surrogate measure for exposure and transportation in Equation 2) are both inversely related to BJW. Furthermore, exposure to *HoC* and fan level are of about of equal importance in explaining just world beliefs as the respondents' expressed importance of religion (the relative importance of each factor is indicated by the standardized regression

Chapter 4

Table 4.1. Study 1 BJW Regression Results for *HoC* (Study 1)

	Equation 1	*Equation 2*	*Equation 3*
HoC Exposure	−.23*		.59*
	(−.11)		(.28)
HoC Fan Level		−.05*	
		(−.10)	
HoC Exp X Identification			−.04*
			(−.40)
Importance of Religion	.13*	.13*	.13*
	(.13)	(.14)	(.13)
Male	.01	.01	−.02
	(.003)	(.01)	(−.01)
Adjusted R²	.029	.027	.034

* significant at the .05 level or better, one-tailed test
Numbers in parentheses are the standardized regression coefficients.

coefficients in the table). And, as was the case for *GoT*, the impact of the show is much greater for those who have a tendency to identify with others (equation 3); indeed, it is only among those who identified with the characters that exposure to the show is associated with a lower belief in a just world. This is as expected, since Frank and Claire Underwood not only contribute to the multiple injustices in their world, their behavior and expressed beliefs also make it clear that they do not believe the world is just. Audiences who identify with these two characters may be adopting the cynical view of Frank and Claire. If audience members identify with any of the characters who exhibit a better nature, their it-is-an-unjust-world lesson comes when the character they identify with is, as is the fate of most of the "good" characters, destroyed by Frank's and/or Claire's machinations.

To further test the relationship between *HoC* and respondents' feelings about whether ends justify the means, I regressed the level of agreement with the statement "sometimes good people have to do bad things in order to attain a greater good" on exposure to the shows or fan level and gender. I present the results in table 4.2. Both simple exposure to *HoC* and fan levels (the way we modeled transportation in this study) are significantly related to believing that the ends justify the means for both shows.

Finally, to extend the analysis to the more specific political attitudes such as those regarding welfare, criminal justice, conservatism, and the use of deadly force (as hypothesized in figure 4.1), I ran a series of regressions (full results available upon request) statistically assessing the relationship between BJW, ends-versus-means, and all the specific attitudes identified in the model. The results can be found in figure 4.1. And, as previous research-

Table 4.2.   *HoC* Ends/Means Regressions
(Study 1)

	HoC	*HoC*
Exposure	.54*	
	(.17)	
Fan Level		.15*
		(.21)
Male	.50*	.46*
	(.16)	(.14)
Adjusted R²	.059	.072

* significant at the .05 level or better, one-tailed test

ers have found, the tendency to believe the world is just was related to lower support for welfare spending and higher support for punitive criminal justice and terrorism policy, suggesting that the effect of *HoC* may go beyond affecting how just their audiences view the world or the extent to which ends justify the means, but also indirectly affect specific political attitudes as well.

STUDY 2

The second study to test the impact of *HoC* was an online experiment carried out in tandem with the second *Game of Thrones* experiment reported on in the previous chapter. As such, the details of the methodology of this study can be found in that chapter. To briefly rehash, my students and I recruited subjects for the experiment using Facebook, Twitter, and email. Students in the research seminar along with students in my "American Political System" class were asked to disseminate social media messages to attract study subjects (students in my classes were instructed to just recruit subjects and to not participate in the study themselves). Colleagues at Texas A&M and the University of Richmond also distributed the recruitment messages.

Enough people volunteered to create five groups of about 50 subjects. I sorted the subjects who volunteered by whether they were UVM students, their gender, and their exposure to *HoC*. Then I randomly assigned subjects using an interval selection process with a random start into one of five groups for the experiment (two of the groups were used exclusively for the *Game of Thrones* study I reported on in chapter 3). Subjects in two of the groups were asked to watch 6 episodes of *HoC* (26 subjects assigned to this condition completed the study) or *The Newsroom* during a one-week period (27 subjects completed this condition); another group was not asked to watch anything (38 subjects). For the comparison group we picked HBO's *The Newsroom* because it was an overtly political show, but one that was the opposite of *HoC* on just world and ends-justify-means themes. In *The Newsroom* producer Aaron Sorkin's gives television news the same treatment he gave the White House in *The West Wing*. The cast of characters always seem to be striving to do the right thing in *The Newsroom*, and are, to a large degree, successful. The upstanding morals the cast exhibits through their actions and in the dialogue is the polar opposite of Frank and Claire Underwood. It would be very out of character for the characters in *The Newsroom* to follow the ruthless end-justifies-means behavior exhibited by the Underwoods, and the notion that pursuing admirable goals is worth the struggle is at the very heart of *The Newsroom*.

After the week during which we asked our subjects to watch *HoC* or *The Newsroom* was over, I emailed all subjects a link to a questionnaire. The questionnaire included questions about how many episodes the subject actually watched, manipulation check questions that asked about characters and the events of the shows (these questions included pictures of the characters so as to re-evoke themes of the program through the imagery), and measures of the key dependent variables and control variables (see Appendix 2 for the questionnaire). To measure belief in a just world and attitudes about ends justifying means we used the same questions as used in the survey in Study 1. In this study, we used a number of items from Green and Brock's narrative transportation scale to measure the extent to which subjects were transported by the show we asked them to watch (see previous chapter for a discussion of this measure).[11]

In figures 4.5 and 4.6, I present the simple breakdowns of the results. While those assigned to *HoC* scored lower on the BJW scale than the subjects who we asked to watch the comparison show and the group that we did not asked to watch any show, the differences in the means were not statistically significant. On whether the subjects believed the ends justify the means, the subjects who were asked to watch *HoC* scored significantly higher on this question than those who watched *The Newsroom* and the watch-nothing control group.

To test whether those who were transported or identified with a character were more affected by exposure to the shows, I ran a series of regressions, regressing BJW and ends/means on exposure to *HoC*. In this analysis, I modeled the effects of transportation and identification with interaction variables, multiplying the level of transportation/identification times exposure to show. I put the results in table 4.3 and 4.4. The results for BJW lend support to the hypothesis that exposure to *HoC* reduces the tendency to believe in a just world—the coefficients for exposure to the show and for fan level are negative and statistically significant. The interaction term for transportation

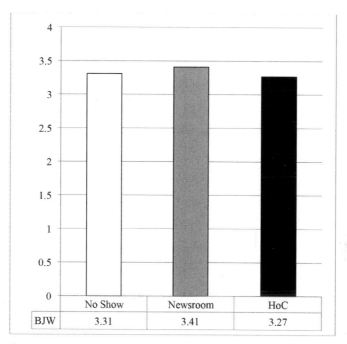

Figure 4.5. Mean BJW score for experimental and control groups in Study 2.

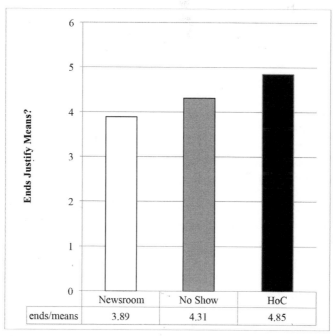

Figure 4.6. Mean score on ends justify means question by experimental group for Study 2.

Table 4.3. BJW Regressed on Experimental Manipulations and
Conditioning Effects of Transportation and Identification (Study 2)

	HoC v. NR	HoC v. Control
Exp. Group	–.97*	–1.17*
	(–.54)	(–.61)
Exp. Group X Transportation	.04*	.04*
	(.80)	(.76)
Exp. Group X Identification	–.09	–.09
	(–.28)	(–.27)
Adjusted R²	.023	.030

* significant at the .05 level or better, one-tailed test

Table 4.4. Ends Justify Means Regressed on Experimental
Manipulations and Conditioning Effects of Transportation and
Identification (Study 2)

	HoC v. NR	HoC v. Control
Exp. group	–.18	–.60
	(–.06)	(–.21)
Exp. Group X Transportation	.01	.01
	(.08)	(.09)
Exp. Group X Identification	.22*	.22*
	(.44)	(.47)
Adjusted R²	.017	.117

* significant at the .05 level or better, one-tailed test

suggests that the effect of the shows on BJW weakened slightly as transportation increased. This result seems puzzling since narrative transportation theory suggests that the impact of the shows should be strengthened
by transportation. For a discussion of these contradictory findings, see the
previous chapter. The interaction term for identification and exposure was
not statistically significant.

The regression results for the impact of the experimental manipulations
and the interaction terms for attitudes about ends and means found that as
identification increased (measured on a scale of 0 to 10) support the notion
that "sometimes good people have to do bad things in order to attain a greater
good" increased. This finding corroborates the findings of Study 1 and seems
fitting given that any identification with the main characters (and the fact that
Frank Underwood addresses the audience on occasion is likely to enhance
this) means identifying with characters who are absolutely ruthless, for whom
the ends justify any means.

STUDY 3

In Study 3 we attempted to go beyond the belief in a just world and attitude on ends justifying means in assessing the relationship between exposure to *HoC* and cynicism. The study was a cross-sectional anonymous survey, carried out as a class research project with my "Politics & the Media" students in the 2015 spring semester.[12] We launched the survey shortly after the release of the third season of *HoC*. The students and I pretested a series of questions designed to measure exposure to *HoC*, levels of cynicism, attitudes about political institutions, and what respondents believed to be the most important issue facing the US, as well as the belief in a just world (BJW) questions. The questionnaire also included the questions to measure narrative transportation and identification used in Study 2 (for the core questions see appendix 4). For this project, we also included two questions measuring the perceived realism of the portrayal of government and politicians in *HoC*. We asked respondents these questions on perceived realism thinking that, because this was a show set in modern-day Washington, acceptance of the realism of the show would play a role in whether viewers internalized the lessons of the show. We then agreed that the students would utilize their social media contacts to distribute the link to the survey. To entice participants to complete the survey, respondents could submit their email to be included in a drawing for one of two $50 Visa cards. The sample size was 914.

I will turn first to one of the central foci of the previous two studies—the relationship between viewing *HoC* and the belief in a just world. In order to assess the impact of exposure to *HoC* I ran a multivariate analysis, regressing BJW on exposure to *HoC*, a series of interaction terms designed to measure the conditioning impact of transportation, identification and realism, the importance of religion, and gender. I present the results of that analysis in table 4.5. As reported in the table, exposure to *HoC* is associated with a lower BJW score, though the significance level just misses the .10 level (the standardized regression coefficient, however, puts exposure to *HoC* on par with the importance of religion as an explainer of the variation in BJW as it was in the results of Study 1). The relationship between exposure to the show and a reduction in just world beliefs was stronger for those who thought the show is a realistic portrayal of politicians.

Given the cynical nature of *HoC*, we also tested to see whether the cynicism would show up in the audience of the show. We used two different measures of cynicism. One was a question that I designed for a previous study that read as follows:

When it comes to disagreements between people over how things are, which of the following statements comes closer to what you believe? It is impossible to know which claims are accurate because studies and evidence can be manipulated to prove whatever someone wants to prove. It is possible to know which claims are accurate based on a careful assessment of the research and evidence.

The purpose of the question is to distinguish cynics from skeptics (the cynical response is the first option). I present the breakdown of responses to this question and exposure to the show in figure 4.7. Compared to those who have had no exposure to *HoC*, those who have seen at least some of it evinced a significantly higher level of cynicism and lower level of skepticism. While this specific component of the study of *HoC* cannot establish a causal link (since it was not part of the experiment in Study 2 and is only supported by this survey), this finding, in combination with the results from the research in chapter 7, does show that the audience for *HoC* are more cynical than the audiences for *The Daily Show* and *The Colbert Report* (who tend to evince more skepticism than cynicism). Since audiences for all three of these political shows likely overlap, these findings hint at differing causal effects from watching explicitly political shows with divergent messages on cynicism and skepticism. It could be due to a framing effect—*HoC's* more cynical portrayal of politicians and government versus *The Daily Show* and *The Colbert Report*'s more skeptical approach—that primes different considerations among audiences, or it could be that the programs actually shift attitudes on government and politicians. The answer will have to be left for future research to settle.

Table 4.5.   BJW Regressed on Exposure to
HoC and Control Variables (Study 3)

	BJW
HoC Exposure	−.29**
	(−.14)
HoC X Transportation	.01**
	(.17)
HoC X Identification	.03
	(.06)
HoC X Realism: Government	.09
	(.06)
HoC X Realism: Politicians	−.12**
	(−.09)
Importance of Religion	.13*
	(.13)
Male	−.08
	(−.03)
Adjusted R^2	.018

* significant at the .05 level or better, one-tailed test
** significant at the .11 level, one-tailed test

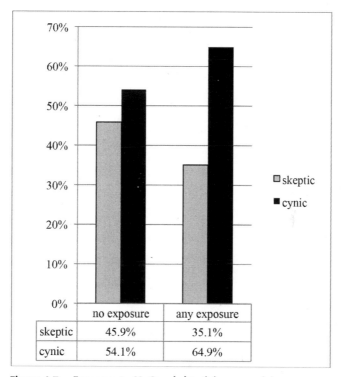

	no exposure	any exposure
skeptic	45.9%	35.1%
cynic	54.1%	64.9%

Figure 4.7. Exposure to *HoC* and skepticism v. cynicism.

To test the relationship between exposure to *HoC* and cynicism further, I created two indexes of cynicism out of the questions we asked, one regarding people's motives and the other cynicism about government. The index of cynicism about people's motives is an additive scale, the sum of a number of items that asked respondents their level of agreement with statements such as "It is safer to trust nobody" and "I think most people would lie to get ahead" (see the first three statements in Q68 in appendix 4). The index of cynicism about government was the sum of respondents reactions to the standard "How much of the time do you think you can trust the government in Washington" and the statement "I don't think public officials care much about what people like me think." I regressed these measures of cynicism on exposure to *HoC*, a series of interaction terms designed to measure the conditioning impact of transportation, identification and realism, and gender. The results can be found in table 4.6. Exposure to *HoC* was associated with increased cynicism about people's motives only for those who indicated they identified with a character, a finding similar to the findings in Study 1. Exposure to *HoC* was actually related to lower levels of cynicism about government, but only for

Table 4.6. Cynicism about People's Motives and Government Regressed on Exposure to *HoC* and Control Variables (Study 4)

	Cynicism of People	Cynicism of Government
HoC Exposure	.06	−.43*
	(.02)	(−.20)
HoC X Transportation	−.02*	−.002
	(−.23)	(−.04)
HoC X Identification	.08*	−.06*
	(.11)	(−.13)
HoC X Realism: Government	.17	.12**
	(.07)	(.08)
HoC X Realism: Politicians	.17	.33*
	(.08)	(.25)
Male	.17	.20*
	(.04)	(.09)
Adjusted R^2	.010	.038

* significant at the .05 level or better, one-tailed test
** significant at the .11 level, one-tailed test

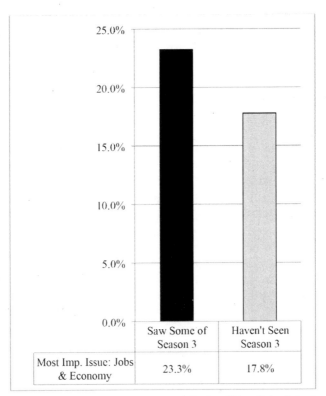

	Saw Some of Season 3	Haven't Seen Season 3
Most Imp. Issue: Jobs & Economy	23.3%	17.8%

Figure 4.8. Exposure to season 3 of *HoC* and identifying jobs & the economy as the most important issue facing the US.

those who did not think the show was a realistic portrayal of government and politicians; respondents who did think *HoC* realistic expressed greater cynicism about government. This makes perfect sense and serves as a reminder that when researchers are dealing with overtly political shows set in current times, one has to be careful when testing for media effects of those shows on attitudes that are too closely tied to the explicitly political content. That is, as argued in chapter 1, the closer the attitudes are to the explicit political content—like trust in government—the greater the likelihood that audiences will be alert to the messages and possibly dismiss the messages.

Finally, given the prominence of some political issues used as plot devices for *HoC*, we decided to see if *HoC* had an agenda-setting effect on its audience. In season 3 the most prominent issue is jobs and the economy—President Underwood goes to any length to get his program, America Works, implemented in order to revitalize the economy and give every American a job. To test for an agenda-setting effect on this issue we compared those who saw at least some of season 3 with those who did not on the question of what the respondents thought was the most important issue facing the US. In figure 4.8 I show the results for the percent of those who selected "jobs & the economy." A statistically significant larger percentage of respondents who had seen at least some of season 3 choose "jobs & the economy," indicating that the show had an agenda-setting effect on its audience.

CONCLUSION

As I argued in chapter 1, the types of political effects overtly political shows are likely to have are more subtle than what one might expect. Instead of having an effect on partisanship or ideology, shows like *House of Cards* are more likely to affect audiences' perspectives in ways that can inform ideology and partisanship—like the belief in a just world—or attitudes that determine the levels of participation, such as person's level of cynicism, or on what issues people think are important. The studies I reported on in this chapter provide some evidence that these areas are indeed areas where overtly political shows may shape how we see the political world.

The findings of the relationship between *House of Cards*, the belief in a just world, and the belief that the ends justify the means are similar to those that the studies of *Game of Thrones* uncovered. The fact that two disparate programs that share common lessons with regard to these two perspectives should increase our confidence in the results. The inconsistent finding regarding the effect of transportation in both studies does raise some concerns and points to an area that needs additional research. This could be a consequence of using a surrogate for transportation in the first studies for both *GoT* and

HoC—level of fandom as an indication of immersion—as opposed to Green and Brock's battery of questions. The Green and Brock measure was associated with BJW in the wrong direction. As mentioned in chapter 3, this could indicate that transportation is a threshold state as opposed to one of degree that one can measure with a scale (as Slater et al. speculated).[13] If that is the case, research that finds a way to measure when subjects cross that threshold of transportation would be beneficial. It could also have been an artifact of the different designs, but since Slater et al. ran into the same puzzle, I do not think that is necessarily the case.

Two of the three *HoC* studies and two of the three *GoT* studies found, as theorized, that the extent to which someone identifies with a character in the story was important to the stories having the hypothesized effects. The theory of identification argues that when you identify with the character you take on the character's perspectives and may carry those perspectives with you when you leave the narrative.[14] The quality acting and the storytelling techniques—like Frank's conversations with the audience—increase the likelihood of identification with the characters of these shows and could explain why those who identify with the characters share their perspectives. I do think additional research is needed on this point, however. It strikes me that those who identify with the characters could do so because they already share their perspectives—especially in the case of *HoC* and the ends-justify-the-means attitude, which is such a dominant trait of both Frank and Claire. The obvious solution for future research would be to include a pretest measure for the dependent variables if it could be done without telegraphing the intent of the experiment. For the research presented here, how convinced you are that it was the series that affected the end-justify-the-means perspective depends on your assessment of the strength of the theory of identification and the previous research findings regarding the dynamic of identification. At the very least, I believe that the shows reinforced this perspective for those who identified with a character.

NOTES

1. Portions of this chapter appeared previously in a paper presented at the 2015 Annual Meeting of the Midwest Political Science Association, April 16–19, Chicago, IL, and coauthored with Sarah Weichselbaum, Hayley Aydelott, Evyn Banach, Matthew Donovan, Allie VanSickle, and Jack Vest.

2. Derek Thompson, "Is *House of Cards* Really a Hit? The people reading about TV and the people watching TV are living in two separate worlds," *The Atlantic*, February 24, 2014, accessed July 29, 2014 http://www.theatlantic.com/business/archive/2014/02/is-i-house-of-cards-i-really-a-hit/284035/.

3. IMDB, *"House of Cards* Awards," accessed August 30, 2017, http://www.imdb.com/title/tt1856010/awards.

4. "Chapter 14," season 2, episode 1, released February 14, 2014.

5. See Geoffrey Baym, *From Cronkite to Colbert: The Evolution of Broadcast News* (New York: Oxford University Press, 2009).

6. See, John W. Dearing and Everett Rogers, *Agenda-Setting* (Thousand Oaks, CA: Sage, 1996); and, Shanto Iyengar and Donald R. Kinder, *News that Matters: Television and American Opinion* (Chicago: University of Chicago Press, 1987).

7. Andrew R. Holbrook and Timothy G. Hill, "Agenda-Setting and Priming in Prime Time Television: Crime Dramas as Political Cues," *Political Communication* 22, no. 3 (2005): 277–95.

8. The students who helped with this study included Marissa Bucci, Mac Cleary, Daniel Cmejla, Nicholas Ingersoll, Kelly Joyce, Anastasia Kopp, Luca Piccin, Macie Rebel, Connor Seitchik, Emma Stern, Ashley Szilvassy, Nicholas Usen, Sarah Weich-selbaum, Matthew West, and Lauren Willigan.

9. Jordan M. Carpenter, Melanie C. Green, and Jeff LaFlam, "People or Profiles: Individual Differences in Online Social Networking Use." *Personality and Individual Differences* 50, no. 5 (April 2011): 538–41.

10. Fandom was calculated by adding the affirmative responses to the series of questions about immersion into the show. See Q69 and Q74 in Appendix 1.

11. Melanie C. Green and Timothy C. Brock, "The Role of Transportation in the Persuasiveness of Public Narratives," *Journal of Personality and Social Psychology* 79, no. 5 (2000): 701–21.

12. There were 94 students in the class.

13. Michael D. Slater, Donna Rouner, and Marilee Long, "Television Dramas and Support for Controversial Public Policies: Effects and Mechanisms," *Journal of Communication* 56 (2006): 235–52.

14. Keith Oatley, "Emotions and the Story Worlds of Fiction," in *Narrative Impact: Social and Cognitive Foundations*, eds. Melanie C. Green, Jeffrey J. Strange, and Timothy C. Brock (Mahwah, NJ: Lawrence Erlbaum Associates, Inc., 2002), 39–69.

Chapter 5

Sci Fi

The previous two chapters tested the impact of two different individual shows—one fantasy and one political fiction. [1] As I argued in chapter 1, one can look beyond individual shows, movies, or books for politically relevant content that may have an effect on audiences. One may look for the common themes/lessons that appear repeatedly in our stories. Or, one may examine entire genres of storytelling for their own unique subset of politically relevant messages which arise from the very nature of the genre. In this chapter I examine the politically relevant content of one genre—science fiction—and report on a study my students and I conducted on the impact of such lessons. [2]

THE POLITICALLY RELEVANT CONTENT
OF A GENRE: SCIENCE FICTION

The Dangers of Technology

While the genre of science fiction has allowed us to imagine the seemingly impossible, out to the edges of space-time, it also typically offers a cautionary tale of the dangers of technology. Indeed, a subgenre of science fiction, dystopian science fiction, usually involves technology run amok in some way. Sometimes, it is the artificial intelligence that we create which rises up and destroys us, such as the robots in the works of Isaac Asimov, HAL in *2001: A Space Odyssey*, the Cylons in the *Battlestar Galactica* series, and Skynet in the *Terminator* movies. Other times, in other dystopian science fiction stories, humans ruin their own future and/or destroy themselves with the technology they have developed. Humans destroy themselves with nuclear weapons in the original *Planet of the Apes* movies, with an experimental drug in the newer version of the series. We engineer viruses that destroy us in *Twelve Monkeys*, and the direct wiring of the internet in our brains makes us mindless consumers in the book *Feed*. In the many different zombie movies and television shows, the zombies are usually a product of some science gone awry. And, the dangers of technology are not just to humans, sometimes humans' pursuit of technology leads to the ruin of other races/planets, as in *Avatar*.

It isn't just dystopian science fiction that includes such cautionary lessons about technology. Even in more optimistic tales of the genre humans are often endangered by technology. In what is one of, if not *the* most optimistic imagined futures of science fiction, the *Star Trek* series, humans have rebounded after World War III nearly destroys the planet. This post-nuclear war scenario seems to be a stock part of science fiction stories that are set in earth's future, perhaps a leftover of the twentieth-century beliefs that nuclear war was close to a historical certainty. Additionally, in the second installment of the series, *Star Trek: The Next Generation*, one of the biggest challenges the crew of the Enterprise must confront is the Borg, a cyborg species, a hybrid of organic-based life forms and machines. It is a species in which individuality is extinguished in a hive-like collective (each Borg "drone" is plugged into the collective, not unlike humans who are so attached to their devices and social media today), and whose goal is to assimilate (and effectively destroy) all other species in order to add the biological and technological distinctiveness of the new species to the Borg collective. In what is probably the other most optimistic science fiction series—the BBC's *Doctor Who* series—the Doctor confronts similar technology-gone-awry races such as the Daleks and the Cybermen. Both the Daleks and the Cybermen are the result of misguided attempts to improve life through technology that, instead, end up destroying critical aspects of what it is to be "human."

Whether it is a component of the main plotline or it just appears in selected episodes, the lesson that technology can lead to ruin is a staple of science fiction. Consequently, watching or reading science fiction means a high likelihood of exposure to a lesson about the dangers of technology, and those who watch a lot of it, fans of science fiction, are likely to be exposed to repeated lessons along these lines.

Now, back to political reality. In the early decades of the twenty-first century the rapid advancement of technology has been and will increasingly be a part of the realm of politics—government regulation, promotion, and/or use of new and emerging technologies. Think about the space program, or the development of military technology (such as weaponized drones and robots), or privacy in the cybernetic world, cyber warfare, and government financing for and regulation of research in genetics and artificial intelligence. How we as a society support and use technology and how we deal with its consequences are all questions that those who control governments will determine. Public opinion on the value and danger of technology, in turn, will play a role in those governmental decisions. These very issues surrounding technologies and the manner in which we as a society handle them are the *sine qua non* of science fiction. As a result, science fiction stories help the public imagine the problems that may arise from technology in a way that is much more powerful than hypothetical arguments. When science fiction stories or games transport us all, the effects of Narrative Transportation kick in—we see, in concrete and powerful images, what will happen, in an emotionally engaging journey whose lessons we carry with us when we leave the narrative and return to the real world. This line of reasoning is what led us to raise the question, Do the tales about technology from science fiction affect how we perceive technologies in the real world and shape our notions of what governments should and should not do when it comes to technological advancements? That is, is it possible that the fictional lessons regarding technology affect the public's awareness of and attitudes toward technology in a way that could shape public policy on the subject and, ultimately, future scientific advances and how they are used? The work of Charli Carpenter on the effects of science fiction on attitudes about autonomous military weaponry is the only piece published to date that explores this question.[3]

THE UNIFYING EFFECT OF EXTERNAL THREATS: SCIENCE FICTION, POLITICAL TOLERANCE, AND DIVERSITY

The history of humanity is one of endless conflict within the species between various tribes, nations, racial, ethnic, and religious groups. Those conflicts delineate and lead to identification with in-groups ("my side") and out-groups ("the enemy"). What would happen if, all of a sudden, we were confronted with an entirely new species of intelligent/sentient life? Would such a discovery alter perceptions of the in-groups and out-groups in such a way that all humans become the in-group and the other form of intelligent life the out-group, increasing acceptance of human diversity and reducing the conflict among humans? Producers, writers, and directors of science fiction have often played around with this question in their stories. In the movie *Independence Day*, for example, all humanity unites to fight the invading alien species; the movie goes so far as to portray the Iraqi Republican Guard (this is a mid-1990s film when this force was deemed the enemy) working alongside US and UN fighters to attack the common alien enemy.

While earth's scientists have made great progress in finding evidence of planets circling distant stars, evidence that increases the probability of the existence of other sentient life, science fiction and fantasy bring such possibilities to life in our imaginations. Indeed, it is a given in most science fiction that we humans are not alone in the universe. The same can be said for the fantasy genre, which stories often involve hidden worlds with other sentient beings—elves, dwarves, wizards, witches, dragons, goblins, orcs, faeries, and so on—either co-existing within our world—as with the Wizarding world of *Harry Potter*, the Fae world of *Lost Girl*, or a world of vampires, werewolves, and ghosts in numerous stories such as *Being Human* and *True Blood*—or in some parallel existence in the past or future. What effect does exposure to this imagining that we, humans, are not alone have? Does it make us more accepting of those humans who are different and increase our levels of political tolerance? There are some hints that this may be the case. In one of her experiments on the authoritarian dynamic, Karen Stenner found some evidence that being exposed to the possibility of other sentient life increased subjects' tolerance by redefining the out-group for those predisposed to authoritarianism.[4] And, other research has found that exposure to the *Harry Potter* fantasy series was associated with greater acceptance of those perceived as different and higher levels of political tolerance.[5]

In sum, the very nature of science fiction is such that any story in the genre is likely to contain lessons and perspectives that have the potential to affect political attitudes, lessons about the dangers of technology, and perspectives that shape how we as humans see ourselves. Given that people tend to equate technology with science, we will explore one additional possible effect of science fiction, and that is whether exposure to science fiction leads people to see the world through the lens of science. The theoretical discussion in chapter 2 maps out why we would expect the lessons and perspectives of science fiction to influence the important politically relevant attitudes. In the remainder of this chapter, I discuss a study that my students and I conducted as a preliminary test of these arguments.

METHODS

The hypotheses we derived from the discussion of the politically relevant content of science fiction and theories about media effects were:

H_1: Exposure to science fiction that negatively depicts technology will be more likely to increase reservations about the dangers of advancing technology.

H_2: Exposure to science fiction will enhance acceptance of diversity.

H_3: Exposure to science fiction will increase political tolerance.

H_4: Exposure to science fiction will lead to greater likelihood of seeing the world through the lens of science.

The study included two components—an experiment and a survey administered to students at the author's university. The subjects for the experiment were students in the author's introductory American politics class.[6] I randomly assigned students in the class into experimental and control groups (70 subjects in each).[7] The experimental group was shown an episode of *Doctor Who*, "The End of the World."[8] In the episode, The Doctor (who is the last of a space-time traveling alien race known as the Time Lords) and his companion travel

> 5 billion years into the future to view a cataclysmic event: the destruction of the Earth. They're on an orbiting space platform with a group of invited guests who seem to travel from one cataclysmic event to another. There are uninvited guests as well in the form of spider-like mechanical robots that seem to multiply at will and are obviously bent on causing destruction. The spiders soon dispose of the Steward and gain control of the orbiting platform's mainframe.[9]

We chose the episode because it included elements of technology gone awry and because it included other forms of intelligent life (in fact, Rose, The Doctor's traveling companion, is one of only two human to witness the end of the earth). We showed the control group an episode from a popular sitcom, *How I Met Your Mother*, "Swarley." We chose it because this series was a typical sitcom, devoid of any politics, technology, or issues of tolerance.[10] At the start of the screenings we told the subjects of both groups "[w]e are interested in your reactions to entertainment shows and we would also like to know a little bit about your political views." We then screened the episodes and had the subjects fill out a short questionnaire (see Appendix 5). We supplemented the experiment by administering the questionnaire to a number of other classes at the university.[11]

The questionnaire included items to indicate whether respondents were fans of science fiction. We asked respondents how often they chose science fiction books, television shows, and movies. We also asked participants whether they considered themselves a fan of science fiction on a five-point scale. Furthermore, we asked whether the possibilities of time travel, the idea of alternate realities, the possibility of intelligent life on other planets interested the participant in order to assess subjects' interest in components of science fiction stories.

In order to measure participant's attitudes toward diversity we utilized an ANES-style "feeling thermometer." The questions asked participants to gauge their feeling toward for four different target groups who have experienced discrimination—Muslims, Blacks/African Americans, undocumented immigrants, and homosexuals—from 100 degrees for "warm/positive feeling" to 0 degrees "cold/negative feeling." In order to measure political tolerance, we utilized a modified version of Sullivan, Piereson, and Marcus' tolerance measure. First we asked participants to select the group that they liked least—atheists, homosexuals, Muslims, fascists, and communists. We then asked a number of questions gauging the participant's tolerance toward the group that they selected.

We asked several questions about participant's feelings toward technology. One question asked where participants would place themselves in regard to new and emerging technologies on a scale of *very comfortable, comfortable, neutral, uncomfortable,* and *very uncomfortable.* Another question we created asks about the work of a professor that has led to the development of robots that have learned to follow accelerated patterns of evolution. The question led with the statement

> University of Vermont scientist Josh Bongard has developed robots that are able to mimic certain aspects of actual evolutionary patterns. The robots change their body forms while learning how to walk and, over generations, evolve to speed up the learning process. How would you categorize your response to an advance such as evolving robots? [Options: I view such advances as potentially more dangerous than beneficial. I view these advances as potentially more beneficial than dangerous.]

Given the centrality of scientific findings to some political disputes, we also asked respondents to place themselves on a scale regarding their acceptance or rejection of scientific conclusions in the following format:

> There are some scientific theories that try to explain the existence of our world and ourselves, such as the Big Bang Theory and Evolution. These theories are overwhelmingly endorsed by the scientific community, and yet some people consider them to be controversial for a variety of reasons. If you would consider these viewpoints opposite ends of a scale with those who accept these scientific conclusions on one end and those who reject the conclusions at the other, where would you place yourself?

Results

Following exposure to the two different programs, the experimental and control groups did not differ on acceptance of diversity or tolerance. On the matter of technology, however, we did find significant differences between the groups on whether they viewed technological developments like the creation of evolutionary robots as dangerous or beneficial—a higher percentage of those who watched the episode of *Doctor Who* found such developments dangerous (see figure 5.1). The differences between the experimental and control groups held even while controlling for subjects' religious belief and place subject grew up in (the two characteristics on which the experimental and control group differed). The results of this analysis can be found in table 5.1.

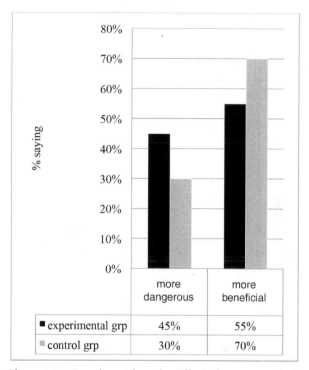

	more dangerous	more beneficial
■ experimental grp	45%	55%
▩ control grp	30%	70%

Figure 5.1. Experimental results: Effect of exposure to science fiction episode v. sitcom episode on concern about technology.

Table 5.1. Logistic Regression assessing the impact of experimental manipulation while controlling for differences between the experimental and control groups

	b
Experimental Condition (*Dr. Who* Episode)	–.69*
Belief in God Scale	–.38*
Grew Up in Small Town/Rural	.09
Percent Predicted Correctly	65.2

* significant at the .05 level or better, one-tailed test

Interestingly, when we compare science fiction fans with nonfans on the questions of technology using the survey data from the study, we find the opposite of the experiment—a slightly larger proportion of science fiction fans (though not statistically significantly) voiced comfort with emerging technologies and think that scientific advances like evolutionary robots are more beneficial than dangerous (see figure 5.2). After giving it some additional

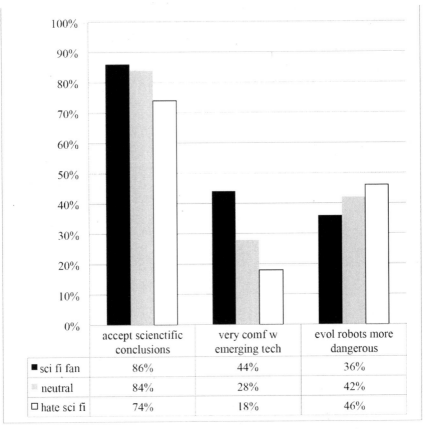

Figure 5.2.   Attitudes toward science and technology by sci fi fan level (from survey).

thought, it occurred to us that the contradictory finding may be due to the fact that, despite the morality lesson about the dangers of technology in a lot of science fiction, the final outcome of most science fiction stories is usually one in which the problems caused by the dangers of technology are overcome by the protagonists—the storytelling-convention-mandated just world, happy ending. So, one exposure to science fiction (like attending a block buster movie) might, as we found, heighten the fear of technology while repeated exposure reassures that despite problems that may arise, humans will persevere in the end.

While the experimental results were limited to heightening fear of advancing technology, we did find some additional associations between respondents' levels of science fiction fandom and attitudes about science, diversity, and tolerance that hint at possible long-term effects (see table 5.2). One measure of science fiction fandom—how frequently respondents choose

Table 5.2.   Multiple Regression Results of Survey Responses (responses includes those from experimental subjects and classroom survey respondents)

	Group Feeling Thermometer	Political Tolerance	Reject Scientific Conclusions
Choose Sci Fi	.162*	.122**	—
Interest in Sci Fi components	—	—	−.112*
Authoritarianism	−.423*	−.470*	—
Openness to experience	—	—	
Grew up rural area	−1.098*	—	
Grew up suburbia	−1.074*	—	
Grew up small city	−.914*	—	
Religion unimportant	—	—	−.349*
Conservative Ideology	—	—	.098*
Type of reader	—	.196	—
Race (white)		.830*	
Adjusted R-square	.044	.034	.164
N	356	345	347

* significant at the .05 level or better, one-tailed test
** significant at the .10 level, one-tailed test

science fiction books, movies, or television shows—was associated with feeling warmer toward the various groups we listed (even when controlling for authoritarian predisposition[12] and what type of area the respondents grew up in[13]) and with higher levels of tolerance (even when controlling for authoritarian predisposition, race, and whether the respondent was an avid reader growing up). Another measure of fandom—interest in the components of science fiction—was associated with a greater likelihood of accepting scientific conclusions (even when controlling for ideology, and the importance of religion). These findings are not rigorous enough to make any bold conclusions—they are based on a questionnaire filled out at a single university and, while the relationships remain even after controlling for some important variables, establishing causality is out of the question with a survey. Nonetheless, the findings on diversity and tolerance do echo that found in the research on the impact of the *Harry Potter* series.

CONCLUSION

My main purpose in including this chapter was to draw attention to the potential value of a genre-based study of entertainment media.[14] As argued in chapter 1, genres share common storytelling conventions, plot devices, and lessons that could shape political perspectives through the repeated exposure to such components across specific movies, television shows, or books. The study I presented here hints at the benefit of that sort of approach.

In this specific study, the findings on the effects of science fiction suggest interesting differences in the effects of short-term and long-term effects of exposure to an entertainment media genre. The short-term exposure to lessons about the danger of technology in the experiment heightened concerns about technology. To a certain degree, the conditions of the experiment reported here parallel the situation when blockbuster science fiction movies, such as *Avatar* or *Jurassic World*, attract an enormous audience that includes those who are not necessarily fans of science fiction. Such exposure to science fiction may have a different effect than the long-term exposure of someone who consumes a great deal of science fiction through, say television shows or book series. The implications of these findings for the politics surrounding technology pose some interesting questions. Future studies of the effects of science fiction that include questions about government regulation and use of technology could explore such implications further.

While the experiment did not find any impact of science fiction on attitudes about diversity and political tolerance, the study here represents only one experiment using one episode of a television show. Given Stenner's finding[15] and the findings of the research on *Harry Potter*[16] in the fantasy genre, I do believe that this area merits additional research.

NOTES

1. Portions of this chapter appeared previously in a paper entitled "The Effects of Science Fiction on Politically Relevant Attitudes," presented at the 2013 Annual Meeting of the Midwest Political Science Association, April 11–14, 2013, with Michael Gibson, Evan McDaniel, and Alex Rosenblatt.

2. This study was developed with the author's senior research seminar class in the fall 2011 semester; students in the class who contributed to the development and implementation of this project were William Andreycak, Ben Brownstein, Fernando DeOleo, Adam Elias, Michael Gibson, Matthew Holleb, Katherine Ida, Alison Kelly, Sara Lindstrom, Evan McDaniel, Patrick Milliken, Scott Olsen, Emily Pijanowski, Alexandra Raymond, Alexander Rosenblatt, Jordan Tahami, Julia Wejchert, and Jordan White.

3. Charli Carpenter, "Does Science Fiction Affect Political Fact? Yes and No: A Survey Experiment on 'Killer Robots,'" forthcoming, *International Studies Quarterly*.

4. Karen Stenner, *The Authoritarian Dynamic* (Cambridge: Cambridge University Press, 2005).

5. Anthony Gierzynski and Kathryn Eddy, *Harry Potter and the Millennials: Research Methods and the Politics of the Muggle Generation* (New York: The Johns

Hopkins University Press, 2013); Loris Vezzali, Sofia Stathi, Dino Giovannini, Dora Capozza and Elena Trifiletti, "The greatest magic of Harry Potter: Reducing prejudice," *Journal of Applied Social Psychology* 45, no. 2 (February 2015): 105–21.

6. This was a separate class from the research seminar in which the students contributed to the design of the project. The experiment was approved by the author's school's Institutional Review Board.

7. The experimental and control groups did not differ significantly on any demographic characteristic (gender, race, ethnicity), though there were more (6) subjects who grew up in suburbia in the control group.

8. Originally aired on April 2, 2005.

9. IMDB, http://www.imdb.com/title/tt0436992/episodes?season=1&ref_=tt_eps _sn_1.

10. Season 2, episode 7, originally aired November 6, 2006.

11. This approach is similar to the methodology followed by Jody Baumgartner and Jonathan S. Morris in their study "The Daily Show Effect: Candidate Evaluations, Efficacy, and American Youth," *American Politics Research* 34, no. 3 (May 2006): 341–67.

12. For this measure we used a modification of new measure that asks respondents the preferred modes of child rearing—here it is reduced to word choices. See Karen Stenner, *The Authoritarian Dynamic* (Cambridge: Cambridge University Press, 2005), for development and use of this measure.

13. We used a series of dichotomous variables for rural, small city, and suburban areas; so, the base of comparison in this model is those who grew up in cities.

14. For an additional discussion of the value of such an approach, see Calvert W. Jones, "It's the End of the World and They Know It: How Dystopian Fiction Shapes Political Attitudes," paper selected for presentation at the Southern Political Science Association Annual Meeting, San Juan, Puerto Rico, January 9, 2016.

15. Stenner, *The Authoritarian Dynamic*.

16. Gierzynski and Eddy, *Harry Potter and the Millennials*; Vezzali, et al., "The Greatest Magic of *Harry Potter*."

Chapter 6

Villains of Science Fiction, Fantasy, and Superhero Genres

The previous studies focused on individual shows or genres.[1] Another way to approach entertainment media's political effects is to focus on character types that are common in stories. Stories require protagonists, supporting characters, and antagonists. Within these sets of characters, an observant person can find similar types that appear across different narratives—the hero who always does the right thing, the goofy sidekick, or the evil villain, to name a few. Over time, one might also be able to track trends in character types, trends that may reflect changes in the media and culture.

In the early decades of the twenty-first century the fragmentation of television media audiences, the proliferation in the means for the delivery of television media content, and the accompanying proliferation of television production companies (such as Netflix, Hulu, and Amazon), has allowed for the development of shows that are more varied and more experimental than in the past. Freed of the need to target audiences broadly, production companies have been rolling out shows that are much more complex in both narrative structure and in their characters. Heroes can be more complex, with a mix of both light and dark sides. Narratives can follow the stories of multiple characters, resulting in more complex plots and richer characters. The story antagonists can be more complicated and portrayed in more nuanced ways as well. The stories that television tells now offer a much more complex and nuanced understanding of the good "guys" and bad "guys" than shows of the past. This trend is carrying over to movies and games, too. Take *Captain America: Civil War* for an example of a formerly straitlaced hero showing a darker side. And, while some of this reflects changes in our culture, as argued in chapter 2 when entertainment media pick up on such cultural threads, it has the potential to spread those changes more broadly in a culture. In this

109

chapter, I discuss research focusing on one such cultural changes—the portrayal of villains in fiction—and how that change in entertainment media may affect the culture's perspectives on what to do about those who do bad things in the real world.

FICTIONAL AND REAL WORLD VILLAINS

Fictional stories require antagonists. The news, because its producers now tell it to us in story form, also requires antagonists.[2] Is it possible that the portraits of antagonists in the former affect perceptions of, and attitudes toward those who are cast as antagonists in the later?

In science fiction, fantasy and superhero genres, antagonists are much more than just an adversary for the protagonists, they are some combination of extremely wicked, clever, powerful, egomaniacal, bloodthirsty and brutal villains. Villains in these genres come in many different forms and any storyline may include a number of different villain types. There are the singular villains, like Sauron of *The Lord of the Rings*, Voldemort of the *Harry Potter* series, or Cluny the Scourge of *Redwall*, who are pure evil and whose single-minded purpose is domination and destruction. There are the individual villains who are painted in a more complex way, such as Magneto of *X-Men*, whose experience in a World War II concentration camp drives his distrust of, and ultimately his preemptory violence against regular humans, the Ice King in *Adventure Time*, and the vampires, werewolves, and ghosts in the BBC series *Being Human* who struggle against their afflictions in an attempt to hold onto their humanity while confronted with intolerance and human "monsters." Villains also come in groups (Klingons in *Star Trek*, Daleks in *Doctor Who*, the Others in *Lost*) who may be either evil like Sauron (Daleks and the aliens in *Independence Day* would fit this category) or more complex (Klingons and the Others), motivated by concerns that while not justifying the villains' actions, may at least be understandable in some way. Sometimes the nature of a villain (or villains) evolves as the story progresses, usually going from one-dimensional evil characters to tragic figures or, at least, more complex characters, as we learn more about them. This is perhaps best illustrated by the tale of Darth Vader. Other examples include the Klingons of the *Star Trek* world and the Cylons of the world of *Battlestar Galactica*. In surveying the nature of villains in science fiction, fantasy, and superhero stories, it seems that villains can be categorized based on three dimensions—whether they are singular villains or a group, whether the villains are portrayed as simply pure evil or more complex, and, finally, based on that which motivates the villain(s). As discussed in chapter 1, my students and I analyzed the frequency of the types of villains in science fiction, fantasy, and superhero genres; I summarized the results of that analysis in figures 1.2 and 1.3 in chapter 1. We found that 57 percent of villains in these genres could be considered complex villains versus 43 percent pure evil. The one villain motive that outstripped all others was the thirst for power. Whether the makeup of fictional villains is indeed changing, as I speculated in the introduction to this chapter is a question for future research.

Clearly, as the results of the analysis of villain types indicates, those who watch/read/play stories in these genres come to know a variety of villain types. These fictional villains have the potential to shape perceptions of real world "villains" in a number of different ways. Audience members who identify with the protagonist who has to confront the villain(s) may, when they leave the narrative, take with them notions about the nature and motives of fictional villains that may then carry over to real world "villains." The story narratives also offer different models of villains and give us lessons in what leads to the development of villains. As argued throughout this book, when a story transports us we are likely to incorporate the story's models and lessons about villains into our understanding of villains in general. It follows, then, that fictional villains may affect the development of our understanding of real world villains—criminals and terrorists. Taking this a step farther, if fictional villains affect how we understand real world "villains," then it is very possible that fiction will affect attitudes regarding government policies to combat real world "villains." Previous research has found that fictional crime shows can affect attitudes about the criminal justice system and the death penalty.[3] Those studies focused on the way the criminal justice system was portrayed and the empathy viewers felt for the protagonist. The research in this chapter seeks to add to our understanding of the impact of fiction on attitudes about criminal justice and also terrorism by focusing on different genres and on the portrayal of the villains themselves.

METHODS

To test the impact of fictional villains on attitudes regarding government policy to deal with real world villains, my students and I devised and conducted an online experiment in the fall of 2012.[4] The purpose of this study was to test how exposure to different types of villains from science fiction, fantasy, and superhero stories might affect attitudes about criminal justice and terrorism. Our hypotheses were that exposure to villains who were portrayed as pure evil and motivated by solely evil causes would elicit harsher, more punitive attitudes about how to deal with crime and terrorism. In order to test this hypothesis, we designed the experiment to prime the different models of villains by showing photos of villains from films, television shows, and video games. We then asked a series of questions to see whether invoking different models of villains would result in differences in attitudes about criminal justice and terrorism policy. Because mental imagery has been found to "re-evoke story themes and messages when recalled,"[5] we expected the photos to do just that with regard to the nature of villains. We also attempted to measured long-term exposure to villains based on subjects' recall of the typical villain motives.

We set up the experiment with four experimental conditions and one control condition (I programmed the Qualtrics survey tool used for this study to randomly assigned subjects to one of these groups when subjects clicked on the link for the survey). Subjects in each of the experimental conditions were shown a series of pictures of villains from science fiction, fantasy, and superhero genres and asked to click a box if they recognized the villain and could describe the villain to a friend. One group (n = 77) was shown singular or individual villains portrayed as pure evil. Included in this group were Sauron from *The Lord of the Rings* series, Emperor Palpatine from *Star Wars*, Voldemort from the *Harry Potter* series, the Joker from *The Dark Knight*, Ganondorf in the game *Legends of Zelda*, the White Witch from *The Chronicles of Narnia*, and the alien from *Alien* (we labeled each photograph to assist respondents in recognizing the villains). Another group (n = 58[6]) was shown individual villains portrayed as more complex. Included in this group were Magneto of *X-Men*, Gollum/Smeagol from *The Lord of the Rings*, Loki from *The Avengers*, Cersei Lannister from *Game of Thrones*, Andrew Ryan from *Bioshock*, Ms. Coulter from *Golden Compass*, Cobb, from the film *Inception*, and Nero from the 2009 *Star Trek* movie. The third group (n = 64) was shown pure evil villain groups: the Borg of *Star Trek*, *Matrix* Agents, Nazi Zombies, *Star Wars* Storm Troopers, Daleks from *Doctor Who*, President Snow/ Government in *The Hunger Games*, the aliens from *Independence Day*, and the Hydra from *Captain America*. And, subjects in the fourth experimental (n = 58) group were shown photos of villainous groups that were portrayed as being more complex: Cylons from *Battlestar Galactica*, the Others from *Lost*, *Star Trek* Klingons, the Covenant from the game *Halo*, the Company from the TV show *Heroes*, and the Corporate Military in *Avatar*. If respondents did not recognize any of the photos, they were dropped from the analysis (since it is unlikely we primed their schema regarding villain types). Subjects in the fifth group, a control group, did not see any pictures and instead the program took them directly to the questionnaire (n =74).

To measure how much exposure to pure evil villains respondents have had over time we created a measure based on the responses to a question asking respondents "Thinking about the movies/videos/television shows you watch and books you read, what do you recall tends to be the main motivation for the villain?" We created two categories from the responses to this question: one category for evil motives including greed, power, and destruction (we left out insanity because in a way that is more complex by definition) and the other category for respondents who picked the motives other than greed, power, and destruction.

The questions we used to measure attitudes about terrorism included one that asked, "Do you agree or disagree with the following statement: The best way to deal with the threat of terrorism is to hunt down and kill all the terrorists?" And, "Would you regard the use of torture against people suspected of involvement in terrorism as acceptable or unacceptable?"[7] To measure attitudes regarding criminal justice, we asked respondents for the opinions on the death penalty and whether they agreed with the statement "people who commit violent crimes can be rehabilitated and reenter society without endangering the public." To see the full questionnaire turn to appendix 6.

We recruited subjects for the study through Facebook—students in the research seminar set up an event on Facebook and invited about 1,000 of their friends, providing the link to the Qualtrics pages that contained the experiment, resulting in the number of subjects in each group reported above.

RESULTS

In figure 6.1 I present respondents' views on "the best way to fight terrorism" question for the experimental groups that were shown pictures of pure evil villains (either singular or group), those shown more complex victims, and the control group. Subjects in the complex villain condition were significantly less likely than those in the pure evil condition or the control group to support the idea that the best way to fight terrorism is to hunt down and kill the terrorists. This finding lends support to the hypothesis that how fictional villains are portrayed can affect attitudes about real-life villains. Despite the random assignment of subjects to the experimental and control groups, the groups were not exactly equal with regard to gender and Republican Party identification, so, I ran a multiple regression analysis to control for these variables and for the authoritarian predisposition.[8] I put the results in table 6.1. Even when controlling for these factors, the respondents in the experimental groups that were shown pictures of complex villains remained less likely (though, at a .09 significant level, one-tailed test) to agree with the statement that the best way to fight terrorism is to hunt down and kill the terrorists.

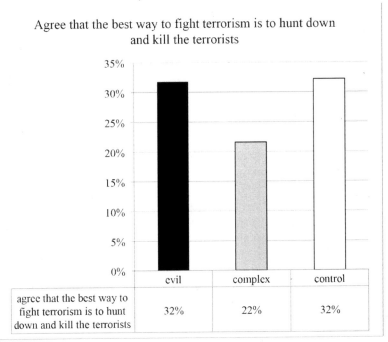

Agree that the best way to fight terrorism is to hunt down and kill the terrorists

	evil	complex	control
agree that the best way to fight terrorism is to hunt down and kill the terrorists	32%	22%	32%

Figure 6.1. Attitude about fighting terrorism by type of villain (evil individual or group, versus complex individual or group) and control group. Percent agree strongly and agree somewhat.

Table 6.1. Multiple regression analysis, responses to the question about the best way to fight terrorism (higher scores disagree with the statement) regressed on groups shown complex villains, the control group, authoritarianism, and dummy variables for males and Republicans

Variables	b (standardized regression coefficients)
(Constant)	3.20
Complex Villain Pictures Group	.13**
	(.08)
Republican	−.35*
	(−.13)
Male	−.28*
	(−.17)
Authoritarianism Predisposition	−.18*
	(−.20)
Control Group	.02
	(.01)
Adjusted R-square	.09

* significant at the .05 level or better, one-tailed test
** significant at the .10 level or better, one-tailed test

In figure 6.2 I present the responses to the question regarding the acceptability of using torture against people suspected of terrorism for the experimental and control groups. While a larger percentage of the group shown pure evil villains (of either the group or individual sort) responded that they regarded the use of torture as acceptable, the difference with the other groups is within the margin of error.

In figure 6.3 I show subjects' attitudes on the death penalty broken down by whether subjects were shown pictures of evil villains, complex villains, or no pictures at all. The significant aspect of these results is in the percentage of subjects who answered "don't know." A larger percentage of subjects who were shown complex villains selected the "don't know" option, suggesting that priming respondents with complex villains may have introduced some uncertainty on their opinions regarding this issue. Further support for the notion that the types of villains can affect opinions on the death penalty can be found in figure 6.4 where I compare respondents based on what they recall being the main motives of the antagonists in their entertainment media. Those who cited motives that we coded as reflecting pure evil villains were more likely to support the death penalty. These findings did not remain significant, however, when we tested the relationships using multivariate logistic regression to control for party identification, gender and authoritarian predisposition.

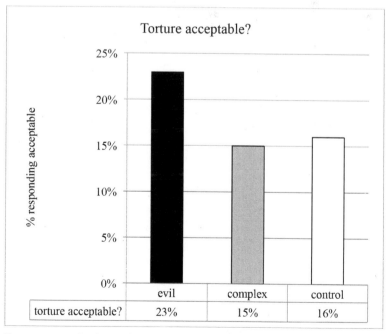

Figure 6.2.   Attitudes on the use of torture by experimental and control groups.

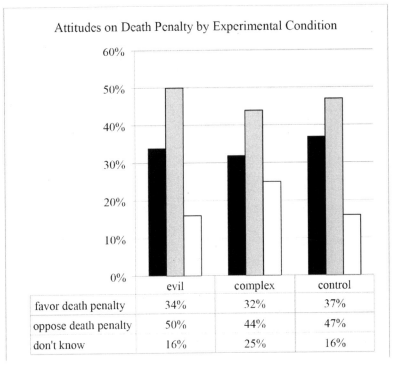

Attitudes on Death Penalty by Experimental Condition

	evil	complex	control
favor death penalty	34%	32%	37%
oppose death penalty	50%	44%	47%
don't know	16%	25%	16%

Figure 6.3. Opinion on the death penalty by experimental and control groups.

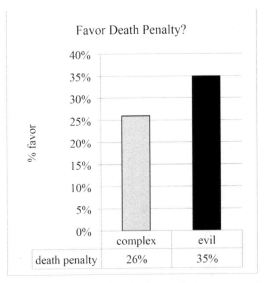

Favor Death Penalty?

% favor

	complex	evil
death penalty	26%	35%

Figure 6.4. Support for death penalty by motives of entertainment media respondents consume.

CONCLUSION

The findings of the experimental study discussed in this chapter show the potential effect that character types found in entertainment media may have on attitudes about how best to deal with criminals and terrorists. Subjects of this study responded differently to questions about criminal justice and terrorism policy depending on whether they were assigned to the group shown simply evil villains versus those assigned to the groups who were primed with images of complex villains. While the findings of the experiment were not as strong as we might have hoped—some of the differences barely met standards of statistical significance while other differences did not—the results, being based on an experiment, do provide an indication that the fictional villains we are exposed to can influence how we think about dealing with real world villains. If the trend toward greater complexity and nuance in character portrayal discussed in the opening of this chapter is real, audiences will see more complex fictional villains, which, as this study suggests, may have consequences for public opinion on criminal justice and terrorism policies. It is certainly an area worthy of additional research.

NOTES

1. Portions of this chapter appeared previously in a paper entitled "The Effects of Science Fiction on Politically Relevant Attitudes," presented at the 2013 Annual Meeting of the Midwest Political Science Association, April 11–14, 2013, with Michael Gibson, Evan McDaniel, and Alex Rosenblatt.

2. For a discussion of the importance of narratives to modern news media coverage see Alison Dagnes, *Politics on Demand: The Effects of 24-hour News on American Politics* (Santa Barbara, CA: Praeger, 2010); Kathleen Hall Jamieson and Paul Waldman, *The Press Effect: Politicians, Journalists, and the Stories that Shape the Political World* (Oxford: Oxford University Press, 2003); and, Gadi Wolfsfeld, *Making Sense of Media and Politics: Five Principles in Political Communication* (New York: Routledge, 2011).

3. Michael D. Slater, Donna Rouner, and Marilee Long, "Television Dramas and Support for Controversial Public Policies: Effects and Mechanisms," *Journal of Communication* 56 (2006): 235–52; and, Diana C. Mutz, and Lilach Nir, "Not Necessarily the News: Does Fictional Television Influence Real-World Policy Preferences?" *Mass Communication and Society* 13, no. 2 (2010): 196–217.

4. This study was developed with the author's class in the fall 2012 semester; students in the class who contributed to the development and implementation of this project were Jake Brudney, Antonia David, Mitchell Hansen, Kevin Kennedy, Frederick Knight, Eric Schwarzbach, Sarah Simmons, David Thal, and Erik Tidmon.

5. Jordan M. Carpenter and Melanie C. Green, "Flying with Icarus: Narrative Transportation and the Persuasiveness of Entertainment," in *The Psychology of*

Entertainment Media: Blurring the Lines Between Entertainment and Persuasion, edited by L. J. Shrum (New York: Routledge, 2012), 175.

6. The sample size of each group varied slightly based on the number of respondents who completed the survey after clicking the link.

7. I used both the question on fighting terrorism and the torture question successfully in the study of the *Harry Potter* effects, see Gierzynski and Eddy, *Harry Potter and the Millennials*.

8. Again, we used Stenner's measure modified for college students (see previous chapter).

Chapter 7

News Parody Shows, Cynicism, and Skepticism

Aside from one show in the political fiction genre, *House of Cards*, most of this book has been devoted to the political effects of "pure entertainment" media.[1] Any discussion of entertainment media effects on politics would fall short, however, if it ignored the group of news parody television shows that use politics to fuel their comedy. Such shows have their origin in *Saturday Night Live's* "Weekend Update" segment, but the format truly blossomed when Jon Stewart took over Comedy Central's *The Daily Show* and when one of his show's cast, Stephen Colbert, created *The Colbert Report*. In 2018, *The Daily Show* still operates with host Trevor Noah, and Stephen Colbert has moved over to host CBS's *The Late* Show, but, it is TBS's *Full Frontal with Samantha Bee*, HBO's *Last Week Tonight with John Oliver*, along with the revival of *Saturday Night Live's* "Weekend Update," that carry on what Stewart and Colbert began with their popular Comedy Central shows.

Despite the fact that this group of shows target the inanity of politics of both the left and right—see, for example, Samantha Bee's coverage of Bernie Sanders and Donald Trump supporters in 2016—the news parody shows have been accused of having a liberal bias. Whether they do have a liberal bias is of little interest to me, because, as I wrote in chapter 1, entertainment programs are not likely to shift someone's ideology or partisanship, especially when they suspect that there is a political bent to the show. The real potential for news satire shows to affect political perspectives comes in areas audiences don't think of as political effects, because you *can* be affected by the messages you are not on the lookout for. With regard to news satire shows, their real potential lies in their ability to affect audiences' views about the overall nature of the political system and the media, as well as how audiences understand the nature of political discourse. The research I discuss in this chapter explores the ways *The Daily Show with Jon Stewart* and *The Colbert Report* may have influenced such perspectives.[2]

CYNICAL OR SKEPTICAL EFFECTS?

Unlike the question of the political effects of pure entertainment media, the question regarding the political impact of news parody shows has attracted some scholarly attention. Scholars, however, have been divided over the effects of news parody shows. There are those that argue that the negative and mocking coverage of the political system and the news media pervasive on news parody shows engenders cynicism among these program's audiences.[3] Others suggest that these news parody shows are actually positive forces in political discourse, encouraging skepticism (as opposed to cynicism) and providing coverage that promotes accountability from politicians and the mass media.[4]

A cynic distrusts people and institutions, they dismiss arguments and evidence, assuming all arguments and evidence are tainted with the bias of whoever it is that is making the argument or offering the evidence. Someone who is skeptical withholds judgment until they have assessed the argument and facts based on standards of reason and evidence. Cynics are dismissive, and their cynicism gives them an excuse not to participate in political life or give it any serious attention. Skeptics, on the other hand, have the cognitive tools that allow them to see the value in participating in political life. Thus, whether news parody shows provoke greater cynicism or skepticism has important implications for the politics of a democratic society.

To date, the only effects research on this question have come down on the side of the argument that these shows promote cynicism. In an experiment and a survey, Baumgartner and Morris found evidence that *TDS* engenders cynicism.[5] In particular, they found that exposure to video segments of *TDS* resulted in more negative evaluations of the politicians featured in the segment than exposure to a video about that politician from a segment of *CBS Evening News*. Baumgartner and Morris also found that exposure to *TDS* (in both their experiment and their survey) was associated with lower levels of external political efficacy—the attitude regarding government responsiveness to citizens. It is relevant to the study here to note that Baumgartner and Morris also found a *positive* relationship between *TDS* exposure and *internal* political efficacy—the sense that one has political power. This aspect of their findings suggests that it may be that exposure to *TDS* engendered skepticism not cynicism, since cynics are unlikely to have that sense of being politically powerful. Finally, participants in Baumgartner and Morris' study whom the researchers exposed to a clip from *TDS* expressed greater distrust in the news media than those who were shown a clip from the *CBS Evening News*. This finding, too, could be interpreted as a skeptical (and deservedly so) reaction to the media since much of *TDS* focuses on the real failings of television news.

Baumgartner and Morris' experiment was based on a onetime and brief exposure to *TDS*. Another set of researchers, Guggenheim et al., found a relationship between systemic cynicism and the frequency of exposure to *The Colbert Report* (*TCR*) and *TDS* over time.[6] Additionally, other researchers found that *TDS* and *TCR's* satirical parody of the media and its coverage of politics was related to increased cynicism toward the media.[7] While these research pieces lend evidence that the news parody shows may engender cynicism, the fact that these pieces fail to distinguish between cynicism and skepticism, means that it is unclear which effect the shows actually have.

While there is no media effects research evidence to support the argument that news parody shows engender skepticism as opposed to cynicism, there are some strong theoretical arguments (and some content analysis) to support the case for skepticism. Geoffrey Baym, in his book *From Cronkite to Colbert*, argued that *TDS* and *TCR* are part of an emerging paradigm of television news, one that blends the rationality of the early days of television news (the Cronkite period) with the postmodern techniques of the current news era. Baym argued that this new paradigm, exemplified by Stewart and Colbert, employs these techniques to satirize and parody the irrational discourse found on the postmodern news programs that dominate the current era of news.

TDS regularly parodied standard aspects of news programs through the fake credentials of the *TDS* reporters (the "Senior Election/Terrorism Correspondent," or the "Senior Black Correspondent"), "on-site reporting" which was done with a green screen next to Stewart's desk, and drawing attention to the stock narratives of the news. Jon Stewart's amazing staff mined the video archives and produced endless sets of video comparisons showing politicians contradicting themselves. Stewart's interviews with politicians were long enough, and Stewart smart enough (he clearly did his homework), that he was able to get politicians off their talking points and have a reasoned and substantive discussion of important policy issues. Colbert's imitation of cable news constantly parodied the irrational and substance free nature of cable news shows. His "Word" segment, in particular, highlighted the shortcomings of news and political discourse in our current period. Indeed, his "Word" segment "Truthiness" not only coined a new word for what you feel is right regardless of the facts, it is also encapsulates much of what is wrong with political discourse in the first decades of the twenty-first century.[8] In the process of using politics for comedy in these ways, Baym argued that Stewart and Colbert actually modeled a form of reasoned discourse and parodied irrational discourse in ways that, if adopted by audiences, would fuel a skeptical, not cynical, approach to politics.[9]

A content analysis of *TDS* conducted by Brewer and Marquardt lends support to Baym's arguments.[10] Brewer and Marquardt examined the framing used to discuss government and politics on *TDS*. They argued that the framing commonly employed by Stewart on *TDS* was one built around issues. According to Brewer and Marquardt, Stewart's use of "issue framing," which portrays government and politics as a battle over public policy, may engender greater political trust among audience members and encourage citizens to make political judgements based on policy.[11]

Whether news parody shows such as *TDS* and *TCR* engender cynicism or skepticism has been a bit difficult to tease out because researchers did not use measures that could differentiate between these concepts. Cynicism has traditionally been measured using questions that assess respondents' levels of trust in government and the media. For example, according to a 2017 Pew Research Center Poll, just twenty percent of the public said they trusted the federal government to do what is right "just about always" or "most of the time."[12] Measuring trust in the media in a similar manner finds that just 20 percent of Americans in 2017 trust the information they get from the national news organizations "a lot."[13] Distrust, however, can be an indication of cynicism or skepticism. Indeed, distrust is the initial reaction of both cynics and skeptics to attempts at persuasion. The difference is that skeptics follow up the initial distrustful reaction with attempts to weigh the evidence and evaluate the reasoning; cynics' reaction begins and ends with distrust. To address the inability of previous measures to differentiate between cynics and skeptics, I, with some help from my students, devised a number of new measures of cynicism and skepticism and used those measures to reexamine the impact of news parody shows like *TDS* and *TCR*.

LEARNING SKEPTICISM OR CYNICISM

Why should we expect viewers of news parody shows to learn either skepticism or cynicism from such shows? The theory of narrative transportation discussed in chapter 2 most likely does not apply to news parody shows. Audiences are not immersed in a story when watching these types of shows. They are, however, relaxing and laughing and it is perhaps in that state of enjoyment that the lessons these shows put on—about what is rational and factual and what is not—can be learned passively, especially when viewers' defenses are down with regard to this sort of political learning. Additionally, as Baym argued, Stewart and Colbert modeled a skeptical approach to politics; the popularity of the shows' hosts and social learning theory would suggest that there is a good chance that the audience of *TDS* and *TCR* learned the modeled skepticism from Stewart and Colbert.[14] Finally, the repetition of the lessons in reasoned discourse increases the likelihood that these shows could cultivate the same type of thinking in their audiences (especially if, as mapped out in the theory in chapter 2, the exposure to this material comes at the right time for the individual, group, or culture).

THE STUDIES

In order to try and find out whether exposure to *TDS* and *TCR* is associated with skepticism or cynicism, I worked with my students to devise three survey-based studies. One study involved a survey of college students in classes at the University of Vermont; the other two studies were online surveys (one a stand-alone survey, the other I piggybacked on the *Game of Thrones* and *House of Cards* study discussed in chapter 4).

Measures of Exposure to TDS and CR

In order to measure exposure to *TDS* and *TCR* we designed measures to assess the frequency and length of exposure to the shows. Frequency of exposure was measured by asking "How often would you say you watch the following programs?" with *TDS* and *TCR* listed along with a number of other political shows and with the response options of "never," "sometimes," "regularly," and "almost always." We tapped duration of exposure to the shows by asking "How long have you been watching the following television programs?" again with *TDS* and *TCR* listed along with a number of other shows and with the response options "I have never watched it," "for about a year or less," "between one and three years," and for "more than three years" (see appendix 7 for these and the rest of the questions). Taking these two questions, I coded respondents as fans of *TDS* and/or fans of *TCR* if they watched the shows "sometimes" or "often" and have been doing so for "between 1 and 3 years" or "more than 3 years."

Measuring Skepticism versus Cynicism

As discussed above, the problem with assessing whether entertainment media encourage cynicism or skepticism has been due to the fact that the previous studies were conducted with attitudinal measures that did not differentiate between the two concepts. So, the first goal in addressing the question at the heart of this research was to construct ways of measuring skepticism as distinct from cynicism. With the help of my students, I came up with three different ways to measures skepticism and cynicism in general, and two measures of skepticism versus cynicism with regard to the media.

The first way we attempted to measure skepticism was directly with a question I devised that was first described back in chapter 4. The question that reads: "When it comes to disagreements between people over how things are, which of the following statements comes closer to what you believe?" The response options were: "[i]t is impossible to know which claims are accurate because studies and evidence can be manipulated to prove whatever someone wants to prove" and "[i]t is possible to know which claims are accurate based on a careful assessment of the research and evidence." The first response option in this question is designed to appeal to cynics—as argued above, a cynic distrusts people and institutions, they dismiss arguments and evidence, assuming all arguments and evidence are tainted with the bias of whoever it is that is making the argument or offering the evidence. The second option is meant to reflect the skeptic's approach of assessing claims and facts based on standards of reason and evidence.

The other attempts to distinguish between skeptics and cynics were more indirect. One involved creating a variable incorporating levels of participation along with the traditional measure of (dis)trust in government. The standard question used to measure trust ("How much of the time do you trust the government in Washington to do what is right?") is likely to capture both cynics and skeptics in the responses "none of the time" or "some of the time." While both cynics and skeptics will answer that question of trust in government in the same way, skeptics, unlike cynics, will be politically engaged. In other words, skeptics will distrust but participate, cynics will distrust and not participate. So, we presented respondents with a list of political activities—including actions such as voting, contributing money, writing letters to government officials, and working on a campaign—asking them to mark which ones they had done (see appendix 7). I added up the activities the respondents engaged in and multiplied the total by the responses to the standard trust question. The result is a measure where those who distrust government but who were still politically engaged scored higher than those who exhibited distrust and were politically inactive.

The other indirect measure meant to distinguish between skeptics and cynics used conspiracy theory belief as a means of getting at the difference between skeptics and cynics. Conspiracy theory thinking mirrors cynicism in that both the cynic and the conspiracy theorist are dismissive of scientific evidence and facts, believing that all such evidence (other than that they chose to believe in) is tainted with bias. This mode of thinking makes cynics vulnerable to belief in conspiracy theories. To tap conspiracy theory belief, we asked respondents whether they believed some of the common conspiracy theories in circulation at the time of the study.[15] The question we used was as follows: "Within our culture there exist theories about certain historical and scientific events. Some of these theories are listed below. Please indicate whether you believe the theory." We followed this with a list including the theories that the US government staged the 9/11 attacks, the JFK assassination, the moon landing, global warming, and Barack Obama's birth certificate, asking the respondents to indicate that they believe that the conspiracy is true or not (see Appendix 7 for the full question). We tried to balance the question so that there would be options for those on either side of the ideological spectrum, since conspiracy theory thinking is not correlated with any one ideology.[16] I created two categories out of these responses, coding respondents who indicated that they believed one or more of these theories as cynics, the rest skeptics.

In order to separate skeptics from cynics on the media we utilized self-reported media use and attitudes about the media and journalism. The self-reported media use question asked: "Which of the following best describes your use of news media sources?" Respondents could pick from the following:

- I don't really see the point in following the news.
- I follow the news every now and then when something big happens.
- I selectively follow the news, seeking out information on government, politics, and/or international affairs that I think is important to know.
- I watch the news all all the time, watching (either on TV or online) as many different news and talk shows as I can, but I don't have time to read too many news stories.
- I follow the news all the time in all forms, watching a lot of television news shows, listening to radio talk shows, and regularly reading news articles online or in print.

The third option, "I selectively follow the news," was the option we thought skeptics would most likely select. It reflects the skeptics' desire to actively seek out information along with the sense that skeptics would have that there is information that is "important to know." Cynics' dismissive attitude toward information would make it unlikely that they would select this option.

Finally, we thought that a better way to get at cynical versus skeptical attitudes about the media would be to collect separate opinions about media organizations and journalists. Media organizations in the United States and the journalists who work for those organizations have different incentives, or motives behind what they do. Media organizations are business entities whose bottom line profit motive drives them to enhance the entertainment quality of the news in order to attract viewers or readers. Journalists are professionals who are driven to get at the truth, providing as accurate a picture of reality as possible.[17] We believe that skeptics would be aware of this dichotomy, while cynics' attitude about biases would make them distrustful of both. So, in order to tap into attitudes about the trustworthiness of the media, we modified the standard question that is frequently used to assess the public's confidence in institutions. In addition to asking how much confidence respondents had in media organizations, we also asked how much confidence they had in journalists.

Controls

We included a number of questions in the survey in order to control for some audience characteristics that might be related to fandom of *TDS* and *TCR* as well as skepticism. Since the samples for these studies were generated by students in political science classes we thought it important to control for exposure to political science material. Studying political science would likely instill a level of skepticism, not cynicism, in students and cynical individuals would likely dismiss the value of studying politics. So we asked respondents if they majored or minored in political science. We asked respondents to specify their gender, thinking that males might prove to be more cynical. And, finally, we asked a series of questions designed to measure need for cognition in order to rule out a possible spurious relationship between need cognition, viewership of *TDS* and *TCR*, and skepticism. The question used to measure need for cognition asked respondents the extent to which respondents they thought certain attributes were characteristic of them, including whether they think "it's important to grapple with complex issues," "form opinions about everything," and "only think as hard" as they "have to," and (see Q19 in Appendix 7 for all seven attributes).

Survey Methods

Using various combinations of these measures, my students and I ran three different surveys in order to gather evidence with regard to the nature of the effect of *TDS* and *TCR*. One study was a survey administered in classes to a little more than 400 undergraduate students at the author's school.[18] The second study was an online survey I developed with my 2013 Politics & the Media class. The students distributed the link to the questionnaire in a variety of ways—tweeting it, posting it on Facebook (in a variety of different ways), emailing it, and posting it on email distribution lists. As an inducement, we offered respondents an opportunity to enter a drawing to win a $50 gift card. A little over 500 people completed this survey.[19] And, finally, the third study was run with the help of the students in my 2014 Politics & the Media class[20] and was part of the *Game of Thrones* and *House of Cards* survey used for Study 1 discussed in chapters 3 and 4 (see chapter 3 for the methodology of this survey). The sample size for this third study was just under 1,000 respondents. These are, obviously, not random samples. Our sampling methods, however, should not pose a problem since our interest is in the relationship between exposure to *TDS* and *TCR* and levels of cynicism versus skepticism, and not in using the data for descriptive purposes.

RESULTS

Comparisons between fans of *TDS* and *TCR* and those who had no or minimal exposure to those shows on the different measures of skepticism versus cynicism can be found in figures 7.1 through 7.3. As shown in each of those figures (representing the different measures of skepticism versus cynicism)

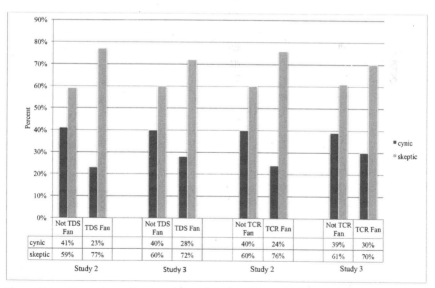

	Not TDS Fan	TDS Fan	Not TDS Fan	TDS Fan	Not TCR Fan	TCR Fan	Not TCR Fan	TCR Fan
cynic	41%	23%	40%	28%	40%	24%	39%	30%
skeptic	59%	77%	60%	72%	60%	76%	61%	70%
	Study 2		Study 3		Study 2		Study 3	

Figure 7.1. Percentage of respondents choosing the cynical versus skeptical response to the question: "When it comes to disagreements between people over how things are, which of the following statements comes closer to what you believe? It is impossible to know which claims are accurate because studies and evidence can be manipulated to prove whatever someone wants to prove. Or, It is possible to know which claims are accurate based on a careful assessment of the research and evidence."

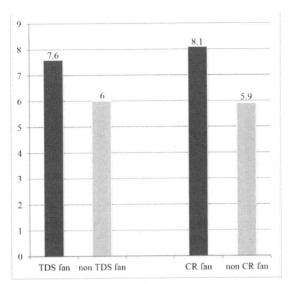

Figure 7.2. Percentage of respondents choosing the cynical versus skeptical response to the question: "When it comes to disagreements between people over how things are, which of the following statements comes closer to what you believe? It is impossible to know which claims are accurate because studies and evidence can be manipulated to prove whatever someone wants to prove. Or, It is possible to know which claims are accurate based on a careful assessment of the research and evidence."

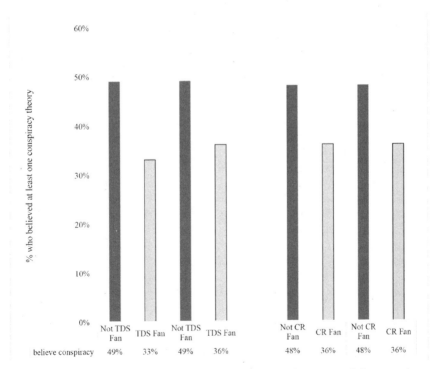

Figure 7.3. Percent of respondents who believed in at least one of the conspiracy theories by TDS and TCR fandom.

those who watched *TDS* and *TCR* at least some of the time, for at least one year (who we categorized as fans), consistently evinced greater skepticism and less cynicism than those only minimally exposed to the shows or not at all. Fans of *TDS* and *TCR* were more likely than nonfans to express the belief that "it is possible to know which claims are accurate based on a careful assessment of the research and evidence" (figure 7.1). In the classroom survey, fans were more likely than nonfans to score high on the distrust and participation measure (figure 7.2). Fans of *TDS* and *TCR* were less likely than nonfans to indicate that they believe in a conspiracy theory in the two on-line surveys (figure 7.3).

When it comes to the use of and attitudes toward the media, exposure to *TDS* and *TCR* was associated with both measures of media skepticism. As shown in figure 7.4, *TDS* and *TCR* fans were more likely than nonfans to

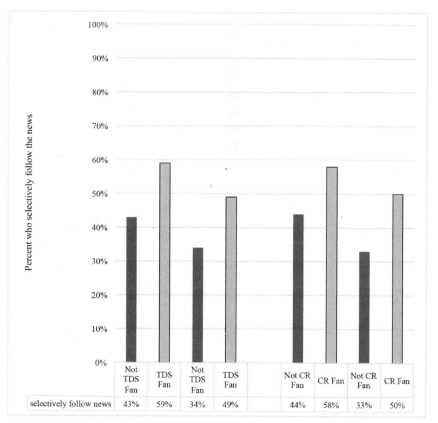

	Not TDS Fan	TDS Fan	Not TDS Fan	TDS Fan	Not CR Fan	CR Fan	Not CR Fan	CR Fan
selectively follow news	43%	59%	34%	49%	44%	58%	33%	50%

Figure 7.4. Percentage (under the age of 34) who "selectively follow the news, seeking out information on government, politics, and/or international affairs that I think is important to know" by fandom of TDS and TCR.

indicate that they "selectively follow the news in order to find information about government and politics that they deemed important." As expected, there was no relationship between exposure to *TDS* and *TCR* and confidence in media organizations; but, also as expected, *TDS* and *TCR* fans were less likely than nonfans to lack confidence in journalism (see figures 7.4 and 7.5).

To more vigorously test the relationship among *TDS*, *TCR*, and skepticism and rule out possible alternative explanations for these findings, I ran a series of multivariate analyses (either regression or logistic regression) with the control variables discussed above—whether the respondent majored in political science, their gender, and their level of need for cognition. The results of these tests can be found in tables 7.1, 7.2, and 7.3. The results of these multivariate analyses indicate that even when controlling for these factors, fans of *TDS* and *TCR* were significantly more likely than nonfans to score high on the direct measure of skepticism—the response to the question "When it comes to disagreements between people over how things are, which of the following statements comes closer to what you believe?" The same held true for one of the indirect measures—the measure created by multiplying responses to the trust in government question with the number of political ac-

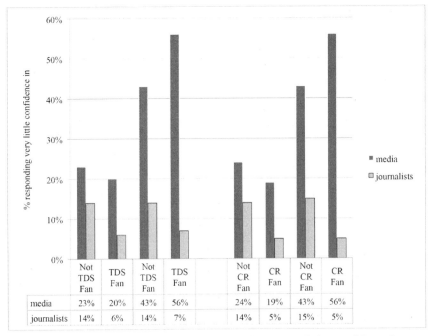

	Not TDS Fan	TDS Fan	Not TDS Fan	TDS Fan	Not CR Fan	CR Fan	Not CR Fan	CR Fan
media	23%	20%	43%	56%	24%	19%	43%	56%
journalists	14%	6%	14%	7%	14%	5%	15%	5%

Figure 7.5.   Percent (under age of 34) saying they have "very little" confidence in news media organizations and journalists by *TDS* and *TCR* fandom.

tivities respondents reported engaging in. And, finally, as shown in table 7.3, after controlling for need for cognition, political science majors, and gender, *TDS* and *TCR* fans were more likely than nonfans (at a statistically significant level) to show skepticism in the media through their media use, that is, they were more likely to say they selectively follow the news.

The findings reported here, when added to the findings of previous research on the impact of *TDS* and/or *TCR* and the results of the *House of Cards* study in chapter 4, provide some evidence in support of the argument that *TDS* and *TCR* promote skepticism of politics and the media among their

Table 7.1. Logistic regression, dependent variable skepticism as measured by question asking "When it comes to disagreements. . . . " Response "It is possible to know which claims are accurate based on a careful assessment of the research and evidence" code 1, cynical response coded 0

	Study 2	Study 3	Study 2	Study 3
(Constant)	−1.52	−.12	−1.52	−.15
TDS exposure	.58*	.42*	—	—
TCR exposure	—	—	.53*	.30*
Need for Cognition	.07*	.02	.07*	.03*
Political Science Major/Minor	.40	−.10	.50	−.13
Male	.33	.47*	.36*	.48*
% predicted correctly	66.3	64.5	66.0	64.7

* significant at the .05 level or better, one-tailed test

Table 7.2. Regression analysis, regressing skepticism (as measured by distrust X number of political activities) on need for cognition, political science major, gender, and *TDS* or *TCR* exposure

	b (standardized b)	b (standardized b)
(Constant)	1.03	1.04
TDS exposure	.20*	—
	(.17)	
TCR exposure	—	.22*
		(.19)
Need for Cognition	.49*	.48*
	(.15)	(.15)
Political Science Major/Minor	2.09*	2.05*
	(.21)	(.21)
Male	−1.26*	−1.30*
	(−.13)	(−.14)
Adjusted R-square	.12	.13

* significant at the .05 level or better, one-tailed test

Table 7.3. Logistic Regression, dependent variable selective use of
the news

	Study 2	Study 3	Study 2	Study 3
(Constant)	−1.20	−2.72	−1.25	−2.71
TDS exposure	.61*	.57*	—	—
TCR exposure	—	—	.37*	.57*
Need for Cognition	.04*	.08*	.04*	.08*
Political Science Major/Minor	−.46	.03	−.31	.03
Male	.04	.17	.11	.17
% predicted correctly	57.0	62.1	55.2	62.1

* significant at the .05 level or better, one-tailed test

audiences, not cynicism. A previous *experimental* study revealed a causal link between exposure to *TDS* and cynicism;[21] here we have shown that perhaps what was deemed cynicism may have instead been skepticism. The fact that the findings of Study 3 in chapter 4 found exposure to *House of Cards* (*HoC*) was related to greater *cynicism* (the opposite of the findings here for *TDS* and *TCR*) also hints at a causal relationship between exposure to all three of these shows and levels of skepticism versus cynicism. The reason to suspect that the shows are indeed having an effect is that explicitly political shows are likely to attract similar audiences. If that is the case, then the differences between the audiences of *TCR* and *TDS* and *HoC* would be due to the shows' different lessons. Confirmation of this suspicion will have to await experimental research.

CONCLUSION

In his book, *From Cronkite to Colbert*, Baym argues that *The Daily Show* and *The Colbert Report* represent an emerging new paradigm for television "news." It is a paradigm that employs satire to mock the dominant cynical postmodern paradigm of television news in the early years of the twenty-first century. It does so while exhibiting the characteristics of the more rational and fact-based approach to television news evident in the early decades of television. In other words, *TDS* and *TCR* represent a paradigm of political discourse that models a more skeptical (as opposed to cynical) approach to news and politics. My students and I suspected that Baym was correct, and that the various ways Jon Stewart and Stephen Colbert modeled skepticism would be reflected in the attitudes of the audiences of the two shows. Using three different surveys and a variety of measures designed to distinguish between skepticism and cynicism, we found just that. More of those categorized as fans of *TDS* and *TCR*, in contrast to nonfans, answered our questions in the manner expected of skeptics not cynics. Because we employed survey designs (as opposed to an experimental design), we cannot claim to have found a causal relationship between viewing *TDS* or *TCR* and skepticism. One piece of previous research, however, has demonstrated a causal connection between *TDS* and cynicism, albeit using measures incapable of differentiating between cynics and skeptics.[22] The multivariate analysis of data from these studies, however, does provide some additional evidence suggesting a causal relationship by ruling out some obvious alternative explanations. The fact exposure to *TDS* and *TCR* was associated with higher levels of skepticism while exposure to *House of Cards* was associated with higher levels of cynicism (see chapter 4) offers another bit of evidence that could indicate different causal effects of these shows. Still, the question as to whether news parody shows do indeed engender more skepticism versus cynicism will have to be left to future, experimental research. The continued popularity of news parody shows, such as *Full Frontal with Samantha Bee* and *Last Week Tonight with John Oliver*, means that additional inquiry into the specific effects of such shows is of value to understanding the impact of such forms of entertainment on audiences' political views.

NOTES

1. Some of the data discussed in this chapter were discussed previously in "Skepticism or Cynicism: Attitudinal Impacts of *The Daily Show* and *The Colbert Report* on Young Americans," presented at the 2012 Annual Meeting of the Midwest Political Science Association, Chicago, Illinois, with Will Andreycak.

2. Some of the research presented in this chapter was completed in collaboration with William Andreycak, a University of Vermont honors student who completed an honors thesis on this subject under my supervision. Other parts of the research were completed with the help of the students in my spring 2013 Politics & the Media class (POLS137): including Emma Allen, Benjamin Beaudoin, Aaron Bernstein, Chelsea Bernstein, Walker Cotton, Andrew Dalessandro, Katie Dzerovych, Grace Emerick, Kasey Emmons, Nick Farley, Casey Gates, Kyle Goebel, Victor Hartmann, Becky Hayes, Anthony Jordick, Kelly Joyce, Katie Kimball, Caitlin Lowe, Padraic Mackin, Maura McGovern, Kinley Mehra, Lauren Morlino, Kyle Mountain, Eric Murray, Siobhan Neela-Stock, Gregory Nyhan, Ivy O'Connor, Clarke Reiner, Clara Richmond, Kamran Rosen, Clancy Rugg, Natasha Sprengers- Levine, Anna Stuart, Olivia Taylor, Andrew Varelas, Justin Wagner, Lauren Willigan, Russel Zintel.

3. See Jody Baumgartner and Jonathan S. Morris in their study "The Daily Show Effect: Candidate Evaluations, Efficacy, and American Youth," *American Politics Research* 34, no. 3 (May 2006): 341–67; S. Robert Lichter, Jody C. Baumgartner, and Jonathan S. Morris, *Politics is a Joke! How TV Comedians Are Remaking Political*

Life (Boulder, CO: Westview Press, 2015); and, Roderick P. Hart and Johanna Hartelius, "The Political Sins of Jon Stewart," *Critical Studies in Media Communication* 24, no. 3 (August 2007): 263–72.

4. See Geoffrey Baym, *From Cronkite to Colbert: The Evolution of Broadcast News* (New York: Oxford University Press, 2009); Chad Painter and Louis Hodges, "Mocking the News: How The Daily Show with Jon Stewart Holds Traditional Broadcast News Accountable," *Journal of Mass Media Ethics* 25, no. 4 (2010): 257–74; Anthony Gierzynski and Kensington Moore, "The New Guard: Entertainment Talk Shows and the Not-so-fake News," in Morgan E. Felchner (editor), *Voting in America* (Westport, CT: Praeger, 2008), 165–73; and, Anthony Gierzynski, *Saving American Elections: A Diagnosis and Prescription for a Healthier Democracy* (Amherst, NY: Cambria Press, 2011).

5. Baumgartner and Morris "The Daily Show Effect."

6. Lauren Guggenheim, Nojin Kwak, and Scott W. Campbell, "Nontraditional News Negativity: The Relationship of Entertaining Political News Use to Political Cynicism and Mistrust," *International Journal of Public Opinion Research* 23, no. 3 (2011): 287–314.

7. Joseph N. Cappella and Kathleen Hall Jamieson, *Spiral of Cynicism: The Press and the Public Good* (New York: Oxford University Press, 1997).

8. Season 1, Episode 1, originally aired October 17, 2005, accessed October 27, 2017, http://www.cc.com/video-clips/63ite2/the-colbert-report-the-word—truthiness.

9. Gierzynski and Moore make a similar argument in their chapter, "The New Guard: Entertainment Talk Shows and the Not-so-fake News."

10. Paul R. Brewer and Emily Marquardt, "Mock News and Democracy: Analyzing the Daily Show," *Atlantic Journal of Communications* 15 (December 2007): 249–67.

11. Cappella and Jamieson, *Spiral of Cynicism*.

12. Pew Research Center, "Public Trust in Government Remains Near Historic Lows as Partisan Attitudes Shift," May 3, 2017, accessed October 20, 2017, http://www.people-press.org/2017/05/03/public-trust-in-government-remains-near -historic-lows-as-partisan-attitudes-shift/.

13. Pew Research Center, "Americans' Attitudes About the News Media Deeply Divided Along Partisan Lines," May 10, 2017, accessed October 20, 2017, http:// www.journalism.org/2017/05/10/americans-attitudes-about-the-news-media-deeply -divided-along-partisan-lines/.

14. Albert Bandura, "Social-Learning Theory of Identificatory Processes," in *Handbook of Socialization Theory Research*, edited by David A. Goslin (Chicago: Rand McNally, 1969).

15. I devised this measure with help from my students for our study of the effects of the *Harry Potter* series that I reported on in *Harry Potter and the Millennials*.

16. See Joseph E. Uscinski and Joseph M. Parent, *American Conspiracy Theories* (Oxford: Oxford University Press, 2014).

17. See Alison Dagnes, *Politics on Demand: The Effects of 24-hour News on American Politics* (Santa Barbara, CA: Praeger, 2010); and, Kathleen Hall Jamieson

and Paul Waldman, *The Press Effect: Politicians, Journalists, and the Stories that Shape the Political World* (Oxford: Oxford University Press, 2003).

18. University of Vermont Honors Student Will Andreycak administered these surveys to my classes and others as part of his honors thesis project, which I supervised. We presented the results of this sample and that of the second study in this chapter in our paper "Skepticism or Cynicism: Attitudinal Impacts of the *The Daily Show* and *The Colbert Report* on Young Americans" at the 2012 Annual Meeting of the Midwest Political Science Association, Chicago, Illinois.

19. Because the age distribution of the respondents was skewed toward younger respondents, I only used only the 460 respondents under the age of 34 when I ran the analysis.

20. There were about 100 students in the section of this class.

21. Baumgartner and Morris "The Daily Show Effect."

22. Baumgartner and Morris "The Daily Show Effect."

Chapter 8

Fictional Leaders and Support for Female Candidates

The 2016 contest for US president between Hillary Rodham Clinton and Donald Trump not only offered a choice between a woman and a man for the first time in US history, but also a choice between starkly contrasting styles of leadership that are, interestingly enough, also connected to gender in the public's mind.[1] People value different qualities or traits in leaders. The leadership traits valued by the public can be divided into those that are stereotypically associated with women—such as empathy, compassion, honesty, willingness to listen to others—those stereotypically associated with men—decisiveness, assertiveness, self-confidence, independence—and those that the public sees as equally descriptive of both genders—intelligence.[2] The extent to which a politician exhibits the leadership traits desired by the public will affect the support for that candidate, which given the preference for stereotypical masculine traits in leaders, works against women running for executive offices, especially on issues concerning national security. The simple response to that problem is to have female candidates exhibit more traditional male traits—act tougher, more decisive, and with emotional detachment. Yet, because there is a normative component associated with gender, women who violate those normative conceptions of femaleness by adopting stereotypical male traits are evaluated negatively and distrusted.[3] Since female candidates cannot get out of this double bind by their own actions, the hope for greater gender equality in leadership positions depends on a change in the traits the public thinks are important in a leader to include more traits stereotypically associated with women and the elimination of normative gender stereotypes. There is some evidence that a change in public's notions of what makes a good leader has already begun,[4] but this trend will need to continue in order to attain improved gender equality in leadership.

To understand how notions of leadership can change, one has to understand how our notions, or schema, of leadership develop in the first place. Social

learning theory leads us to believe that the leadership models that we are
exposed to during our life would play the most important role in the development of our role schema of leaders.[5] That is, the traits exhibited by successful leaders that we observe throughout our political socialization will be the
traits that we come to associate with good leadership. The fact that, up to this
point in time, most political leaders have been men means that observations
of real world leaders have likely been reinforcing the masculine notions of
leadership. As more women win leadership posts the conceptions of leadership should become less biased toward masculine traits; but, progress in this
direction (the proportion of women as leaders) has been slow.

There is, however, an alternative source of leadership role models that
could accelerate the shift away from the masculine-centric view of leadership—the fictional world. Indeed, the fictional worlds of entertainment media
offer a growing variety of women as leaders and leadership role models—
think Hermione Granger from the *Harry Potter* series, Katniss Everdeen of
The Hunger Games series, Vin from Brandon Sanderson's *Mistborn* series,
Rey from *Star Wars: The Force Awakens* and *The Last Jedi*, and Princess
Bubblegum from *Adventure Time*. Given previous research on the power of
fictional narratives, there is good reason to expect that these fictional role
models can have an effect on notions of leadership that is equal to or greater
than the real world ones. Add to that the fact that the public consumes much
more entertainment media than news media in this modern media environment and one can see the potential influence of fictional leaders.

In order to test whether fictional leaders can change our notions of leadership
and by extension support for women as leaders, I return in this chapter to the
potential impact of character types as a source of entertainment media political effects (as discussed in chapter 1). Recall that in chapter 6 I reported on
research that found the portrayal of one group of characters—villains—affected
attitudes about criminal justice and fighting terrorism. In this chapter I follow
that approach to entertainment media effects testing the effect of the portrayal
of another group of characters—leaders—on the traits people associate with
good leadership and, ultimately, support for women in leadership positions. To
that end, I present the results of two experiments that offer a first cut at examining the impact of this group of fictional characters, leaders.

FICTIONAL LEADERS AND THEIR EFFECTS
ON THE TRAITS VALUED IN LEADERS

Up until recently (and, certainly continuing in many outlets today) entertainment media offered limited roles for women—the vamp, the fatal attraction,
the girl next door, the mother, and the crone.[6] Additionally, successful leaders

in popular fictional worlds tended to be those who exhibit masculine traits, especially in the more popular genres where leadership matters the most—those involving intense action and individual heroes. While female characters and fictional leaders exhibiting less masculine-centric traits have by no means gained parity in the entertainment media, change is taking place, change that could affect the public's views on real world leadership and the women who seek to occupy those leadership positions.

The critically acclaimed reboot of *Battlestar Galactica* (2004–2009) had one of the most diverse set of roles for female characters of its time—including, among others, a hotshot pilot (who in the 1970s version of the show was a male character), a mechanic, a variety of deck officers and security personnel, a rebel leader of the Cylons (Cylons are a form of artificial intelligence created by the humans), and a president. (This diversity may be responsible for the show's high level of appeal to female viewers, who typically represent a much smaller portion of the audience for science fiction shows than they did for this one.) The character of President Roslin (played by Mary McDonnell) in *Battlestar Galactica* offers a perfect illustration of an alternative view on both leadership and gender. In the story, Roslin assumes the presidency after the Cylons kill all of the cabinet members above her in line to the presidency in their attack on the human race. Roslin was the Secretary of Education, and the military leaders in the series often demean her for just being a "schoolteacher." Roslin, however, proves to be a formidable leader—she negotiates, listens, collaborates, and persuades, as opposed to commands (though she does command at times as well). She was a strong female leader who exhibited stereotypical female traits that were portrayed as strengths in a way not typical for television or movies in the United States.

While *Battlestar Galactica* was a critically acclaimed series, its reach (in terms of audience) was not great. That cannot be said of the *Harry Potter* and *Hunger Game* series, the seventh and eighth episodes of the *Star Wars* series, *Rogue One*, *Game of Thrones*, or the 2017 *Wonder Woman* movie. These immensely popular series/movies all showcased female and male characters in leadership roles that exhibited traits that are stereotypically considered feminine. The *Harry Potters* series not only included Hermione and other important female characters whose strength came, in many ways, from traits typically associated with women (it is no exaggeration to say that Hermione held the group of Harry, Ron, and herself together through it all), but it also included a male protagonist—Harry—whose stereotypical female traits proved to be strengths, such as the empathy he showed for all creatures. Katniss Everdeen's compassion, empathy, and emotionality are portrayed as her core strengths in the *Hunger Games* series, traits echoed in one of her male counterparts, Peeta (who, among the male characters, is portrayed the most positively). And, Rey, of *The Force Awakens* and *The Last Jedi*, and Jinn of

Rogue One, like Leia of the earlier parts of the *Star Wars* saga, also evince compassion and empathy as part of the strength of their characters.

These characters (and others similar to them) are not the typical characters in entertainment media, but they do offer alternative models of leadership and of the value of what have been stereotypically deemed feminine traits in the role of leadership. The lessons regarding the value of these traits help to form or add to our role schema of leadership. And, if these different notions of the traits that are important in leaders do become part of our schema of leaders, it is possible for entertainment media to not only contribute to the development of different role conceptions of leadership, but also to prime certain traits over others. Before I turn to a discussion of the test of such a hypothesis, a little explanation of why we expect fiction to have such an influence is in order.

Once again, I refer the reader back to the discussion of Narrative Transportation Theory in chapter 2. When people are transported by stories, they are likely to learn the lessons of those stories including lessons about what makes for a good leader and how women are supposed to act. In other words, we take leadership characters as role models for leaders and "learn" what works and what doesn't work from the perspective of the character. And, female characters in stories inform our stereotypes of women. The power of fictional leaders and the portrayal of women in entertainment to shape one's views is likely to be at its highest during adolescence and the formative years of political socialization; but, since one's schema of leadership is not one of those perceptions that people are very aware of, or emotionally vested in, views on leadership should be susceptible to influence from fictional models at any time in one's life. In sum, being transported by a story increases the likelihood that fictional models, especially those viewed during adolescence and the formative years of political socialization, can have an impact as real world perceptions as argued by Social Learning Theory.[7]

In the case of the research that is the focus of this chapter, imagine following a story in which the protagonist successfully uses empathy and compassion in negotiating to resolve a major conflict within the storyline. According to narrative transportation theory, while immersed in the story we will come to accept the protagonist's approach as an effective way to lead (as narrative transportation theory argues, it is hard to counterargue the concreteness of what happens in a story, especially when we have become immersed in, and accept the story's reality). Additionally, it is unlikely that we even *think* about the fact that the story is presenting us with a certain perspective on leadership. When we leave that narrative world, we unknowingly carry that perspective with us to the real world. Through this process, fictional characters inform our schema of leadership and the traits that we look for in potential leaders.

In addition to the characteristics of transportation that suggest a powerful effect for stories, a companion process, identification, provides another reason to expect that exposure to stories could lead to belief change. When one identifies with a character in a narrative, they come to see the events of the story from the perspective of that character. Identification "involves losing track of one's own identity and then subsequently adopting the character's goals and perspectives as one's own."[8] Identification makes it even more likely that when we exit a narrative we will come away from it with altered perspectives, including on the traits we value in a leader.

In sum, narrative transportation theory, its companion process of identification and the extent research utilizing the two theories, in addition to Social Learning Theory, all provide a clear expectation that the fictional narratives of popular entertainment can have an effect on the traits that people perceive as valuable to leadership. When we are transported to fictional worlds and identify with the characters of those worlds, we will come away from those fictional worlds with a conception of leadership that includes the traits that are demonstrated as effective in the story.

RESEARCH DESIGN

To test whether fictional portrayals of leaders can affect the traits audiences associate with good leadership, the students in my senior seminar, "The Political Effects of Entertainment Media," and I designed an online experiment in 2015 that we ran twice.[9] Students in two of my classes recruited subjects for the first experiment via Facebook, Twitter, and email with a message that included a link to the study page in Qualtrics.[10] Once subjects clicked on the link they were taken to the Qualtrics survey page, which I had programmed to randomly assign subjects to one of four experimental conditions. I list the number of subjects who participated in each experimental group in figure 8.1. In each condition the subjects were asked to watch a brief video clip chosen to emphasize either stereotypical female or male traits in leaders in order to test the impact of such portrayals on which traits subjects valued in leaders. It is important to note that we theorize that exposure to different models of fictional leadership has the potential to effect the value the public assigns to different leadership traits through both a short-term and long-term effect. The long-term effect would occur from repeated exposure to models of leadership over an extended period time, lessons from which would contribute to the development of individuals' role schema of leadership. Alternatively, long-term effects could be the product of fiction's influence over time.[11] That said, we do not test the long-term effect here and leave that question to future research. What we can test is the immediate impact of a fictional portrayal of leadership and the ability of that portrayal to influence audiences' conception of leadership or, to borrow from schema theory, prime different components of existing role schema of leaders.

The clips we chose for the experimental conditions varied in the gender of the main characters in the clip and in the gender related traits they exhibited. We had two videos with lead female characters, one exhibiting stereotypical male leadership traits and the other stereotypical female leadership traits; and, we had two videos with lead male characters, alternating the leadership traits as we did with the clips focusing on female characters.

For the female character exhibiting stereotypical female traits treatment group, we chose an excerpt from *The Hunger Games: Mockingjay—Part I*. *The Hunger Games* series is a story set in a dystopian future where an oppressive government rules the peoples of thirteen different "districts." As an instrument of control, the government runs "The Hunger Games"—a battle to the death between randomly selected children from each of the districts, staged in a reality-show manner. After surviving her first Hunger Game and forcing a rule change that allowed her district partner, Peeta, to also survive, Katniss becomes the reluctant symbol of a rebellion against the oppressive regime headed by President Snow. By the beginning of *Mockingjay—Part I* the districts are engaged in a civil war with the central government. The clip we chose from that movie shows Katniss visiting a hospital in District 13. In the video, Katniss exhibits a great deal of empathy and compassion (stereotypical female traits) for the wounded in the hospital. When the hospital comes under fire by the air force of the Capital, she helps to take down a couple of the jets and then makes an emotional and defiant speech directed at President Snow.

For the female character exhibiting stereotypical male leadership traits treatment group, we selected a clip from *Battlestar Galactica: Razor*. *Razor* tells the story of the Battlestar Pegasus during and after the attack of the Cylons (robots that humans had created). Admiral Helena Cain, in charge of the Pegasus at the time of the attack, and a junior officer, Lt. Kendra Shaw, offer clear-cut cases of female leaders exhibiting stereotypical male traits. Admiral Cain is cold, tough, and decisive—in the clip she is shown ordering a blind jump to light speed to escape total destruction of her ship in the Cylon assault. Lt. Shaw admires and emulates Cains traits and, among other things, is shown in the clip running a weapons training exercise like a stereotypical male drill sergeant.

For the experimental condition with a male exhibiting stereotypical male traits we chose a scene from the 2009 *Star Trek* movie. Captain James T. Kirk is the archetypical male leader—decisive, aggressive, calm and self-confident. The clip shown this group follows Kirk and Spock as they infiltrate a Romulan ship to rescue Captain Pike and steal a futuristic ship. Kirk and Spock fight their way through the ship aggressively, confident in the chances they take and decisive in their handling of the situation. The end of the clip shows them destroying the Romulan ship and Kirk issuing a daring and decisive order necessary to save the Enterprise.

In the fourth experimental condition—male character exhibiting stereotypical female traits—subjects were shown a clip from *Doctor Who*, "The Zygon Inversion."[12] In the clip, The Doctor, talks two hostile sides down from a cataclysmic war, emotionally appealing to both sides, relating his experiences in the Time War, and showing empathy and forgiveness.

All of the clips came from the same genre—science fiction—and all involved war. All of the videos were comprised of compelling scenes designed to transport the subject into the story. Following the clips, subjects filled out a questionnaire (see appendix 7 for the core questions). The first questions were a couple of simple trivia questions about the clip (accompanied by pictures of the characters in order to make the recall easier) to measure the extent to which subjects paid attention to the clips. We include only those subjects who got both trivia questions correct. After those questions, we asked a couple of questions about war in order to distract from the intent of the study.

Since our main interest was to determine whether a fictional portrayal of successful leadership utilizing different gender associated traits affected how much subjects valued those traits, we listed a series of traits and asked "please indicate the extent to which you think the quality is important in a leader," with four response options ranging from "not important in a leader" to "essential in a leader" (Q5 in appendix 7). The traits included a mix of traits, some associated with women and some with men and others with neither gender. We also asked respondents (in a different question) whether those same traits were "generally more true of men or more true of women." To measure support for female candidates we asked a number of trial heat questions involving candidates in the 2016 presidential nomination contest and the question "If your party nominated a woman for President, would you vote for her if she were qualified for the job?"

[For the second experiment,] we used the same clips, but added a fifth group—a control group that was not asked to watch any clip (in this experiment we were aided by the help of Heather Yates, who coauthored a conference paper on these studies). The subjects for this experiment were drawn from introductory courses in political science at the University of Vermont and the University of Central Arkansas and offered extra credit for their participation. Subjects were randomly assigned to one of the five groups and then asked to fill out a questionnaire similar to the first experiment, but including additional measures to assess the subjects' feelings about female leaders (a

feeling thermometer that assessed feelings toward a number of leaders including the female Justices currently on the US Supreme Court, see Q79). Because
of the low number of respondents for this experiment (see figure 8.2 for the
number of subjects in each experimental group), we included all subjects who
got at least one of the manipulation check (trivia) questions correct.

RESULTS

Experiment 1

We created an additive score of the subjects' ratings of the importance of
stereotypical female traits—compassion, empathy, emotionality, and a willingness to consider the thoughts of others—and stereotypical male traits—
decisive, self-confidence, and assertiveness. We calculated the mean on
these two trait scales and compare the different experimental groups on both
in figure 8.1. The average scores for the importance of the female-associated
traits were higher for the two groups that watched videos in which those
traits were shown to be effective and positive. The difference between the

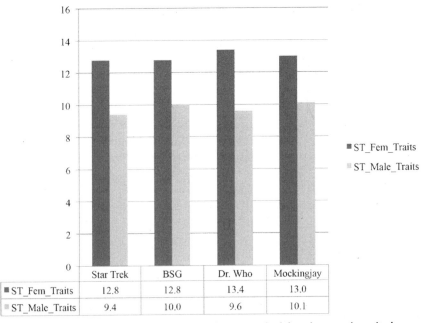

	Star Trek	BSG	Dr. Who	Mockingjay
ST_Fem_Traits	12.8	12.8	13.4	13.0
ST_Male_Traits	9.4	10.0	9.6	10.1

Figure 8.1. Average score on importance of stereotypical female or male traits by experimental group for Experiment 1.

subjects in the *Doctor Who* group and the *Battlestar Galactica: Razor* (*BSG*) group on this measure were statistically significant. Male-associated traits were rated, on average, higher for the *BSG* group, but interestingly, not the *Star Trek* group. In fact, we found that the *Mockingjay* group actually rated male-associated traits higher. This may be due to the fact that Katniss also exhibited some of these male-associated traits in the clip—aggressiveness and decisiveness in taking down a jet fighter.

Because we used an experimental design (with random assignment of subjects), we can conclude that the differences in the rating of the gender-related traits after the experimental manipulation (watching the video) were caused by the video. In the terms of this study, the results mean that we found support for the notion that fictional portrayals of leaders can affect the importance people ascribe to leadership traits, at the least on a short-term basis. To provide an additional check on those findings, that is to test whether some other variables were responsible for the difference between the experimental groups, I ran a series of multivariate analyses. The purpose of these analyses was to determine via statistical analyses whether the relationship between the experimental manipulation and the value subjects assigned to stereotypical female traits in leaders was due to some other factor that may have been unevenly distributed among the experimental groups. I did this for gender (a dichotomous variable labeled "male" for whether the respondent was a male), ideology, and exposure to entertainment media that we deemed as promoting female traits in leaders (*How to Get Away with Murder*, *Scandal*, *Parks and Recreation*, and *Doctor Who* for TV programs, *The Hunger Games* and *Harry Potter* series for books). Because of our limited sample size, I could not put all variables into the statistical model at once, so I ran a series of equations inserting these variables in pairs or individually. Table 8.1 contains the results of the analysis. Only subjects who got both manipulation-check questions correct were included in the analysis.

The takeaway from the analysis is that the impact of portraying female traits positively in the *Doctor Who* clip remained significant even when controlling for these other variables. This result gives us additional confidence (beyond the fact that this was an experiment, not a survey) in concluding that it was the video clip that caused the increase in the importance subjects assigned to stereotypical female traits. We also ran an additional analysis to test for the conditioning impact of narrative transportation by including interactive measures of the experimental groups and the level of transportation. Transportation did not enhance the impact, which may be due to the fact that we ran the analysis with only those who got both manipulation-check questions correct (that is, the manipulation-check questions may have filtered out those who were not transported).

Table 8.1. Sum of stereotypical female traits rated as important in a leader regressed on experimental conditions, and various control variables

	Experiment 1			Experiment 2
	Model 1	Model 2	Model 3	Model 1
(Constant)	13.19	12.40	11.95	14.23
Doctor Who Clip	.98*	.94*	.97*	1.06*
	(.23)	(.22)	(.22)	(.18)
Mockingjay Clip	.68	.59	.64	.46
	(.15)	(.13)	(.14)	(.08)
Star Trek Clip	.39	.38	.41	.40
	(.08)	(.07)	(.08)	(.07)
Male	−.41	−.41	−.45	−.21
	(−.09)	(−.08)	(−.10)	(−.05)
Ideology	−.237*	—	—	−.65*
	(−.14)			(−.34)
Read either HP or HG more than once	—	.32 (.08)	—	—
Frequency of viewing Scandal, How to Get Away w/ Murder, P&R, and Dr Who	—	—	.08 (.10)	—
Adjusted R-square	.03	.04		.12

* Significant at the .05 level or better, one-tailed test.
Note: Table entries are regression coefficients with standardized regression coefficients reported in parentheses. The group that watched the clip from BSG is the baseline for the comparison in the model.

To assess whether the gender-related leadership traits or gender stereotypes had an effect on willingness to support a female candidate we analyzed the relationship between leadership traits and gender stereotypes on two separate measures: a measure of support for Hillary Clinton and the responses to the question "If your party nominated a woman for president, would you vote for her?" For the Clinton measure, we added up the number of times in the trial heat questions that the respondents said they would vote for Hillary Clinton; for the generic question we recoded the variable so that a "no" was 0, "don't know 1," and "yes" 2. The results for the generic question were insignificant (most likely due to the lack of variation in the response to this question—over 80 percent of respondents said "yes" so there was little in the way of variation in this measure to explain in the first place). The results for the measure of support for Hillary Clinton can be found in table 8.2.

The importance of stereotypical female traits in a leader was not significantly related to support for Clinton. So, the video clip was unable to move attitudes on Clinton through changes in the value of female associated traits. This could be due to the unique reaction to Hillary Clinton among the respondents and Clinton's own public persona—because of the importance of mas-

Table 8.2. Support for Hillary Clinton regressed on the value of female traits in leaders, male and female stereotypes, gender, and Republican identification

Variables	b (standardized regression coefficient)
(Constant)	2.45
Female traits important to leaders	−.05
	(−.07)
Male stereotype	−.18*
	(−.15)
Female stereotype	−.001
	(−.001)
Male	.03
	(.13)
Republican	−1.41*
	(−.27)
Adjusted R-square	.09

* Significant at the .05 level or better, one-tailed test.

culine traits in leaders for the public she has had to show such traits, which has then caught her up in the double bind of violating normative gender stereotypes. The effects on a different female candidate (or at a different stage of the election) might find a different result. It is interesting to note that the subjects who scored high on associating stereotypical male traits with males (that is, hold a gender stereotype) were significantly less likely to support Clinton, suggesting that Clinton had fallen prey to the double bind.

In sum, the first experiment demonstrated the ability of an example of leadership from a fictional character in a video clip to change how important gender related traits are to leadership. While this is possibly a temporary effect, it does possibly show that younger people (the bulk of the subjects in the study) have role schema of leaders that either can be influenced by entertainment media, or have schema of leaders that includes those traits typically associated with women that can be primed by a work of fiction.

Experiment 2

The average score for the female and male related leadership traits from the second experiment can be found in figure 8.2. While the results parallel those in the first experiment with regard to the *Doctor Who* video (being the most likely to boost the value of stereotypical female traits), none of the differences reach statistical significance. The lack of statistical findings may be due to the small number of subjects in each category.

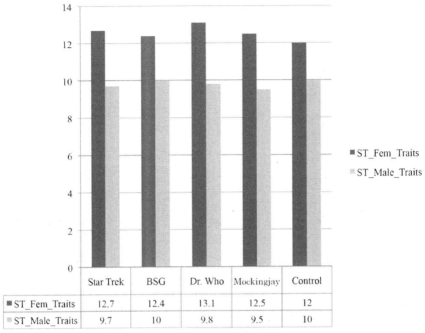

	Star Trek	BSG	Dr. Who	Mockingjay	Control
■ ST_Fem_Traits	12.7	12.4	13.1	12.5	12
■ ST_Male_Traits	9.7	10	9.8	9.5	10

Figure 8.2. Average score on importance of stereotypical female or male traits by experimental group for Experiment 2.

When I ran multivariate analyses to examine the relationship closer, I found, as in the first experiment, that the impact of watching the *Doctor Who* video was related to assigning a higher importance to those traits stereotypically associated with women when controlling for gender and ideology, and that the relationship was statistically significant (see last column in table 8.1). None of the relationships held for Model 2 and 3 in Experiment 2, so I do not present those results. The replication of some of the findings in Experiment 1 for Model 1 increases confidence that the *Doctor Who* video led to an increase in the value respondents assigned to stereotypical female traits for leaders.

Finally, for the subjects in Experiment 2 I tested the link between the value assigned for gender related traits and evaluations of four female leaders— Hillary Clinton and the three female Justices on the US Supreme Court. The point here is simply to take the findings of the experiment the next step to see if the differences in how subjects rated gendered stereotypical traits was associated with evaluation of women in prominent leadership positions. I measured the evaluations using the feeling thermometer scores respondents gave

Table 8.3. Sum of feeling thermometer scores for women leaders (Hillary Clinton and the 3 women on the US Supreme Court) regressed on value of female associated traits, male associated traits, male gender, and ideology

Variables	b (standardized regression coefficient)
(Constant)	166.08
Female Traits	5.73*
	(.18)
Male Traits	1.24
	(.03)
Male	−11.96
	(−.08)
Ideology	−15.97*
	(−.29)
Adjusted R-square	.14

* Significant at the .05 level or better, one-tailed test.

to each, summing those feeling thermometer scores to make one variable. I present the results of the regression analysis in table 8.3. In this analysis of evaluations of female leaders (when it isn't just Hillary Clinton), the relationship between how much the respondents valued stereotypical female traits in leaders was positively and significantly related to the feelings toward these women leaders, even when controlling for ideology and male gender.

CONCLUSION

The purpose of the research in this chapter was to demonstrate that the portrayal of leadership by fictional characters could affect the traits we value in real world leaders. In both experiments it was the *Doctor Who* video (in which The Doctor uses empathy and forgiveness in an emotional appeal to two adversaries at the brink of war) that led to an increase in the importance of stereotypical female traits in a leader. It is interesting to note that the significant effect occurred in the experimental condition involving a man effectively using traits typically associated with women (especially given that the new Doctor—the thirteenth Doctor—for the 2018 season will be a woman). The failure to find that the experimental condition in which a female leader portrayed stereotypical female traits could be due to the fact that in the clip for that condition—that of Katniss in *Mockingjay II*—included a scene in which Katniss evinced some stereotypical male traits in addition to the stereotypical female traits prominent in the clip. One could argue that Katniss evinced stereotypical male traits in the scene during the clip in which she takes down a fighter jet with an explosives-tipped arrow. On the other hand, it may be that public at this point in time is more open to learning about the value of traits associated with women only when they are shown to be effective by a man. One of the students who participated in this project suggested a year later that this might explain part of the appeal of Bernie Sanders over Hillary Clinton for many during the 2016 Democratic nomination contest.[13] Future research would do well to look further into this dynamic as well as investigate the long-term effects of entertainment media on what the public values in leaders.

NOTES

1. The research in this chapter was previously presented in a paper, "Fictional Leaders, Leadership Stereotypes and Evaluations of Women in Leadership Positions," presented at the Annual Meeting of the Midwest Political Science Association, April 7–10, 2016, with Heather Yates.

2. Alice H. Eagly and Steven J. Karau, "Role Congruity Theory of Prejudice Toward Female Leaders," *Psychological Review* 109, no. 3 (2002): 573–98; Pew Research Center, "Women and Leadership," January 14, 2015, accessed March 24, 2016 http://www.pewsocialtrends.org/2015/01/14/women-and-leadership/.

3. Eagly and Karau, "Role Congruity Theory of Prejudice Toward Female Leaders"; Anne M. Koenig, Alice H. Eagly, Abigail A. Mitchell, Tiina Ristikari, "Are Leader Stereotypes Masculine? A Meta-Analysis of Three Research Paradigms," *Psychological Bulletin* 137, no. 4 (July 2011): 616–42.

4. Koenig, Eagly, Mitchell, and Ristikari, "Are Leader Stereotypes Masculine?"; John Gerzama and Michael D'Antonio, *The Athena Doctrine: How Women (And The Men Who Think Like Them) Will Rule The Future* (New York: Wiley and Sons, 2013).

5. Albert Bandura, *Social Foundations of Thought and Actions: A Social Cognitive Theory* (Englewood Cliffs, NJ: Prentice-Hall, 1986).

6. Elizabeth Haas, Terry Christensen, and Peter J. Haas, *Projecting Politics: Political Messages in American Films* second edition (New York: Routledge, 2015).

7. Bandura, *Social Foundations of Thought and Actions*.

8. Jordan M. Carpenter and Melanie C. Green, "Flying with Icarus: Narrative Transportation and the Persuasiveness of Entertainment," in *The Psychology of Entertainment Media: Blurring the Lines Between Entertainment and Persuasion*, edited by L. J. Shrum (New York: Routledge, 2012), p. 181.

9. The students in the seminar were Hayley Aydelott, Meaghan Blanchard, Austen Carpenter, Brianna Fay, Sean Feenan, Jeffrey Fuller, Aphaia Lambert-Harper, Ceara Ledwith, Ned Liggett, Cam Panepinto, and Adrian Willing.

10. The message used to make the appeal was as follows: "My class at the University of Vermont and our professor are recruiting subjects for an online study. Please

consider volunteering. All subjects need to do is to watch a video clip (clips range from 9 to 16 minutes) and fill out a brief survey (about 10 minutes). Those who fully participate in the study can enter into a drawing for one of several cash prizes (we are giving away four $25 visa cards and one $100 visa card). If you are interested in participating in this study, follow this link: [hyperlink to survey]."

11. Markus Appel and Tobias Richter, "Persuasive effects of fictional narratives increase over time," *Media Psychology* 10, no. 1 (2007): 113–34.

12. Season 9, original airdate November 7, 2015.

13. Meaghan Blanchard.

Conclusion

How we perceive and react to the political is a product of many factors. Our personalities—that cluster of fundamental traits—determine, to an extent, how we interact with the world and the political values and beliefs we internalize about that world.[1] That exposure to the political world is channeled through, and filtered by the agents of our socialization—family, peers, schools, community, news *and* entertainment television, movies, books, and video games.[2] The political being who arises from those processes moves through an environment full of lessons, stereotypes, information and feelings, much of which has some relevance to politics and thus impinges on our thoughts and feelings about the political in a variety of ways. Entertainment media dominates the environment through which people move in the early decades of the twenty-first century. As I write, the options for entertainment media seem endless, especially compared to the media environments of the past. When I was in my adolescent years our options were limited to four broadcast channels (five if the atmospheric conditions were conducive), the movie theaters, and, of course books. Now, in addition to those options, I can watch a host of movies and television shows from streaming companies like Netflix, Hulu, and Amazon, or peruse YouTube, watch the Chicago Cubs using an app on my phone, or browse endless websites. The dominance of entertainment media in this era means that in order to understand public opinion and political behavior fully, we need to understand the role that entertainment media plays.

The purpose of this book has been to examine the role that entertainment television shows, movies, books, and video games play in how we see and react to the political world. The pursuit of that goal started with mapping out the theoretical arguments for entertainment media's political effects. As discussed in chapter 1, theorizing about entertainment media effects starts with developing an understanding of where to look for potential political effects. After identifying the content most likely to have a political effect, I turned to the theoretical arguments that explain *how* that content can affect political views—the process of belief acquisition from the transported state that characterizes consumption of stories and the context (individual, group and cultural) *when* entertainment media has the opportunity to influence the transported individuals. I then presented research on the politically relevant effects of both pure entertainment and explicitly political shows—*Game of Thrones*, *House of Cards*, *The Daily Show*, and *The Colbert Report*—genres, and character types using a variety of different methods and designs, experimental and correlational.

While significant, the effects of the entertainment media presented here (and in the extant literature on media effects) are often small, but that doesn't mean they are unimportant. Given the multitude of other factors driving political opinions and the cacophonous political environment through which individuals move in time, it is surprising that we are able to detect any media effect. That is, the complexity of human beliefs and the diversity of the factors involved in developing those beliefs means that the relationship between entertainment media exposure and political beliefs may be muddied by all the other things going on in people's lives. The theory provided in chapter 2 should give the reader some sense of where entertainment media would fit in the universe of factors affecting political development. Research designed within the context of such a theory should optimize the chances of finding such effects if they exist, but cannot fully eliminate problems associate with the complexity of human beliefs. For these reasons and others, the coefficients that indicate a relationship between media and opinions should not be taken as an upper limit on the actual importance of entertainment media. Coefficients may underestimate the magnitude of a relationship between two variables for a number of reasons.[3] Underestimation of media effects may occur if the impact of the media being studied is stronger for some individuals than for other (that is, when there is a wide variation in effect among subjects). My conversations with fans of the *Harry Potter* series following the release of *Harry Potter and the Millennials* and testimonials offered up at talks I have given on my research provided anecdotal evidence of very powerful effects of fiction on some individuals. One individual, for example, told a story of how their aunt came to accept their transgendered sexuality only after having read the *Harry Potter* series, with their aunt openly attributing her change in acceptance to the series. A published illustration of this high level of effect can be found in Ronald D. Moore' testimonial in an op-ed piece he wrote for *The New York Times* (Moore was the writer/producer for *Battlestar Galactica* and several of the *Star Trek* series). Moore declared:

[W]hen the starship Enterprise first settled into orbit around Planet M-113 on Sept. 8, 1966. . . . I could not have known it at the time, but "Star Trek" would literally change my life. . . . *Star Trek* painted a noble, heroic vision of the future, and that vision became my lodestar. As I grew into adolescence, the show provided a handy reference against which to judge the questions that my young mind began to ask: What is the obligation of a free society toward the less fortunate? . . . What does it mean to be human?[4]

The coefficients produced by various means of analysis provide the researcher with the *mean* effect of exposure on belief, masking the fact that the media exposure may have had more of an impact on certain groups or individuals. A fully specified theory that models interaction effects would minimize this problem, but the potential for underestimating effects remains.

The importance of media may also be underestimated because statistical models cannot truly measure the magnitude of reinforcing effects, and, media effects often operate to reinforce opinions shaped by other factors. And, as argued by Slater, reinforcing effects *are* important.[5] Finally, most statistics used to measure media effects assume a linear relationship—that the impact increases with each additional unit of exposure—when media effects may occur as a threshold effect or plateau after a certain amount of exposure. If the media effects are not linear, the coefficients produced by the analysis may underestimate the media effect.

While the studies I presented each have their individual weaknesses, the fact that each study consistently finds a relationship between the politically relevant lessons of the entertainment programs studied and the audiences of those shows—a relationship that is found in experiments that provide evidence of a causal linkage and in correlational research where the associations remain significant while controlling for other known predictors of the politically relevant views—leaves me confident that there is indeed evidence here that entertainment media play a role in how we see the political world. Add the research in this volume to the findings of previous research on entertainment media effects conducted using experimental, natural experiments, and survey designs, and one cannot help but see that there is something to the notion that entertainment media help shape public opinion.[6] And, as such, it is an area worthy of even more scholarly attention.[7]

POTENTIAL AREAS OF RESEARCH ON ENTERTAINMENT MEDIA EFFECTS

Most of the research in this book focused on, or used science fiction, fantasy, superhero, and political genres. This fact reflects the geeky tastes of this author, but there are some advantages to studying science fiction, fantasy and superhero genres for its political effects—the fantastical settings of these stories reduces the likelihood that audiences will be on guard for political messages. Most people would not think, for example, that what happens in a fictional twenty-third century story could have an effect on audiences' political views in the twenty-first century. As a political science scholar, the appeal of political shows is obvious. Still, in political entertainment media the key is to look for political effects outside of ideology and partisanship, such as how such shows might affect skepticism versus cynicism. That said, other entertainment genres clearly *do* hold potential for entertainment media effects (and I leave studying these effects to scholars with other tastes in entertainment). Take crime genres. Slater, Rouner, and Long, found that exposure to a single episode of *Law & Order* in an experiment led to increased support death penalty regardless of ideology.[8] Mutz and Nir found that the portrayal of the justice system in *Law & Order* affected peoples view about the real justice system.[9] These findings, along with our work discussed in chapter 7, suggest that the portrayal of criminals (or villains), police, and the criminal justice system in any genre may influence public attitudes about criminal justice and the best way to deal with real world villains.

War movies hold the potential for some obvious political effects, but so does any story that portray militaries and war. The portrayal of militaries can range from the heroic to the corrupt or inept, militaries can be shown as defenders of a democratic system, tools of an oppressive regime, or rebels fighting against that oppressive regime. Horror movies often contain morals that could promote conservative beliefs—in many of these stories, like *Halloween*, sexual promiscuity is often followed by the brutal murder of the promiscuous couple. And, then there is the embedded sexual morality of the *Twilight* series (and the entire vampire genre), where passion and sex gets you a condition where you are tortured by an eternal craving.

With a former reality-show star occupying the White House, it is clear that, as illustrated by Trump's reality-show behavior, those shows, too, contain politically relevant lessons. What is it, after all, that allow the contestants to survive? Self-serving behavior? Teamwork? Strong, decisive leadership? And do we internalize such lessons, too? It would be interesting to see whether attitudes toward Trump are related to acceptance of the behavior displayed within these shows among those who consume reality television.

Entertainment geared toward youth has common themes that could affect political perspectives. The *Harry Potter* series, *The Hunger Games* series, the *Divergent* series, all contain a wealth of politically relevant lessons, some that have been explored,[10] others still worthy of looking into. Avenues of research may include the effect that relationship between the young characters in such stories and authority figures has on attitudes about authority. Or, the effect of the frequent portrayal of adults as incapable of handling the problems of the world and the subsequent need for the young characters to step up to do what the grownups cannot or will not do. I suspect this theme of incompetent adults and the need for youth to take charge has added to the empowerment of youth in politics in recent years, such as surge in voter turnout among young adults in the 2008 election or the positive activism of students spurred by their peers at Marjory Stoneman Douglas High School.

There is a huge segment of entertainment media which engrosses millions that could be explored for its political messages—sports, with its fandom creating in-groups and out-groups, the diversity of players, and its hierarchical nature that likely engenders greater deference to authority (not to mention the platform it provides for political expression). If our (scholars') goal is to develop a complete picture of that which shapes the perspective of citizens, and if we (citizens) are to have a clearheaded understanding of how we come to believe what we do (and why others believe differently), we all need to keep asking such questions and doing the research that can provide us with the answers.

While I make scattered references to video games throughout the book, I have not directed my attention fully to the potential this form of entertainment has for shaping political views. The fact that in many of the games the player *is* the character means that identification and transportation may be even more powerful, leading to greater or different effects than books, television, and movies. As with those other sources of entertainment media, the effects are not likely to be overtly political and instead may shape politically relevant beliefs in areas that the player won't expect. Take guns. We have all been alerted to the potential that first-person shooter games may have on levels of violence (and there has been a lot of research on this point[11]), but how do these games affect users' views about the utility of guns as a tool and a form of protection—the need a "good guy" has for a gun? In other words, do these games act as pro-gun advertisement to the benefit of the gun industry? On another subject, how do multiplayer games affect notions of cooperation and conflict resolution? What impact do they have on attitudes about gender? On social capital?

I will stop here because I cannot possibly identify and/or list all the potential avenues of research on the effect of entertainment media on political views. Additional areas of entertainment media effects research can be found in chapter 1 along with the framework meant to provide a map for the search for entertainment media's political effects.

IMPLICATIONS

The findings I reported on here and the other extant research findings on entertainment media's political effects have implications beyond adding to our understanding of how people see the political world. The fact that entertainment media can shape public opinion has, as I have alluded to throughout this volume, implications for public policy because it influences the support for, or opposition to certain policies. As shown in chapters 3 and 4, this is the case for the role that entertainment media has in just world beliefs, which then affect a variety of policies including support for anti-poverty programs and affirmative action.[12] Public opinion on how to combat real world villains can be influenced by fictional villains (as shown in chapter 6) or by the portrayal of the justice system in crime shows.[13] Entertainment can affect engagement in politics depending on whether it promotes cynicism, à la *House of Cards* (as shown in chapter 4), or skepticism as *The Daily Show* and the *Colbert Report* appear to have done (as shown in chapter 7). And, the types of candidates that garner our support can be influenced by the leaders we see in fictional worlds (as shown in chapter 8).

Unfortunately, these findings also mean that entertainment media can be intentionally used to manipulate public opinion. This has been the fear of segments of society on both the left and the right: the Christian groups that fear fictional stories—say those portraying witchcraft and wizardry in a positive light—may weaken their children's' religious beliefs; the concerns that liberal Hollywood or, on the other hand the corporate sector is brainwashing America in one direction or another; the fear that leads groups to ban or even burn books that are seen as immoral or antithetical to their belief systems. The general conclusions of the research on entertainment media—that entertainment media can influence politically relevant views—can be used by such segments of society to justify their attempts to ban or in other ways attack entertainment media producers. This despite the fact there is no evidence to show that the types of effects uncovered in this body of research are intentional, nor is it likely that the writers and producers of entertainment are aware of the potential impact their entertainment has on the public along the lines identified in the research.

Many of the effects that this research has identified are ones that most people would deem positive—seeing the injustice in the world, reductions in bigotry and intolerance, a more skeptical approach to criminal justice and politics in general, and a more open mind to different forms of leadership. The positive effects identified by the research might lead some to argue that it would be good to intentionally use entertainment to achieve such desirable attitudes. It strikes me that there are several dangers to this line of thought. One danger is that while there may be a near-consensus on the positive nature of many of these effects, intentionally designing entertainment to further expand the reach of such beliefs may actually backfire. The second danger is that once you open the door to such manipulations, you also open the door to the promotion of harmful perspectives. It doesn't take much imagination to see how certain political interests might benefit by producing entertainment that makes the public more cynical and thus less engaged in politics. Or entertainment that draws attention to certain issues and frames those issues in certain ways. Or entertainment that makes us less accepting and tolerant as many movies and television shows did for a large segment of the twentieth century (from the obvious *Birth of a Nation* to the racism evident in the portrayal and lack of casting of nonwhites throughout entertainment in that century).

Whether you think entertainment should be used to promote positive values or not, the potential to intentionally use entertainment media to manipulate the public remains a possibility. Such is the cost of knowledge, but that knowledge can also be used to limit those costs. The ability to counteract intentional manipulation and the negative effects of entertainment media comes, after all, from an awareness of the role that entertainment plays in shaping our perspectives on politics. With an awareness of the potential ways entertainment can affect our politics, we may be able to guard against it (though such an awareness may, as one of my students told me, also spoil one's enjoyment of entertainment). Such an awareness does have the added benefit of humbling us with regard to the righteousness of our beliefs. By drawing our attention to the fact that our beliefs and attitudes are not the product of some rational calculus, but instead the result of a cluster of influences, some of which are not even real, one barrier to productive political discourse may be eliminated.

NOTES

1. Jeffery J. Mondak, *Personality and the Foundations of Political Behavior* (New York: Cambridge University Press, 2010).

2. M. Kent Jennings and Richard G. Niemi, "The Transmission of Political Values from Parent to Child," *American Political Science Review* 62 (1968): 169–84; M. Kent Jennings, Laura Stoker, and Jake Bowers, "Politics across Generations: Family Transmission Reexamined," *Journal of Politics* 71 (2009): 782–89.

3. For an extended discussion on why small coefficients in media effects research does not mean unimportant effects, see Elizabeth M. Perse, *Media Effects and Society* (Mahwah, NJ: Lawrence Erlbaum Associates, Inc., 2001), pp. 10–14.

4. Ronald D. Moore, "Mr. Universe," *The New York Times*, Op-Ed, September 18, 2006.

5. Michael D. Slater, "Reinforcing Spirals: The Mutual Influence of Media Selectivity and Media Effects and Their Impact on Individual Behavior and Social Identity," *Communications Theory* 17 (2007): 281–303.

6. See the Introduction and the notes for that chapter for the extent research on entertainment media effects.

7. Others who have made this argument include Diana C. Mutz and Lilach Nir, "Not Necessarily the News: Does Fictional Television Influence Real-World Policy Preferences?" *Mass Communication and Society* 13 (2010): 196–217; Kenneth Mulligan and Philip Habel, "The Implications of Fictional Media for Political Beliefs," *American Politics Research* 41, no. 1 (2013), 122–46; and, R. Lance Holbert, "A Typology for the Study of Entertainment Television and Politics," *American Behavioral Scientist* 49, no. 3 (2005): 436–53.

8. Michael D. Slater, Donna Rouner and Marilee Long, "Television Dramas and Support for Controversial Public Policies: Effects and Mechanisms," *Journal of Communication* 56 (2006): 235–52.

9. Diana C. Mutz and Lilach Nir, "Not Necessarily the News: Does Fictional Television Influence Real-World Policy Preferences?" *Mass Communication and Society* 13 (2010): 196–217

10. Anthony Gierzynski and Kathryn Eddy, *Harry Potter and the Millennials: Research Methods and the Politics of the Muggle Generation* (New York: The Johns Hopkins University Press, 2013); Loris Vezzali, Sofia Stathi, Dino Giovannini, Dora Capozza and Elena Trifiletti, "The greatest magic of Harry Potter: Reducing prejudice," *Journal of Applied Social Psychology* 45, no. 2 (2015): 105–21; and Calvert W. Jones, "It's the End of the World and They Know It: How Dystopian Fiction Shapes Political Attitudes," paper selected for presentation at the Southern Political Science Association Annual Meeting, San Juan, Puerto Rico, January 9, 2016.

11. Elizabeth M. Perse provides an overview of this research in her book, *Media Effects and Society* (Mahwah, NJ: Lawrence Erlbaum Associates, Inc., 2001).

12. Rubin and Peplau, "Who Believes in a Just World," Appelbaum, Lennon and Aber, "When Effort Is Threatening," and Vicky M Wilkins and Jeffrey B. Wenger, "Belief in a Just World and Attitudes Toward Affirmative Action," *Policy Studies Journal* 42 (2014): 325–43.

13. Slater, Rouner, and Long, "Television Dramas and Support for Controversial Public Policies"; Mutz and Nir, "Not Necessarily the News."

Appendix 1

Questions for Study 1

Q71 Which of the following statements characterizes your familiarity with the HBO series *Game of Thrones*? [1]

- ◦ I have never seen *Game of Thrones*, nor have I read any of the series *A Song of Ice and Fire*.
- ◦ I have seen at least some of *Game of Thrones*.
- ◦ I have seen the show and read at least some of the books.
- ◦ I have read the books, but not seen the TV show.

Q69 We would like to ask a few more specific questions about the HBO TV series *Game of Thrones*. Please tell us whether the following statements are true for you.

- ◦ I watch *Game of Thrones* as soon as it airs.
- ◦ I have watched all the episodes of *Game of Thrones*.
- ◦ I have read books in the series *A Song of Ice and Fire*.
- ◦ I can name almost all of the characters in *Game of Thrones*.
- ◦ In anticipation of the new season, I re-watched previous episodes.
- ◦ I have the music soundtrack to *Game of Thrones*.
- ◦ I talk about the show with people.
- ◦ I have posted about *Game of Thrones* on social media (Facebook, Twitter, etc.).

Q45 Please tell us why you have not watched all of the *Game of Thrones* series.

- ◦ I haven't had the time yet, but plan to watch it all when I have the chance.
- ◦ I like the show, but I don't have time to watch all of it.
- ◦ I found I did not like the show because (please type in your response below).

Q56 We'd like to get your feelings about some of the characters in *Game of Thrones* using what is called a feeling thermometer. Ratings between 50 degrees and 100 degrees mean that you feel favorable and warm toward the character. Ratings between 0 degrees and 50 degrees mean that you don't feel favorable toward the character and that you don't care too much for that character. You would rate the character at the 50 degree mark if you don't feel particularly warm or cold toward the character. If you want to make a rating of 0, you must click on the slider. If you don't recognize the character, just skip to the next character. Characters listed for rating: Cersei Lannister, Arya Stark, Jon Snow, Theon Greyjoy, Daenerys Targaryen, Little Finger, Stannis Baratheon, Tyrian Lannister, Sandor Clegane, and Ned Stark.

Q72 What got you to start watching *Game of Thrones*?

- Because everyone was talking about it.
- Because I usually watch HBO shows.
- Because I like fantasy shows.
- Because I read the books.
- Because my friends were watching it.
- Because my family was watching it.
- Because I saw clips posted on social media.
- Because of media coverage of the show.
- Other. (Please tell us what that was)

Q75 Which of the following statements is true regarding your exposure to the Netflix series *House of Cards*.

- I have not seen any of the episodes.
- I have seen some of the episodes.
- I have seen all of the episodes.
- I have watched all of the episodes and at least some of the episodes more than once.

Q74 We would like to ask a few more specific questions about the Netflix series *House of Cards*. Please tell us whether the following statements are true for you.

- I have watched all the episodes of *House of Cards*.
- I binge-watched *House of Cards* (watched a number of episodes all at once).
- In anticipation of the new season of *House of Cards*, I re-watched previous episodes.
- I talk about the show with people.
- I have posted about *House of Cards* on social media (Facebook, Twitter, etc).
- I would vote for Frank Underwood in an election.

Q46 Please tell us why you have not watched all of the episodes of *House of Cards*.

- I haven't had the time yet, but plan to watch it all when I have the chance.
- I like the show, but I don't have time to watch all of it.
- I found I did not like the show because (please type in your response below)

Q58 We'd like to get your feelings about some of the characters in *House of Cards* using what is called a feeling thermometer. Ratings between 50 degrees and 100 degrees mean that you feel favorable and warm toward the character. Ratings between 0 degrees and 50 degrees mean that you don't feel favorable toward the character and that you don't care too much for that character. You would rate the character at the 50 degree mark if you don't feel particularly warm or cold toward the character. If you want to make a rating of 0, you must click on the slider. If you don't recognize the character, just skip to the next character. Characters listed for rating: Frank Underwood, Claire Underwood, Zoe Barnes, Peter Russo, President Walker, Lucas Goodwin, Freddy Hayes, and Raymond Tusk.

Q76 What got you to start watching *House of Cards*?

- Because everyone was talking about it.
- Because it was a Netflix recommendation.
- Because I like shows about politics.
- Because I watched the BBC series.
- Because my friends were watching it.
- Because my family was watching it.
- Because I saw clips posted on social media.
- Because of media coverage of the show.
- Other. (Please tell us what that was) _____

Q77 Should federal spending on welfare be increased, decreased or stay the same?

- Increased.
- Decreased.
- Stay the same.

Q39 Do you favor or oppose the death penalty?

- Favor.
- Oppose.
- Don't know.

Q43 Would you regard the use of torture against people suspected of involvement in terrorism as acceptable or unacceptable?

◦ Acceptable.
◦ Unacceptable.
◦ No opinion.

Q50 Do you agree or disagree with the following statement: The best way to deal with the threat of terrorism is to hunt down and kill all the terrorists.

◦ Agree strongly.
◦ Agree somewhat.
◦ Disagree somewhat.
◦ Disagree strongly.

Q66 Some people say that people get ahead by their own hard work; others say that lucky breaks or help from other people are more important. Which do you think is most important?

◦ Hard work is most important.
◦ Hard work and luck are equally important.
◦ Luck is most important.

Q67 How much of the time do people get what they deserve?

◦ Always.
◦ Most of the time.
◦ About half of the time.
◦ Once in a while.
◦ Never.

Q23 What is your gender?

◦ Female.
◦ Male.
◦ Transgender.
◦ Gender neutral.
◦ Other.

Q21 Are you or were you a political science major or minor in college?

◦ Yes.
◦ No.

Q54 Are you, or have you been a student at The University of Vermont?

∘ No.
∘ Yes, I am currently a student at UVM.
∘ Yes, I was a student at UVM.

Q25 Below is a 7-point scale on which the political views that people might hold are arranged from extremely liberal to extremely conservative. Where would you place yourself on this scale?

Q58 Please tell us whether you agree or disagree with the following statements. Response options were strongly disagree, disagree, somewhat disagree, neither agree nor disagree, somewhat agree, agree and strongly agree.

∘ When I meet new people, I like wondering how they got to where they are in life.
∘ If someone's actions do not relate to me directly, I generally do not concern myself with why they do what they do.
∘ There is just something intriguing about the insight different people can offer about someone else's motivations and perspective.
∘ I rarely find myself wondering what other people are thinking.
∘ I have a wide range of intellectual interests.
∘ I find philosophical arguments boring.
∘ I would rather keep my options open than plan everything in advance.
∘ Sometimes good people have to do bad things in order to attain a greater good.
∘ If you are not using people, they are probably using you.

Q78 How important is religion in your life—very important, somewhat important, not too important, or not at all important?

∘ Very Important.
∘ Somewhat important.
∘ Not too important.
∘ Not at all important.

NOTE

1. The questions are presented in the order they appeared in the survey, not by the numbering system that Qualtrics assigns the questions.

Appendix 2

Questions for Study 2:
Game of Thrones *Group*

Q71 How many episodes of *Game of Thrones* were you able to watch this past week?[1]

- none
- 1
- 2
- 3
- 4
- 5
- more than 5

Q47 For our research it would be helpful if you told us why you weren't able to watch more than few episodes of *Game of Thrones* this week.

- I ended up being too busy this past week and didn't have the time.
- I had trouble getting access to the show.
- I disliked the show so much that I didn't want to continue watching.
- Other. (Please specify) _____

Q47 Why did you end up disliking the show so much?

- It was boring.
- It was too violent.
- I did not like the genre.
- It was too dark and depressing.
- Other. (Please specify) _____.

Q72 Had you ever seen any episodes of *Game of Thrones* before this past week?

○ Yes, I've seen all or most of the episodes.
○ Yes, I have seen some of the episodes.
○ No, I have not seen any full episodes of this show before.

Q73 On a scale of 0 to 10, where 1 is not at all and 10 is very much so, please tell us the extent to which the following statements were accurate for you when you were watching the show *Game of Thrones*.

○ I enjoyed watching the show.
○ I found myself worrying about what would happen to the characters as I watched.
○ I ended up doing other things while I watched the show.
○ I found my mind wandering while watching the show.
○ The show affected me emotionally.
○ I found myself thinking of ways the narrative could have turned out differently.
○ While I was watching the show, activity going on in the room around me was on my mind.
○ As I watched, I found myself identifying with a character in the show.

Q55 Now we would like to ask you if you remember some specific things about the show.

Q53 What did Daenerys receive as a wedding gift? (Photo of Daenerys)

○ A serpentine bracelet.
○ Dragon eggs.
○ The Crown of the North.
○ A direwolf pelt.

Q49 Do you happen to remember why Sandor Clegane's face was marred? (Photo of Sandor Clegane, "The Hound")

○ He was wounded in battle.
○ He was born disfigured.
○ He was burned by his brother.
○ He was burned by a dragon.

Q56 What gift does Tyrion bring for Bran at Winterfell? (Photos of Tyrion and Bran)

- A rare book on the history of the north.
- A Valyrian steel sword.
- A design for a saddle.
- Delicacies from King's Landing.

NOTE

1. The rest of the questions are the same as used in Study 1 (see appendix 1). The questions are presented in the order they appeared in the survey, not by the numbering system that Qualtrics assigns the questions.

Appendix 3

Questions for Study 3:
The Hobbit *Group Version*

Q71 Were you able to watch *The Hobbit: The Battle of 5 Armies* this past week?[1]

- No.
- Yes.

Q47 How many times have you seen *The Hobbit: The Battle of 5 Armies*?

- Just this once.
- Two times.
- More than two times.

Q73 On a scale of 0 to 10, where 1 is not at all and 10 is very much so, please tell us the extent to which the following statements were accurate for you when you were watching the *The Hobbit: The Battle of 5 Armies*.

- I enjoyed watching the movie.
- I found myself worrying about what would happen to the characters as I watched.
- I ended up doing other things while I watched the movie.
- I found my mind wandering while watching the movie.
- The movie affected me emotionally.
- I found myself thinking of ways the narrative could have turned out differently.
- While I was watching the movie, activity going on in the theater around me was on my mind.
- As I watched, I found myself identifying with a character in the movie.

Q55 Now we would like to ask you if you remember some specific things about the movie.

Q55 Which character kills the dragon Smaug?

- Legolas.
- Bard.
- Bilbo.
- Tauriel.

Q57 Which of the following characters dies in the movie?

- Bard.
- Tauriel.
- Kili.
- Balin.

Q59 What does Bilbo give to Thranduil and Bard?

- A message from Thorin.
- The arkenstone.
- His magic ring.
- The sword of the dwarf kings.

Q66 Some people say that people get ahead by their own hard work; others say that lucky breaks or help from other people are more important. Which do you think is most important?

- Hard work is most important.
- Hard work and luck are equally important.
- Luck is most important.

Q67 How much of the time do people get what they deserve?

- Always.
- Most of the time.
- About half of the time.
- Once in a while.
- Never.

Q46 For our research it would be helpful if you told us why you were not able to watch *The Hobbit: The Battle of 5 Armies* this week.

- ∘ I ended up being too busy this past week and didn't have the time.
- ∘ I have heard of the movie and did not want to watch it.
- ∘ Other. (Please specify) _____.

NOTE

1. The rest of the questions are the same as used in Study 1 (see appendix 1). The questions are presented in the order they appeared in the survey, not by the numbering system that Qualtrics assigns the questions.

Appendix 4

Questions for Study 3:
House of Cards *Group Version*

Q53 What do you think is the most important issue facing the US today?[1]

- Our relations with Russia.
- Jobs and the economy.
- The budget deficit.
- Taxes.
- Health care.
- Crime.
- Inequality.
- Race relations.
- Terrorism.
- The environment and climate change.
- Other _____.

Q9 When it comes to disagreements between people over how things are, which of the following statements comes closer to what you believe?

- It is impossible to know which claims are accurate because studies and evidence can be manipulated to prove whatever someone wants to prove.
- It is possible to know which claims are accurate based on a careful assessment of the research and evidence.

Q68 Generally speaking, would you say that most people can be trusted or that you can't be too careful in dealing with people?

- Most people can be trusted.
- You can't be too careful in dealing with people.

Q41 How much of the time do you think you can trust the government in Washington to do what is right—just about always, most of the time or only some of the time?

- ◦ Just about always.
- ◦ Most of the time.
- ◦ Some of the time.
- ◦ Never.

Q68 Please tell us whether you agree or disagree with the following statements.

- ◦ Most people will use somewhat unfair reasons to gain profit or an advantage rather than lose it.
- ◦ I think most people would lie to get ahead.
- ◦ It is safer to trust nobody.
- ◦ I don't think public officials care much what people like me think.

Q44 We would like to ask you a series of questions about Netflix's series *House of Cards* starring Kevin Spacey and Robin Wright.

Q75 Which of the following statements is true regarding your exposure to the Netflix series *House of Cards*.

- ◦ I have not seen any of the episodes.
- ◦ I have seen a few of the episodes.
- ◦ I have seen all of the episodes of seasons 1 and 2.
- ◦ I have seen all of the episodes of seasons 1 and 2 and at least some of the episodes of season 3.
- ◦ I have seen all of the episodes of all 3 seasons.

Q74 We would like to ask a few more specific questions about the Netflix series *House of Cards*. Please tell us whether the following statements are true for you.

- ◦ I binge-watched *House of Cards* (watched a number of episodes all at once).
- ◦ In anticipation of the new season of *House of Cards*, I re-watched previous episodes.
- ◦ I have talked about the show with people.
- ◦ I have posted about *House of Cards* on social media (Facebook, Twitter, etc).
- ◦ I would vote for Frank Underwood in an election.
- ◦ I have watched all the episodes of *House of Cards*.

Q46 Please tell us why you have not watched all of the episodes of *House of Cards*.

◦ I haven't had the time yet, but plan to watch it all when I have the chance.
◦ I like the show, but I don't have time to watch all of it.
◦ I found I did not like the show because (please type in your response below)

Q67 On a scale of 0 to 10, where 0 is not at all and 10 is very much so, please tell us the extent to which the following statements were accurate for you when you were watching the show *House of Cards*.

◦ I enjoyed watching the show.
◦ I found myself worrying about what would happen to the characters as I watched.
◦ I ended up doing other things while I watched the show.
◦ I found my mind wandering while watching the show.
◦ The show affected me emotionally.
◦ I found myself thinking of ways the narrative could have turned out differently.
◦ While I was watching the show, activity going on in the room around me was on my mind.
◦ As I watched, I found myself identifying with a character in the show.

Q63 Do you think *House of Cards* gives an accurate depiction of how the U.S. government works?

◦ Yes.
◦ No.
◦ Don't know.

Q65 Do you think *House of Cards* gives an accurate depiction of how politicians behave?

◦ Yes.
◦ No.
◦ Don't know.

Q76 What got you to start watching *House of Cards*?

◦ Because everyone was talking about it.
◦ Because it was a Netflix recommendation.
◦ Because I like shows about politics.
◦ Because I watched the BBC series.
◦ Because my friends were watching it.

- Because my family was watching it.
- Because I saw clips posted on social media.
- Because of media coverage of the show.
- Other. (Please tell us what that was.)

Q51 For our research it would be helpful if you let us why you haven't seen any episodes of *House of Cards*.

- I don't have access to the show.
- I have never heard of the show.
- I don't have the time to watch the show.
- I have heard of the show and do not want to watch it.
- Other. (Please specify.)

NOTE

1. The questions are presented in the order they appeared in the survey, not by the numbering system that Qualtrics assigns the questions.

Appendix 5

Questions for Science Fiction Experiment and Survey

Thank you for agreeing to take part in our class research project. Your participation and honest opinions are of utmost importance to the success of our research and will remain completely anonymous. Please answer the following questions by filling out the bubble on the scan form for the option that best fits what you think and feel.

First we would like to know what you thought about the program that you watched today.

How interesting did you find the program?

- Very interesting.
- Somewhat interesting.
- Somewhat boring.
- Very boring.

Below are 4 pairs of words. Please choose the word that appeals to you more or that sounds better to you.

- Independence or respect for elders.
- Curiosity or good manners.
- Obedience or self respect.
- Being considerate or well-behaved.

Please give us your thoughts on the following issues by selecting the options that best reflect your views.

Do you agree or disagree with the following statements?

Women are better than men at problem solving.

- ◦ Agree strongly.
- ◦ Agree somewhat.
- ◦ Disagree somewhat.
- ◦ Disagree strongly.
- ◦ Don't know.

Men are innately leaders whereas women are innately nurturers.

- ◦ Agree strongly.
- ◦ Agree somewhat.
- ◦ Disagree somewhat.
- ◦ Disagree strongly.
- ◦ Don't know.

If you had to pick, which of the following groups would you say you like the least?

- ◦ Atheists.
- ◦ Homosexuals.
- ◦ Muslims.
- ◦ Fascists.
- ◦ Communists.

Considering the group that you picked in the question above, do you agree or disagree with the feeling that members of that group (response options included "agree strongly," "agree somewhat," "disagree somewhat," and "disagree strongly."

- ◦ Should be banned from being president?
- ◦ Should be allowed to teach in public schools?
- ◦ Should be allowed to make a speech in your city/town?
- ◦ Should have their phones tapped by our government?
- ◦ Should be outlawed?

How comfortable are you with new and emerging technologies?

- ◦ Very comfortable.
- ◦ Comfortable.
- ◦ Neutral.
- ◦ Uncomfortable.
- ◦ Very uncomfortable.

Do you agree or disagree with the statement: I like to have the responsibility of handling a situation that requires a lot of thinking.

- Agree strongly.
- Agree somewhat.
- Neither agree nor disagree.
- Disagree somewhat.
- Disagree strongly.

Do you agree or disagree with the statement: I would prefer complex to simple problems.

- Agree strongly.
- Agree somewhat.
- Neither agree nor disagree.
- Disagree somewhat.
- Disagree strongly.

There are some scientific theories that try to explain the existence of our world and ourselves, such as the big bang theory and evolution. These theories are overwhelmingly endorsed by the scientific community, and yet some people consider them to be controversial for a variety of reasons. If you would consider these viewpoints opposite ends of a scale with those who accept these scientific conclusions on one end and those who reject the conclusions at the other, where would you place yourself?

- I accept these scientific conclusions.
- I reject these scientific conclusions.

Imagine the following scenario: Two weeks away from Election Day the media uncover a story about the presidential candidate for whom you were going to vote that suggests that the candidate did something in his/her personal life that, while not illegal nor a reflection of their politics, you found objectionable. What impact would such an objectionable revelation have on your decision to vote?

- It would affect my vote decision.
- It would NOT affect my vote decision.

We'd like to get your feelings about some groups in American society using a version of what is called a feeling thermometer. Using the thermometer to the right how would you rate Muslims? Blacks/African Americans? Undocumented immigrants? Homosexuals?

Thinking about yourself, how characteristic would you say the following statements are about you? (Response options ranged from "extremely characteristic" to "extremely uncharacteristic.")

- I often prefer to remain neutral about complex issues.
- I frequently find myself getting hung up on the little things.
- I often strive to see the bigger picture.

About how many galaxies do you think there are there in the universe?

- One.
- Hundreds.
- Thousands.
- Millions.
- Billions or more.

If the history of the earth were set to the equivalent of one year, about how much of that year do you think would include human beings?

- The last few minutes.
- The last day.
- The last week.
- The last month.
- The last few months or more.

Please indicate whether you agree or disagree with the following statements

- If I feel my mind starting to drift off into daydreams, I usually get busy and start concentrating on some work or activity instead.
- I find philosophical arguments boring.
- I would rather keep my options open than plan everything in advance.

UVM scientist Josh Bongard has developed robots that are able to mimic certain aspects of actual evolutionary patterns. The robots change their body forms while learning how to walk and, over generations, evolve to speed up the learning process. How would you categorize your response to an advance such as evolving robots?

- I view such advances as potentially more dangerous than beneficial.
- I view these advances as potentially more beneficial than dangerous.

Please indicate whether the following things interest you. (Response options "yes" or "no.")

- The possibilities of time travel.
- The idea of alternate realities.
- The possibility of intelligent life on other planets.

Science fiction is entertainment that involves any number of elements including advanced technology, depictions of the future, time travel, or other forms of intelligent life (that is "aliens). Examples include but are not limited to TV shows like *Lost, Battlestar Galactica, Fringe, Doctor Who,* any of the *Star Trek* series, *The X-Files,* movies such as *Avatar, Independence Day, Star Wars, Inception, Super 8, Men in Black, Alien, Transformers, Planet of the Apes,* and books such as *Ender's Game, The Foundation Trilogy, Slaughterhouse Five, Watchmen, Never Let Me Go,* and *Dune.*

When you choose entertainment media, how often do you choose (response options "never," "rarely," "occasionally," and "frequently")

- Science fiction movies?
- Science fiction TV?
- Science fiction books?

On the scale below where "a" represents fans who are/were very much into science fiction and "e" people who hate it, where would you place yourself?

Finally, please answer the following questions about yourself.

Are you a political science major or minor?

- Yes.
- No.

Please indicate your gender

- Female.
- Male.
- Transgendered.
- Gender neutral.
- Other.

Please tell us your age

- 17–18
- 19–20
- 21–22
- 23–25
- 25 or above

How would you characterize the place you grew up?

- In a large city.
- In suburbia.
- In a small city.
- In a rural area.

Outside of the books you were assigned for school, what kind of reader were you when you were younger?

- I was not much of a reader of books.
- I was an occasional reader of books.
- I was an avid reader of books.

How important is religion in your life—very important, somewhat important, not too important, or not at all important?

- Very important.
- Somewhat important.
- Not too important.
- Not at all important.

Do you believe in God or a universal spirit, or not?

- No.
- Yes.

If you answered "yes" to the previous question, please tell us how certain are you about this belief? Are you absolutely certain, fairly certain, not too certain, or not at all certain?

- Absolutely certain.
- Fairly certain.
- Not too certain.
- Not certain at all.

What race do you consider yourself?

- ○ White.
- ○ Black or African American.
- ○ American Indian or Alaska Native.
- ○ Asian.
- ○ Of mixed race or some other race.

Do you consider yourself Hispanic or Latino(a)?

- ○ Yes.
- ○ No.
- ○ I am part Hispanic/Latino(a).

When it comes to politics, do you usually think of yourself as very liberal, liberal, moderate or middle of the road, conservative, or very conservative?

- ○ Very liberal.
- ○ Liberal.
- ○ Moderate.
- ○ Conservative.
- ○ Very conservative.

Appendix 6

Villain Survey

Q33 First we would like to assess how popular some entertainment media are by asking you to identify some of the antagonists from those movies, books, shows and games.[1] Please review the following photos and check the box next to the photo of the antagonists that you recognize well enough to describe to a friend.

- ○ Magneto.
- ○ Gollum/Smeagol.
- ○ Loki.
- ○ Cersei Lannister.
- ○ Andrew Ryan.
- ○ Coulter, from *Golden Compass*.
- ○ Cobb, from the film *Inception*.
- ○ Nero, from *Star Trek*.

Q40 First we would like to assess how popular some entertainment media are by asking you to identify some of the antagonists from those movies, books, shows, and games. Please review the following photos and check the box next to the photo of the antagonists that you recognize well enough to describe to a friend.

- ○ Cylons.
- ○ The Others.
- ○ Klingons.
- ○ The Covenant.
- ○ The Company from the TV show *Heroes*.
- ○ The Corporate Military in *Avatar*.

Q38 First we would like to assess how popular some entertainment media are by asking you to identify some of the antagonists from those movies, books, shows and games. Please review the following photos and check the box next to the photo of the antagonists that you recognize well enough to describe to a friend.

- Sauron.
- Emperor Palpatine.
- Voldemort.
- The Joker.
- Ganondorf.
- The White Witch.
- The alien from *Alien*.

Q39 First we would like to assess how popular some entertainment media are by asking you to identify some of the antagonists from those movies, books, shows and games. Please review the following photos and check the box next to the photo of the antagonists that you recognize well enough to describe to a friend.

- The Borg.
- Matrix Agents.
- Nazi Zombies.
- Storm Troopers.
- Daleks.
- President Snow/Government in *The Hunger Games*.
- Aliens from *Independence Day*.
- The Hydra from *Captain America*.

Q40 Below are questions on a variety of subjects that we are interested in your opinions on. Please answer the questions in a way that best represents your views. Your responses will remain entirely anonymous and never be associated with any identifying information about you.

Q29 Below is a pair of words. Please choose the word that appeals to you more or that sounds better to you.

- Respect for Elders.
- Independence.

Q30 Below is a pair of words. Please choose the word that appeals to you more or that sounds better to you.

○ Curiosity.
○ Good manners.

Q31 Below is a pair of words. Please choose the word that appeals to you more or that sounds better to you.

○ Obedience.
○ Self-respect.

Q32 Below is a pair of words. Please choose the word that appeals to you more or that sounds better to you.

○ Being considerate.
○ Being well-behaved.

Q15 Below is a list of institutions in American society. Please tell me how much confidence you, yourself, have in each one: a great deal, quite a lot, some, or very little. Institutions listed: corporations, the media, congress, religious institutions, the military, the presidency, the courts, and ideological groups.

Q6 We'd like to get your feelings about some political groups and politicians using a version of what is called a feeling thermometer. Ratings between 50 degrees and 100 degrees mean that you feel favorable and warm toward the person or group. Ratings between 0 degrees and 50 degrees mean that you don't feel favorable toward the person or group and that you don't care too much for that person or group. You would rate the person or group at the 50 degree mark if you don't feel particularly warm or cold toward the person. (If you want to make a rating of 0, you must click on the slider.)

○ The Democratic Party.
○ The Republican Party.
○ Barack Obama.
○ Mitt Romney.

Q9 Do you favor or oppose the death penalty?

○ Favor.
○ Oppose.
○ Don't know.

Q14 In general, would you say that most of what government does makes things better or worse for people?

◦ Most of what the government makes things better for people.
◦ Most of what the government makes things worse for people.
◦ Don't know.

Q23 How much of the time do you think you can trust the government in Washington to do what is right—just about always, most of the time or only some of the time?

◦ Just about always.
◦ Most of the time.
◦ Some of the time.
◦ Never.

Q7 For most people, the political world holds political groups that they dislike (for example, but not limited to Fascists, Communists, atheists, religious extremists, etc.). If you had to pick, what political group would you say you like the least?

Q8 Considering the group that you named in the question above, do you agree or disagree with the feeling that members of the group you named . . .

◦ Should be banned from being president?
◦ Should be allowed to teach in public schools?
◦ Should be allowed to make a speech in your city/town?
◦ Should have their phones tapped by our government?
◦ Should be outlawed?

Q16 Outside of the books you were assigned for school, what kind of reader were you when you were younger?

◦ I was not much of a reader of books.
◦ I was an occasional reader of books.
◦ I was an avid reader of books.

Q12 Do you agree or disagree with the following statement: The best way to deal with the threat of terrorism is to hunt down and kill all the terrorists.

◦ Agree strongly.
◦ Agree somewhat.
◦ Disagree somewhat.
◦ Disagree strongly.

Q34 Do you agree or disagree with the following: people who commit violent crimes can be rehabilitated and reenter society without endangering the public.

Q13 Would you regard the use of torture against people suspected of involvement in terrorism as acceptable or unacceptable?

- ○ Acceptable.
- ○ Unacceptable.
- ○ No opinion.

Q17 Below is a 7-point scale on which the political views that people might hold are arranged from extremely liberal to extremely conservative. Where would you place yourself on this scale?

Q18 Generally speaking do you usually think of yourself as a Republican, a Democrat, an independent or what?

- ○ Republican.
- ○ Democrat.
- ○ Independent.
- ○ Other.

Answer if generally speaking do you usually think of yourself as a . . . Independent is selected

Q19 Do you think of yourself as closer to the Republican or Democratic Party?

- ○ Republican.
- ○ Democratic.

Answer if generally speaking do you usually think of yourself as a . . . other is selected

Q20 Do you think of yourself as closer to the Republican or Democratic Party?

- ○ Republican.
- ○ Democratic.

Answer if generally speaking do you usually think of yourself as a . . . Republican is selected.

Q21 Would you call yourself a strong Republican or a not very strong Republican?

- Strong.
- Not very strong.

Answer if generally speaking do you usually think of yourself as a . . . Democrat is selected.

Q22 Would you call yourself a strong Democrat or a not very strong Democrat?

- Strong.
- Not very strong.

Q24 Please complete the following sentence: The main reason why people murder is because murderers are

- greedy.
- jealous.
- just plain evil.
- seeking revenge.
- people who don't know better.
- people who society has marginalized.

Q25 What, in your opinion, is the main reason terrorists exist?

- Because there is evil in the world.
- Because of extremist ideas and religions.
- Because of sense of powerlessness in the face of injustice, inequality, and/or oppression.

Q2 How old are you?

Q36 How would you characterize the place you grew up?

- A large city.
- Suburbia.
- A small city.
- A rural town or rural area.
- Other.

Q3 What is your gender?

- ◦ Female.
- ◦ Male.
- ◦ Transgendered.
- ◦ Gender Neutral.
- ◦ Other.

Q34 What is the highest level of education you have completed?

- ◦ Less than high school.
- ◦ High school / GED.
- ◦ Some college.
- ◦ 2-year college degree.
- ◦ 4-year college degree.
- ◦ Masters degree.
- ◦ Doctoral degree.
- ◦ Professional degree (JD, MD).

Q35 What race do you consider yourself?

- ◦ White.
- ◦ Black or African American.
- ◦ American Indian or Alaska Native.
- ◦ Asian.
- ◦ Of mixed race or some other race.
- ◦ I prefer not to say.

Q37 Do you consider yourself Hispanic or Latino(a)?

- ◦ Yes.
- ◦ No.
- ◦ I am part Hispanic/Latino(a).

Q35 When it comes to movies/videos/television shows to watch or books to read, which do you prefer?

- ◦ Stories involving a conflict between good and evil.
- ◦ Stories involving a conflict between characters where antagonists have more complex motives beyond pure good/evil.

Q36 Thinking about the movies/videos/television shows you watch and books you read, what do you recall tends to be the main motivation for the villain?

- Greed for wealth and riches.
- Power and domination.
- Destruction.
- An idea, philosophy or set of religious beliefs.
- Insanity.
- Jealousy.
- Fear.
- Revenge.

Q37 Thinking about the movies/videos/television shows you watch and books you read, are the villains in those stories typically individuals or groups (governments, corporations, groups of individuals or creatures)?

- Individuals.
- Groups (governments, corporations, groups of individuals or creatures).

Q41 Are you a student at the University of Vermont?

- Yes.
- No.

Q42 Did you grow up in the United States?

- Yes.
- No.

NOTE

1. The questions are presented in the order they appeared in the survey, not by the numbering system that Qualtrics assigns the questions.

Appendix 7
The Daily Show (TDS) *and* The Colbert Report (TCR) *Studies*

Q15 Which of the following best describes your use of news media sources?[1]

- ○ I don't really see the point in following the news.
- ○ I follow the news every now and then when something big happens.
- ○ I selectively follow the news, seeking out information on government, politics, and/or international affairs that I think is important to know.
- ○ I watch the news all the time, watching (either on TV or online) as many different news and talk shows as I can, but I don't have time to read too many news stories.
- ○ I follow the news all the time in all forms, watching a lot of television news shows, listening to radio talk shows, and regularly reading news articles online or in print.

Q14 When it comes to disagreements between people over how things are, which of the following statements comes closer to what you believe?

- ○ It is impossible to know which claims are accurate because studies and evidence can be manipulated to prove whatever someone wants to prove.
- ○ It is possible to know which claims are accurate based on a careful assessment of the research and evidence.

Q6 Within our culture there exist theories about certain historical and scientific events. Some of these theories are listed below. Please indicate whether you believe the theory.

- ○ The US government staged the terrorist attacks of 9/11.
- ○ The Bush administration ignored warnings regarding the terrorist attacks of 9/11.

- There was a conspiracy to assassinate John F. Kennedy.
- Global warming is not occurring.
- The 1969 Apollo moon landing never actually happened.
- Barack Obama's birth certificate is not authentic.

Q7 Please indicate whether you agree or disagree with the statements.

- Sometimes politics and government seems so complicated that a person like me can't really understand what's going on.
- People like me do not have any say about what the government does.

Q8 When you read news articles (either online or in newspapers) how much of the article do you usually get through?

- I don't read news articles.
- I usually skim the article for important points.
- I usually read the first few paragraphs.
- I usually read half the first half of the article.
- I usually read most or all of the article.

Q18 Below is a list of institutions in American society. Please tell me how much confidence you, yourself, have in each one: a great deal, quite a lot, some, or very little. Institutions listed: corporations, news media organizations, journalists, congress, the courts, religious institutions, the military, the presidency.

Q1 How often would you say you watch the following programs? Never, rarely, sometimes, often.

- *The O'Reilly Factor*
- *The Daily Show with Jon Stewart*
- *The Colbert Report*
- *Hardball with Chris Matthews*
- *The Late Show with David Letterman*
- *The Newsroom*

Q2 How long have you been watching of the following television programs? I have never really watched it, for about a year or less, between 1 and 3 years, for more than 3 years.

- *The O'Reilly Factor*
- *The Daily Show with Jon Stewart*
- *The Colbert Report*

○ *Hardball with Chris Matthews*
○ *The Late Show with David Letterman*
○ *The Newsroom*

Q3 Are you or were you a political science major or minor?

○ Yes.
○ No.

Q5 What is your gender?

○ Female.
○ Male.
○ Transgendered.
○ Gender Neutral.
○ Other.

Q20 Below is a 7-point scale on which the political views that people might hold are arranged from extremely liberal to extremely conservative. Where would you place yourself on this scale?

Q17 Outside of the books you were assigned for school, what kind of reader were you when you were younger?

○ I was not much of a reader of books.
○ I was an occasional reader of books.
○ I was an avid reader of books.

Q19 Thinking about yourself, how characteristic would you say the following statements are about you? Extremely characteristic, somewhat characteristic, uncertain, somewhat uncharacteristic, extremely uncharacteristic.

○ I form opinions about everything.
○ I have many more opinions than the average person.
○ I often prefer to remain neutral about complex issues.
○ I only think as hard as I have to.
○ I like to have the responsibility of handling a situation that requires a lot of thinking.
○ It's enough for me that something gets the job done; I don't care how or why it works.
○ It is important to grapple with complex issues.

Q22 How old are you?

Q24 What is the highest level of education you have completed?

- Less than high school.
- High school / GED.
- Some college.
- 2-year college degree.
- 4-year college degree.
- Masters degree.
- Doctoral degree.
- Professional degree (JD, MD).

Q26 Are you or have you been a student at the University of Vermont?

- Yes.
- No.

Answer if are you or have you been a student at the University of V . . . yes is selected

Q28 Have you had any classes taught by Professor Gierzynski?

- Yes.
- No.

NOTE

1. The questions are presented in the order they appeared in the survey, not by the numbering system that Qualtrics assigns the questions.

Appendix 8

Questions for Leadership and Gender Experiment

Q47 Please follow the link below to watch the video. After watching the video please return to the survey page and complete the survey.[1] [Link to Survey]

Q64 Now we would like to ask you a few questions about the clip that you just watched.

Q65 Did the Romulan leader, Nero, accept Captain Kirk's offer of assistance at the end of the clip?

- Yes.
- No.
- Captain Kirk did not offer him assistance.

Q66 Who piloted the ship into a collision course with the Romulan ship in order to blow it up?

- Captain Kirk.
- The Romulan Leader Nero.
- Lieutenant Uhura.
- Spock.
- None of the above: there was no such scene in the video clip.

Q52 Have you seen this movie?

- Yes.
- No.

(Answer if "no" is selected.)

Q80 Did the clip make you interested in seeing more of this 2009 movie, *Star Trek*?

∘ Yes.
∘ No.

Q53 Do you consider yourself a *Star Trek* Fan?

∘ No.
∘ Yes, somewhat.
∘ Yes, very much so.

Q72 Now we would like to ask you a few questions about the clip that you just watched.

Q76 What decision did Admiral Cain make in response to the Cylon attack?

∘ She ordered Lt. Shaw to fire on the attacking Cylon ships with nuclear missiles.
∘ She ordered Lt. Shaw to make a blind jump into light speed.
∘ She ordered Lt. Shaw to disengage the Pegasus from the docking bay and maneuver the ship behind another destroyed Battlestar.
∘ She decided to surrender to the Cylons.

Q77 What did the new commander of the Pegasus do to Lt. Shaw?

∘ He promoted her to commander and made her the Executive Officer (XO) of the Pegasus.
∘ He demoted her to Captain and reassigned her to a civilian ship.
∘ He imprisoned her for insubordination.
∘ He sent her on a covert mission to the *Battlestar Galactica*.

Q54 How much of this TV series *Battlestar Galactica* have you seen before?

∘ none
∘ some
∘ most
∘ all

(Answer if your answer to 254 is "none.")

Q81 Did the clip make you want to see more of the TV series *Battlestar Galactica*?

- ◦ Yes.
- ◦ No.

Q73 Now we would like to ask you a few questions about the clip that you just watched.

Q74 What are the two buttons in the boxes in this clip labeled?

- ◦ Truth and regret.
- ◦ Life and death.
- ◦ Life and consequences.
- ◦ Truth and consequences.

Q75 What button does Bonnie press in the end?

- ◦ Life.
- ◦ Truth.
- ◦ Consequences.
- ◦ Death.
- ◦ She doesn't press any button.

Q57 How much of this TV series, *Doctor Who*, have you seen?

- ◦ None.
- ◦ Some.
- ◦ Most.
- ◦ All.

(Answer if your answer to 257 is "none.")

Q82 Did this clip make you want to see more of the TV series, *Doctor Who*?

- ◦ Yes.
- ◦ No.

Q58 Do you consider yourself a *Doctor Who* fan?

- ◦ No.
- ◦ Yes, somewhat.
- ◦ Yes, very much so.

Q62 Now we would like to ask you a few questions about the clip that you just watched.

Q59 What do the people in the hospital do when they see Katniss has come to see them?

◦ Yell at her to leave and never come back.
◦ Bow at her feet.
◦ Ask if she is going to join them in the fight.

Q63 What powerful decision does President Snow make in the clip you just saw?

◦ To end the war and admit defeat.
◦ To bomb the hospital, and kill the wounded.
◦ To kidnap Katniss and to teach the districts a lesson.

Q50 Have you seen this movie before?

◦ Yes.
◦ No.

(Answer if your answer to 250 is "no.")

Q83 Did this clip make you want to see more of this movie, *Mockingjay Part I*?

◦ Yes.
◦ No.

Q51 Which of the books in *The Hunger Games* series have you read? (Mark all that are true for you.)

◦ None of them.
◦ *Hunger Games.*
◦ *Catching Fire.*
◦ *Mockingjay.*

Q70 Which of the movies in *The Hunger Games* series have you seen? (Mark all that are true for you.)

◦ None of them.
◦ *Hunger Games.*
◦ *Catching Fire.*
◦ *Mockingjay Part I.*
◦ *Mockingjay Part II.*

Q68 You have been randomly selected to simply fill out the following questions. Please click the continue button (>>) below to access the questions and finish the survey.

Q24 On a scale of 0 to 10, where 0 is not at all and 10 is very much so, please tell us the extent to which the following statements were accurate for you when you were watching the video clip.

◦ I enjoyed watching the video clip.
◦ I found myself worrying about what would happen to the characters as I watched.
◦ I ended up doing other things while I watched the clip.
◦ I found my mind wandering while watching the video.
◦ The video affected me emotionally.
◦ I found myself thinking of ways the story in the video could have turned out differently.
◦ While I was watching the video, activity going on in the room around me was on my mind.
◦ As I watched, I found myself identifying with a character in the video.

Q79 Now we would like to ask your opinion on a number of different subjects.

Q55 Please tell us whether you agree or disagree with the following statements.

◦ I expect the United States will fight in another war within the next ten years.
◦ Sometimes the use of military force is necessary.

Q5 Below is a list of personal characteristics or qualities that some people say are important in a leader and other people say are not important. For each, please indicate the extent to which you think the quality is important in a leader. Response options: not important in a leader, somewhat important, very important, essential in a leader.

◦ Decisiveness.
◦ Intelligence.
◦ Compassion.
◦ Empathy.
◦ Self-confidence.
◦ Shows emotion.
◦ Honesty.
◦ Independence.
◦ Assertiveness.

◦ A willingness to consider the thoughts of others.
◦ Logical.

Q79 We'd like to get your feelings about some public officials using what is called a feeling thermometer. Ratings between 50 degrees and 100 degrees mean that you feel favorable and warm toward the person. Ratings between 0 degrees and 50 degrees mean that you don't feel favorable toward the person and that you don't care too much for that person. You would rate the person at the 50 degree mark if you don't feel particularly warm or cold toward the person. (If you want to make a rating of 0, you must click on the slider.)

◦ Barack Obama.
◦ Hillary Clinton.
◦ Bill Clinton.
◦ George W. Bush.
◦ Justice Ruth Bader Ginsburg.
◦ Chief Justice John Roberts.
◦ Justice Sonia Sotomayor.
◦ Justice Stephen Breyer.
◦ Justice Elana Kagan.
◦ Justice Samuel Alito.
◦ Donald Trump.

Q74 Do you personally hope the United States will elect a female president in your lifetime?

◦ Yes.
◦ No.

Q73 Which one of the following statements comes closest to your opinion about women and men as POLITICAL LEADERS?

◦ Men generally make better political leaders than women.
◦ Women generally make better political leaders than men.
◦ In general, women and men make equally good political leaders.

Q38 Below is a pair of words. Please choose the word that appeals to you more or that sounds better to you.

◦ Respect for elders.
◦ Independence.

Q40 Below is a pair of words. Please choose the word that appeals to you more or that sounds better to you.

- Curiosity.
- Good Manners.

Q42 Below is a pair of words. Please choose the word that appeals to you more or that sounds better to you.

- Obedience.
- Self-respect.

Q44 Below is a pair of words. Please choose the word that appeals to you more or that sounds better to you.

- Being considerate.
- Being well-behaved.

Q6 Now we would like to ask about some specific characteristics of men and women. For each one listed below, please tell us whether you think it is generally more true of men or more true of women? Response options: more true of men, more true of women, equally true of both.

- Decisive.
- Intelligent.
- Compassionate.
- Empathetic.
- Self-confident.
- Honest.
- Shows Emotion.
- Assertive.
- Independent.
- Willing to listen.
- Logical.

Q78 Now we would like to ask you some questions about some movies and TV shows you might have seen and some books you may have read.

Q69 How many episodes of the following programs have you watched? Response options: none, some, a lot, all that are available.

- *Scandal.*
- *How to Get Away with Murder.*
- *Game of Thrones.*

- *Parks and Recreation.*
- *Doctor Who.*
- *Veep.*

Q71 How many books in the following series did you read? Response options: none of them, one of them, some of them, all of them, I read them all, and at least some more than once.

- *The Lord of the Rings.*
- *Harry Potter.*
- *The Hunger Games.*
- *Twilight.*
- *Divergent.*

Q71 How often would you say you watch entertainment TV and movies?

- Never or rarely.
- Occasionally.
- Often.
- A lot.

Q79 Outside of the books you were assigned for school, what kind of reader were you when you were younger?

- I was not much of a reader of books.
- I was an occasional reader of books.
- I was an avid reader of books.

Q69 Have you seen the most recent *Star Wars* movie, *The Force Awakens*?

- No.
- Yes, I've seen it once.
- Yes, I've seen it and more than once.

Q8 To finish up, we would like to ask a few questions about yourself.

Q10 What is your gender?

- Female.
- Male.
- Transgender.
- Gender neutral.
- Other.

Q28 Did you grow up in the United States?

- Yes.
- No.

Q14 Generally speaking do you usually think of yourself as a Republican, a Democrat, an independent or what?

- Republican.
- Democrat.
- Independent.
- Other.
- I don't participate in US politics.

[Party ID question followed up with standard questions regarding strength of party affiliation or which party closest to for independents.]

Q26 If your party nominated a woman for president, would you vote for her if she were qualified for the job?

- Yes.
- No.
- Don't know.

Q12 Below is a 7-point scale on which the political views that people might hold are arranged from extremely liberal to extremely conservative. Where would you place yourself on this scale?

Q24 What race do you consider yourself?

- White.
- Black or African American.
- American Indian or Alaska Native.
- Asian.
- Of mixed race or some other race.
- I prefer not to say.

Q26 Do you consider yourself Hispanic or Latino(a)?

- Yes.
- No.
- I am part Hispanic/Latino(a).

Q36 How would you characterize the place you grew up?

- A large city.
- Suburbia.
- A small city.
- A rural town or rural area.
- Other.

Q34 Are you a political science major or minor?

- Yes.
- No.

Q66 What school are you currently attending?

- The University of Vermont.
- The University of Central Arkansas.
- Other. (Please specify) _____.

NOTE

1. The questions are presented in the order they appeared in the survey, not by the numbering system that Qualtrics assigns the questions.

Bibliography

Abraham, Anna, D. Yves von Cramon, and Ricarda I. Schubotz. "Meeting George Bush versus Meeting Cinderella: The Neural Response When Telling Apart What is Real from What is Fictional in the Context of our Reality." *Journal of Cognitive Neuroscience* 20, no. 6 (2008): 965–76.

Adorno, Theodor, Else Frenkel-Brunswik, Daniel J. Levinson, and R. Nevitt Sanford. *The Authoritarian Personality.* New York: Harper & Row, 1950.

Andreycak, William and Anthony Gierzynski. "Skepticism or Cynicism: Attitudinal Impacts of the *The Daily Show* and *The Colbert Report* on Young Americans." Paper presented at the 2012 Annual Meeting of the Midwest Political Science Association, Chicago, IL.

Annenberg Public Policy Center. *"Daily Show* Viewers Knowledgeable About Presidential Campaign, National Annenberg Election Survey Shows." (Philadelphia, PA: Annenberg Public Policy Center, 2004).

Appel, Markus. "Fictional Narratives Cultivate Just-World Beliefs." *Journal of Communication* 58, no. 1 (2008): 62–83.

Appel, Markus, and Tobias Richter. "Persuasive effects of fictional narratives increase over time." *Media Psychology* 10, no. 1 (2007): 113–34.

Appelbaum, Lauren D. "The Influence of Perceived Deservingness on Policy Decisions regarding Aid to the Poor." *Political Psychology* 22, no. 3 (September 2001): 419–42.

Appelbaum, Lauren D., Mary Clare Lennon, and J. Lawrence Aber. "When Effort Is Threatening: The Influence of the Belief in a Just World on Americans' Attitudes toward Antipoverty. *Political Psychology* 27, no. 3 (June 2006): 387–402.

Bandura, Albert. *Social Foundations of Thought and Actions: A Social Cognitive Theory.* Englewood Cliffs, NJ: Prentice-Hall, 1986.

———. "Social-Learning Theory of Identificatory Processes." In *Handbook of Socialization Theory Research*, edited by David A. Goslin, 213–62. Chicago: Rand McNally, 1969.

Baumgartner, Jody, and Jonathan S. Morris. "The Daily Show Effect: Candidate Evaluations, Efficacy, and American Youth." *American Politics Research* 34, no. 3 (May 2006): 341–67.

Baym, Geoffrey. "The Daily Show: Discursive Integration and the Reinvention of Political Journalism." *Political Communication* 22, no. 3 (August 2006): 259–76.

———. *From Cronkite to Colbert: The Evolution of Broadcast News.* New York: Oxford University Press, 2009.

Bolin, Goran. *Media Generations: Experience, Identity and Mediatised Social Change.* New York: Routledge, 2017.

Brewer, Paul R. and Emily Marquardt. "Mock News and Democracy: Analyzing The Daily Show." *Atlantic Journal of Communications* 15 (December 2007): 249–67.

Butler, Lisa D., Cheryl Koopman, and Philip G. Zimbardo. "The Psychological Impact of Viewing the Film *JFK*: Emotions, Beliefs, and Political Behavioral Intentions." *Political Psychology* 16, no. 2 (1995): 237–57.

Cao, X. "Hearing it From Jon Stewart: The Impact of the Daily Show on Public Attentiveness to Politics." *International Journal of Public Opinion Research* 22, no. 1 (2010): 26–46.

Cappella, Joseph N., and Kathleen Hall Jamieson. *Spiral of Cynicism: The Press and the Public Good.* New York, NY: Oxford University Press, 1997.

Carpenter, Charli. "Rethinking the Political Science Fiction Nexus: Global Policy Making and the Campaign to Stop Killer Robots." *Perspectives on Politics* 14, no. 1 (2016): 53–69.

———. "Does Science Fiction Affect Political Fact? Yes and No: A Survey Experiment on "Killer Robots."" Forthcoming, *International Studies Quarterly.*

Carpenter, Jordan M., and Melanie C. Green. "Flying With Icarus: Narrative Transportation and the Persuasiveness of Entertainment." In *The Psychology of Entertainment Media: Blurring the Lines Between Entertainment and Persuasion*, edited by L. J. Shrum, 169–94. New York: Routledge, 2012.

Carpenter, Jordan M., Melanie C. Green, and Jeff LaFlam. 2011. "People or Profiles: Individual Differences in Online Social Networking Use." *Personality and Individual Differences* 50, no. 5 (April 2011): 538–41.

Chong, Dennis, and James N. Druckman. "Framing Theory." *Annual Review of Political Science* 10 (2007): 103–26.

Christensen, Terry, and Peter J. Haas. *Projecting Politics: Political Messages in American Films.* Armonk, NY: M. E. Sharpe, 2005.

Cohen, Jonathan. "Defining Identification: A Theoretical Look at the Identification of Audiences with Media Characters." *Mass Communication and Society* 4, no. 3 (2001): 245–64.

Dagnes, Alison. *Politics on Demand: The Effects of 24-hour News on American Politics.* Santa Barbara, CA: Praeger, 2010.

Dawson, Richard E., Kenneth Prewitt, and Karen S. Dawson. *Political Socialization*, second edition. Boston: Little, Brown and Company, 1977.

Delli Carpini, Michael X., and Bruce A. Williams. "Constructing Public Opinion: The Uses of Fictional and Nonfictional Television in Conversations about the Environment," In *The Psychology of Political Communication*, edited by Ann N. Crigler. Ann Arbor, MI: University Michigan Press, 1996.

Eagly, Alice H and Steven J. Karau. "Role Congruity Theory of Prejudice Toward Female Leaders." *Psychological Review* 109, no. 3 (2002): 573–98.

Feldman, Stanley, and Lee Sigelman. "The Political Impact of Prime-Time Television: 'The Day After.'" *The Journal of Politics* 47, no. 2 (June 1985): 556–78.

Feldman, Stanley, and Karen Stenner. "Perceived Threat and Authoritarianism." *Political Psychology* 18, no. 4 (December 1997): 741–70.

Franklin, Daniel P. *Politics and Film: The Political Culture of Television and Movies*. New York: Rowman & Littlefield, 2017.

Gabriel, Shira, and Ariana F. Young. "Becoming a Vampire without Being Bitten: The Narrative Collective-Assimilation Hypothesis." *Psychological Science* 10 (2011): 1–5.

Gamson, William A. "Policy Discourse and the Language of the Life-World." In *Eigenwilligkeit und Rationalität sozialer Prozesse,* edited by J. Gerhards and R. Hitzler R, 127–44. Opladen, Germany, 1999.

Gerbner, George, Larry Gross, Michael Morgan, and Nancy Signorielli. "Growing Up with Television: Cultivation Processes." In *Media Effects: Advances in Theory and Research*, second edition, edited by J. Bryant and D. Zillmann, 43–68. Hillsdale, NJ: Lawrence Erlbaum Associates, 2002.

Gerrig, Richard J. *Experiencing narrative worlds: On the Psychological Activities of Reading.* New Haven, CT: Yale University Press, 1993.

Gerrig, Richard J., and Deborah A. Prentice. "The Representation of Fictional Information." *Psychological Science* 2, no. 5 (1991): 336–40.

Gerzama, John, and Michael D'Antonio. *The Athena Doctrine: How Women (and the Men Who Think Like Them) Will Rule the Future.* New York: Wiley and Sons, 2013.

Gierzynski, Anthony. *Saving American Elections: A Diagnosis and Prescription for a Healthier Democracy.* Amherst, NY: Cambria Press, 2011.

———. 2014. "Harry Potter Did Help Shape the Political Culture of a Generation." *The Conversation*, August 19, 2014. Accessed March 19, 2015. http://theconversation.com/harry-potter-did-help-shape-the-political-culture-of-a-generation-29513.

Gierzynski, Anthony, and Kathryn Eddy. *Harry Potter and the Millennials: Research Methods and the Politics of the Muggle Generation.* New York: The Johns Hopkins University Press, 2013.

Gierzynski, Anthony, Michael Gibson, Evan McDaniel, and Alexander Rosenblatt. "The Effects of Science Fiction on Politically Relevant Attitudes." Paper presented at the 2013 Annual Meeting of the Midwest Political Science Association.

Gierzynski, Anthony, and Kensington Moore. "The New Guard: Entertainment Talk Shows and the Not-so-fake News," in *Voting in America*, edited by Morgan E. Felchner, 165–73. Westport, CT: Praeger, 2008.

Gierzynski, Anthony, Sarah Weichselbaum, Hayley Aydelott, Evyn Banach, Matthew Donovan, Allie VanSickle, and Jack Vest. "*Game of Thrones, House of Cards* and the Belief in a Just World." Paper presented at the 2015 Annual Meeting of the Midwest Political Science Association, April 16–19, Chicago, IL.

Gierzynski, Anthony, and Heather Yates. "Fictional Leaders, Leadership Stereotypes and Evaluations of Women in Leadership Positions." Paper presented at the Annual Meeting of the Midwest Political Science Association, April 7–10, 2016, Chicago, IL.

Giglio, Ernest. *Here's Looking at You: Hollywood, Film & Politics*, fourth edition. New York: Peter Lang Publishing, Inc., 2014.

Green, Melanie C., and Timothy C. Brock. "The Role of Transportation in the Persuasiveness of Public Narratives." *Journal of Personality and Social Psychology* 79, no. 5 (2000): 701–21.

———. "In the Mind's Eye: Transportation-Imagery Model of Narrative Persuasion," In *Narrative Impact: Social and Cognitive Foundations* edited by Melanie C. Green, Jeffrey J. Strange, and Timothy C. Brock, 315–41. Mahwah, NJ: Lawrence Erlbaum Associates, Inc., 2002.

Guggenheim, Lauren, Nojin Kwak, and Scott W. Campbell. "Nontraditional News Negativity: The Relationship of Entertaining Political News Use to Political Cynicism and Mistrust." *International Journal of Public Opinion Research* 23, no. 3 (2011): 287–314.

Haas, Elizabeth, Terry Christensen, and Peter J. Haas. *Projecting Politics: Political Messages in American Films*, 2nd Edition. New York: Routledge, 2015.

Holbert, R. Lance. "A Typology for the Study of Entertainment Television and Politics." *American Behavioral Scientist* 49, no. 3 (2005): 436–53.

Holbert, R. Lance, Owen Pillion, David A. Tschida, Greg G. Armfield, Kelly Kinder, Kristin L. Cherry, and Amy R. Daulton. "*The West Wing* as an Endorsement of the American Presidency: Expanding the Domain of Priming in Political Communications." *Journal of Communications* 53 (September 2003): 427–43.

Holbert, R. Lance, David A. Tschida, Maria Dixon, Kristen Cherry, Kelly Steuber, and David Airne. "*The West Wing* and Depictions of the American Presidency: Expanding the Domains of Framing in Political Communication." *Communication Quarterly* 53 (2005): 505–22.

Holbrook, R. Andrew, and Timothy G. Hill. "Agenda-Setting and Priming in Prime Time Television: Crime Dramas as Political Cues." *Political Communication* 22, no. 3 (2005): 277–95.

Iyengar, Shanto. *Is Anyone Responsible? How Television Frames Political Issues*. Chicago: University of Chicago Press, 1991.

Iyengar, Shanto, and Donald R. Kinder. *News that Matters: Television and American Opinion*. Chicago: University of Chicago Press, 1987.

Jamieson, Kathleen Hall, and Paul Waldman. *The Press Effect: Politicians, Journalists, and the Stories that Shape the Political World*. Oxford: Oxford University Press, 2003.

Jennings, M. Kent, and Richard G. Niemi. *The Political Character of Adolescence: The Influence of Families and Schools*. Princeton, NJ: Princeton University Press, 1974.

Jennings, M. Kent, and Richard G. Niemi. "The Transmission of Political Values from Parent to Child." *American Political Science Review* 62, no. 1 (March 1968): 169–84.

Jennings, M. Kent, Laura Stoker, and Jake Bowers. "Politics across Generations: Family Transmission Reexamined." *Journal of Politics* 71, no. 3 (July 2009): 782–89.

Jones, Calvert W. "It's the End of the World and They Know It: How Dystopian Fiction Shapes Political Attitudes." Paper presented at the Southern Political Science Association Annual Meeting, San Juan, Puerto Rico, January 9, 2016.

Koenig, Anne M., Alice H. Eagly, Abigail A. Mitchell, Tiina Ristikari. "Are Leader Stereotypes Masculine? A Meta-Analysis of Three Research Paradigms." *Psychological Bulletin* 137, no. 4 (July 2011): 616–42.

Lane, Robert E. "Self-Reliance and Empathy: The Enemies of Poverty: And of the Poor." *Political Psychology* 22, no. 3 (September 2001): 473–92.

Lenart, Silvo, and Kathleen McGraw. "America Watches 'Amerika': Television Docudrama and Political Attitudes." *The Journal of Politics* 51, no. 3 (August 1989): 697–712.

Lerner, Melvin J. "Evaluation of Performance as a Function of Performer's Reward and Attractiveness." *Journal of Personality and Social Psychology* 1 (1965): 355–60.

———. *The Belief in a Just World: A Fundamental Delusion.* New York: Plenum Press, 1980.

Lerner, Melvin J., and Miller, Dale T. "Just World Research and the Attribution Process: Looking Back and Ahead." *Psychological Bulletin* 85, no. 5 (September 1978): 1030–51.

Lichter, Robert S., Jody C. Baumgartner, and Jonathan S. Morris. *Politics is a Joke! How TV Comedians Are Remaking Political Life.* Boulder, CO: Westview Press, 2015.

Mindich, David T. Z. *Tuned Out: Why Americans Under 40 Don't Follow the News.* New York: Oxford University Press, 2005.

Mondak, Jeffery J. *Personality and the Foundations of Political Behavior.* New York: Cambridge University Press, 2010.

Mulligan, Kenneth, and Philip Habel. "An Experimental Test of the Effects of Fictional Framing on Attitudes." *Social Science Quarterly* 92, no. 1 (2011): 79–99.

———. "The Implications of Fictional Media for Political Beliefs," *American Politics Research* 41, no. 1 (2013): 122–46.

Mutz, Diana C. 2016. "Harry Potter and the Deadly Donald." *PS: Political Science and Politics* 49, no. 4 (October 2016): 722–29.

Mutz, Diana C., and Lilach Nir. "Not Necessarily the News: Does Fictional Television Influence Real-World Policy Preferences?" *Mass Communication and Society* 13, no. 2 (2010): 196–217.

Oatley, Keith. "Emotions and the Story Worlds of Fiction." In *Narrative Impact: Social and Cognitive Foundations* edited by Melanie C. Green, Jeffrey J. Strange, and Timothy C. Brock, 39–69. Mahwah, NJ: Lawrence Erlbaum Associates, Inc., 2002.

Painter, Chad, and Louis Hodges. "Mocking the News: How *The Daily Show with Jon Stewart* Holds Traditional Broadcast News Accountable." *Journal of Mass Media Ethics* 25, no. 4 (2010): 257–74.

Perse, Elizabeth M. *Media Effects and Society*. Mahwah, NJ: Lawrence Erlbaum Associates, Inc, 2001.

Pew Research Center. "Women and Leadership." January 14, 2015. Accessed March 24, 2016. http://www.pewsocialtrends.org/2015/01/14/women-and-leadership/.

Pfau, Michael, Patricia Moy, and Erin Alison Szabo. "Influence of Prime-Time Television Programming on Perceptions of the Federal Government." *Mass Communication & Society* 4, no. 4 (2001): 437–53.

Plato. *The Republic*. Translated by Desmond Lee. New York: Penguin, 1974.

Prior, Markus. *Post-Broadcast Democracy: How Media Choice Increases Inequality in Political Involvement and Polarizes Elections*. Cambridge: Cambridge University Press, 2007.

Raney, Arthur A. "Punishing Media Criminals and Moral Judgment: The Impact on Enjoyment." *Media Psychology* 7, no. 2 (May 2005): 145–63.

Rubin, Zick, and Letitia Anne Peplau. 1975. "Who Believes in a Just World." *Journal of Social Issues* 31, no. 3 (July 1975): 65–89.

Sester, Marc, and Melanie C. Green. "You Are Who You Watch: Identification and Transportation Effects on Temporary Self-Concept." *Social Influence* 5, no. 4 (2010): 272–88.

Shrum, L. J., and Jaehoon Lee. "The Stories TV Tells: How Fictional TV Narratives Shape Normative Perceptions and Personal Values." In *The Psychology of Entertainment Media: Blurring the Lines Between Entertainment and Persuasion*, edited by L. J. Shrum, 147–67. New York: Routledge, 2012.

Slater, Michael D. "Reinforcing Spirals: The Mutual Influence of Media Selectivity and Media Effects and Their Impact on Individual Behavior and Social Identity." *Communications Theory* 17 (2007): 281–303.

Slater, Michael D., Donna Rouner, and Marilee Long. 2006. "Television Dramas and Support for Controversial Public Policies: Effects and Mechanisms." *Journal of Communication* 56 (2006) 235–52.

Stenner, Karen. *The Authoritarian Dynamic*. Cambridge: Cambridge University Press, 2005.

Strange, Jeffrey J. "How Fictional Tales Wag Real-World Beliefs: Models and Mechanisms of Narrative Influence." In *Narrative Impact: Social and Cognitive Foundations*, edited by Melanie C. Green, Jeffrey J. Strange, and Timothy C. Brock, 263–86. Mahwah, New Jersey: Lawrence Erlbaum Associates, Publishers, 2002.

Sullivan, John L., James Piereson, and George E. Marcus. *Political Tolerance and American Democracy*. Chicago: University of Chicago Press, 1993.

Thompson, Derek. "Is *House of Cards* Really a Hit? The people reading about TV and the people watching TV are living in two separate worlds." *The Atlantic*, February 24, 2014. Accessed March 7, 2018. http://www.theatlantic.com/business/archive/2014/02/is-i-house-of-cards-i-really-a-hit/284035/.

Uscinski, Joseph E., and Joseph M. Parent. *American Conspiracy Theories*. Oxford: Oxford University Press, 2014.

Van Laer, Tom, Ko de Ruyter, Luca M. Visconti, and Martin Wetzels. "The Extended Transportation-Imagery Model: A Meta-Analysis of the Antecedents and Consequences of Consumers' Narrative Transportation." *Journal of Consumer Research* 40, no. 5 (February 2014): 797–817.

Vezzali, Loris Sofia Stathi, Dino Giovannini, Dora Capozza, and Elena Trifiletti, "The Greatest Magic of *Harry Potter*: Reducing Prejudice," *Journal of Applied Social Psychology* 45, no. 2 (February 2015): 105–21.

Wilkins, Vicky M., and Jeffrey B. Wenger. "Belief in a Just World and Attitudes Toward Affirmative Action." *Policy Studies Journal* 42 (2014): 325–43.

Windolf, Jim. 2014. "The Gathering Storm." *Vanity Fair*, April 2014. Accessed March 7, 2018. http://www.vanityfair.com/hollywood/2014/04/game-of -thrones-season-4.

Wolfsfeld, Gadi. *Making Sense of Media and Politics: Five Principles in Political Communication*. New York: Routledge, 2011.

Young, Dannagal Goldthwaite. "Daily Show Viewers Knowledgeable about Presidential Campaign, National Annenberg Election Survey Shows." Annenberg Public Policy Center, September 21, 2004. Accessed October 20, 2017. http:// cdn.annenbergpublicpolicycenter.org/wp-content/uploads/2004_03_late-night -knowledge-2_9–21_pr2.pdf.

Zillmann, Dolf. "Anatomy of Suspense." In *The Entertainment Functions of Television / Sponsored by the Social Science Research Council,* edited by Percy H. Tannenbaum. Hillsdale, NJ: L. Erlbaum Associates, 1980.

———. "Empathy: Affect from Bearing Witness to the Emotions of Others." In *Responding to the Screen: Reception and Reaction Processes*, edited by Jennings Bryant and Dolf Zillmann, 135–68. Hillsdale, NJ: Erlbaum, 1991.

Index

About the Author

Anthony "Jack" Gierzynski, PhD, is professor and chair of the Political Science Department at the University of Vermont. He has published four other books including *Harry Potter and the Millennials* and *Saving American Elections*, as well as over a dozen articles and book chapters on campaign finance, political parties, and elections. He has been part of research teams awarded grants for election studies from the National Science Foundation and the Joyce Foundation and was an expert witness and consultant in several court cases testing campaign finance laws, including the US Supreme Court case *Randall v. Sorrell*. He is the creator and director of the University of Vermont's Vermont Legislative Research Service.